Reflections of a Surgeon

DR. V. N. SHRIKHANDE

Popular Prakashan
www.popularprakashan.com

Published by
Harsha Bhatkal for
POPULAR PRAKASHAN PVT. LTD.
301, Mahalaxmi Chambers
22, Bhulabhai Desai Road
Mumbai 400 026

First Published 2015
Revised Second Edition January 2016

(4428)
ISBN: 978-81-7991-869-2

Design: Anjali Sawant and Mahendra Ghanekar

PRINTED IN INDIA
by Saurabh Printers (P) Ltd.
Plot No. 67 A-68, Ecotech, Ext. I
Kasna, Greater Noida-201306 (U.P)

About the Author

Dr. Vinayak N. Shrikhande, one of the pioneers in gastrointestinal surgery in India, was born in 1931 in Kolhapur.

He obtained an M.B.B.S (Bombay) in 1953. He had the rare distinction of obtaining F.R.C.S. in England and Edinburgh at the first attempt in 1959.

On returning to India, he played an important role in the Family Planning Programme, by his work on reversing birth control surgery in men, which was recognised all over the world.

He was the former Professor of Surgery at Grant Medical College, Mumbai, and later on Professor and Head of Department of General Surgery, Bombay Hospital Institute of Medical Sciences. He was the first president of the Indian Chapter of the International Hepato Pancreato Biliary Association.

Though he was based in Mumbai, he went to smaller towns to train surgeons so that patients could get better treatment near their homes.

He established Shrikhande Clinic in 1977, in Mumbai, which has become a training centre in gastrointestinal surgery for young surgeons and observers from all over the country and abroad.

He was invited to operate on the President of India, Dr. Shankar Dayal Sharma, at the Army Hospital, New Delhi, in April 1994.

Known as an inspiring teacher, students flocked around him and it is no surprise that he has trained more than 250 surgeons in the last 40 years, some of whom continue to carry out the excellent traditions of surgery. He is a much sought after speaker at various medical conferences all over the country.

A Surgeon's Prayer

Give me work when I am young
Let there be no unexpected death on the operation table
Let no swabs or forceps remain inside the abdomen
Let me not cross a point of no return during an operation
Let there be some help available in a critical situation
Let my skilful hands not make me arrogant
Keep me away from the temptations of money
Let the invisible enemies, the microbes, not infect the patient
Give me the wisdom to quit in time
Give me good health to enjoy the evening of my life.

My Prayer has been Answered:

I am blessed by my profession,
I am 84 years old; full of happy memories.
My life overflows with hidden treasures which
no authority can tax; no one could ever know
that I envy my destiny!

To become a surgeon entails two distinct and sequential phases. The first consists of learning to become a gentleman in its broadest sense, the second is learning the technical skills of the profession. Some have never passed the first phase. They become technicians, not surgeons.

— **James Priestley**
Surgeon, Mayo Clinic
Performed the first ever successful
pancreatic surgery in 1944

... Improper intervention with surgical manoeuvre due either to ignorance of the disease process, greed for money or lack of judgement, lead only to complications.

— **Sushruta, 600 BC**
The Famous Indian Plastic Surgeon

Whatever Dr. Shrikhande has done in his life is with devotion, dexterity and dedication. At the core of his story, therefore, is honesty and fairness that stresses the importance of using both the head and the heart in conducting one's profession.

— **P. S. Deodhar**
Life Fellow IEEE USA, Fellow IE,
Fellow INAE, Dist. Fellow IETE
President, India China Economic and
Cultural Council, New Delhi
Chairman, APLAB Limited
Former Chairman Electronics
Commission, Government of India
Former Advisor to the
Late PM Rajiv Gandhi (1982-1991)

The book is a magnificent collection of his deep insights and wealth of experience, sparkling with wit and wisdom. ...I especially recommend this book to leaders who have the important task of balancing ambition and professional progress with humility and a sense of service to others.

— **Sudhanshu Palsule**
Fellow at Cambridge University, Panelist of Educators of
Duke Corporate Education and Associate Professor
in the Advanced Management Program at INSEAD

More than a reflection, the book is an exhortation to all doctors who are readying to embark on their careers. It tells us that virtues like determination, clarity, hard work and conviction can always help you to win no matter how difficult your circumstances. Once these virtues get to work, all constraints, hindrances and obstacles seem to melt away. Eventually, the world always bows down to capability and performance.

— **Umesh Shrikhande**
CEO; Taproot

Dedication

My parents who taught me by example
how to lead a meaningful life

Suhas, my wife, who has walked along with me

Thousands of patients in India and England
who placed their trust in my hands

Genes that provided me
assets for a surgical career

and

A destiny that took me
to unknown peaks

Acknowledgement

Writing this book has been a very difficult and complicated 'operation' for me. However, I have had help and guidance from many whom I wish to thank. I have had very enthusiastic assistance from Mrs. Bharati Anand, Mrs. Anjali Sawant, Ms. Armaity Motafram and Mrs. Swapna Shinde who spent countless hours with me working on this book.

I am grateful to Mrs. Mrudula Joshi for promptly and willingly editing a part of my book. I have had the unusual privilege of having a qualified editor at home, my granddaughter, Anushree. Furthermore, I am fortunate to receive constructive feedback and invaluable insights from my son-in-law, Anand, and my daughters, Seema and Vasanti. I am touched that my younger granddaughters, Sanjana and Shivani, too contributed in refining this book in the final stages.

I am also thankful to my secretary of twenty-five years, Ms. Thelma Sequeira. I thank Mr. Santosh Samal, who scanned some of the very old photographs and made them available for the book.

I am indebted to Mr. Harsha Bhatkal and Mr. Ramdas Bhatkal for their helpful suggestions and support in spite of their busy schedules. Lastly, I would like to thank the thousands of patients, their families, the nurses, the doctors and the hospital staff for their invaluable support in my professional life. The book is based on real experiences and I have made a few changes in details so that the identity of no patient is disclosed.

Contents

Foreword

About a month ago, Shailesh, Dr. V. N. Shrikhande's son, now himself a distinguished hepatobiliary and pancreatic surgeon at the Tata Memorial Centre in Mumbai, told me that his father had written an autobiography in Marathi which had gone through four editions and received numerous literary awards. Shrikhande Senior had now decided to write a book in English and Shailesh requested me to write the Foreword to this new version. I immediately agreed because I had known of the author for many years as a distinguished surgeon who headed the Bombay Hospital Department of Surgery, who was an excellent raconteur but, above all, was a good human being.

I expected to read a chronological account of a person's road to surgical success and thought it would be easy to write down a few thoughts about what a great doctor Dr. V. N. Shrikhande was.

However when I received the pages by email I was pleasantly surprised. I started reading the book on a Friday and by Sunday had finished it and was absolutely enthralled. The opening page sets the tone of this book which is full of optimism and gratitude of what life has given to the author—work when young, guidance and protection from mistakes during operations, a disdain for money and 'good health to enjoy the evening of his life'. His prayers have been answered.

Dr. Vinayak Shrikhande was born in Kolhapur and had schooling at Belgaum in rather straitened circumstances in a house without electricity. However all this was compensated for by a loving mother and an inspirational father who was a distinguished lawyer and later became a sessions court judge.

He went to Fergusson College in Pune and then Grant Medical College in Bombay where he did not particularly shine and later left for the United Kingdom where he passed the coveted F.R.C.S.

examinations of both Edinburgh and England at his first attempt. Rejecting numerous offers to remain and lead a comfortable life in England, he returned to serve his motherland and by dint of sheer hard work and dedication reached the highest levels in his profession.

His guiding motto was to improve himself every day by practicing the Japanese philosophy of 'Kaizen', and he thus became a skillful surgeon. When he realised that working with both hands would be an asset, he started brushing his teeth, shaving, putting on clothes, using scissors, and even writing, with his left hand.

He was also a voracious reader especially of inspirational books by the good and the great. His guiding philosophy was —in spite of living and working in an environment in which the norm was otherwise, he always maintained the highest ethical standards.

He reached the pinnacle of success when, out of all the surgeons in this country and perhaps abroad who were available, he was chosen and asked to operate on the President of India. He retains a charming modesty about this and his other numerous achievements and now having wound down a little, has recently undergone two major cardiac procedures which he seems to have borne with great equanimity.

However this book is not a chronicle of the events of what has been a very eventful life. Interspersed are numerous anecdotes about Dr. Shrikhande's patients, his triumphs as well as his failures, encounters with surgeons in India and from all over the world. What I found most interesting and stimulating were his meditations on life and happiness. In spite of a speech defect (which I gather is a stammer, although I've never noticed it), he has become an effective and much sought after public speaker.

Dr. Shrikhande's legacy and example to all of us is how a boy from a small town in Karnataka, with a speech defect and not a very outstanding academic record, can reach the dizzying heights of a very competitive profession by sheer hard work, clearly focussed goals, yet always remaining ethical, kind, and compassionate.

This philosophical, anecdotal, and charming autobiography celebrates a life all his colleagues in the medical profession as well as his countrymen should be proud of.

— **Samiran Nundy**
Chairman,
Dept. of Surgical Gastroenterology
and Organ Transplantation,
Sir Ganga Ram Hospital
Editor-in-Chief,
Current Medicine Research and Practice

April 27, 2015
New Delhi

Preface

I have been a surgeon for 5 decades in Mumbai, a city of over 16 million. I was fortunate to work as a Professor of Surgery at the Grant Medical College and G.T. Hospital, a university teaching hospital where we had a large influx of poor patients from all over the country because treatment was free and Mumbai was well-known for excellent medical care. I had opportunities to train undergraduate and postgraduate students for over 4 decades since I was later appointed as a consultant surgeon at Bombay Hospital Institute of Medical Sciences (the premier private hospital in the country where many leading doctors, who were also professors in teaching hospitals, were appointed as honoraries). I retired as a Chief of General Surgery from Bombay Hospital when I was nearing 80.

In addition, in my initial years, I had the privilege to work at Dr. G.M. Phadke's private Colony Nursing Home which gave me an excellent avenue to continue and further my private practice, where the work-ethic and philosophy of the profession was identical to my own. This culminated in the opening of my own set-up, Shrikhande Clinic in 1977, an institution built on the "Small is Beautiful" principle, that has continued to uphold the best traditions of my noble profession.

I have been lucky enough to meet excellent fellow surgeons, many of them from abroad, and be present as an observer when they operated. They in turn have reciprocated by attending my wards and operation theatre.

Diseases brought strangers into my life and some became my friends. Life has been like a kaleidoscope; the way I perceived the world changed with every new experience, however small. This enriching journey has more than compensated for the stress and hectic schedule inherent in a surgeon's life.

During my career as a surgeon, many people wanted me to write a book. However, writing is a taxing and time-consuming activity, and I had no time. This is a paradox in a surgeon's life; either there is less work, so few experiences to write about, or there is heavy load of work and more experiences, but no time to write!

At the age of 78, I finally had the time to spare and wrote a book in Marathi, my mother tongue. It was not supposed to be an autobiography. It was not meant to tell interesting secrets of the lives of my patients. It wasn't written to advertise my success as a surgeon. It was simply a narration of what life had taught me. I have been a part of human drama. A drama where I did not have the luxury of choosing the actors, writing the script or knowing what the end would be. So I never imagined that I could write, or that I would ever write a whole book which would be a bestseller for 12 weeks with 4 editions and 2 reprints in 3 years, 6 literary awards and an audio-book version read out on the All India Radio. It was overwhelming and touching to have such an unexpectedly powerful response.

I received a phone call from an admirer. He said "I am 94 and blind, but I could see your entire life after listening to your book being read out on the All India Radio!" I received scores of letters from people I had never met, and it was especially heartening to hear from young readers who I thought would have little interest in reading about the experiences of someone much older.

I also received letters from respected men from the field of literature. K.J Purohit, a renowned Marathi short story writer wrote "..*Your book will be considered as one of the outstanding autobiographies in Marathi literature...it will guide people in all professions, of all ages, all the time...*"

Mukundrao Kirloskar, Marathi publisher of great repute, wrote, "...*My special interest is autobiographies. I could not complete most of them because they contained irrelevant details which were uninteresting. In fact doctors, advocates, bureaucrats must have, apart from their profession, a social perspective. However, in none of autobiographies I read was this evident.*

Your book is an exception; so much so that while reading your book, I learnt enough about medicine to become almost half a doctor!.. I started keeping notes on your book, which is my common practice, but I gave up halfway, because the notes threatened to become a book in itself! ...I have recommended this book to everyone. Your experience from the profession, your social awareness, the gratitude and integrity with which you worked—also represents my life. Had I written a book, the last chapter would have been the same as in your book...I congratulate you for an outstanding autobiography and your unique contribution to Marathi literature. ..."

Life continues to be full of surprises. What greater contentment can anyone expect?

At the age of twenty, I had decided to be a surgeon. At the age of 25, I had a strong feeling that my decision had been the right one. At 40, I experienced my first real taste of success. But I never once imagined that I would be a writer at the age of 78! In the four years following the publication of the Marathi book, many people urged me to have it translated into English. This English book may draw from the content of the Marathi book, but it is not a translation. It is a fresh attempt with new insights and experiences that I have gained in the intervening years.

> "It is duty incumbent on upright and credible men of all ranks who have performed anything noble or praiseworthy to record in their own words the events of their lives. But they should not undertake this honourable task until they pass the age of forty."
>
> **Benvenuto Cellini**,
> November 3, 1500 to February 13, 1571,
> goldsmith, painter, sculptor, soldier and
> musician of the Renaissance

50 years ago, I moved to the city then known as Bombay, a city 150 times bigger than the small town where I had spent my childhood. Mumbai, as it is known now, is a city dominated by the powerful and the rich. However, there is another side to

Mumbai- the second-largest city in India and the most generous, tolerant, cosmopolitan metro in the country. It not only inspires individuals with humble backgrounds to dream big, but also helps them fulfill those dreams, however absurd they may seem.

Every profession has a social angle, but a humane attitude with social concerns is developed first at home. Genes we cannot change, but character we can cultivate. I was influenced by my parents. My father was an advocate, a professor of law and later a judge. He inculcated in me values of hard work, simplicity, sincerity, commitment to excellence and empathy for the poor and underprivileged. I became a surgeon by choice. I was aware that in spite of my troublesome, heavy tongue, nature had gifted me with skillful hands. As I polished these assets through constant efforts, the awareness of my positives helped and made the drawbacks comparatively irrelevant. Every journey starts with a vision and mine was to be a good surgeon. My father wanted me to be an extraordinary surgeon for an ordinary man. He felt happy that I had remained true to his expectations. I missed him when I was called to New Delhi to operate on the then-President of India, Dr. Shankar Dayal Sharma in 1994.

Destiny helped me to attain a successful position; a position and a life that I would never have imagined. I hope this book will help aspiring surgeons realise what the profession is really about. In surgery there are no runs to score, no matches to win, no records to break, no mountain peaks to scale. It is a long journey in which continuous improvement and innovation should become habits. The 4 years that I spent in the United Kingdom taught me innumerable things that broadened my horizons, one among them being the strong sense of fairness the British abide by even in their everyday life. I have practised ethical surgery and avoided unnecessary investigations and surgical interventions. I have come to realise that any good surgeon with a good pair of hands and a patient's well-being uppermost in his thoughts will always reach the heights of excellence. It is only when the patient's welfare becomes secondary that the exploitation and unethical practices begin to creep in. In addition to continuous hard work, a surgeon must accept difficulties, disappointments, failures and the denial of the simple pleasures of life. It is a vocation for the welfare of the patient who surrenders his most important possession, his life, into the surgeon's hands.

Some of the quotes and references in the book may not be accurate; I am not a student of history nor have I undertaken any special research for this book. These are the impressions and experiences I've gathered throughout the 84 years of my life.

We all know of the "Indian Brain Drain" to other countries. We know that many who left for better opportunities have indeed got them and succeeded. We also know of many who returned to India and made significant contributions to the country's growth and rise of stature in the committee of nations. All such stories have the potential to inspire the youth to choose a right direction in the uncharted seas of profession. I hope that some would feel inspired by this story of a diffident boy from a small town becoming a role model for many young surgeons in India.

Here is my story.

—V. N. Shrikhande

Mumbai
April 27, 2015

In This Book

Had I not been a fighter pilot serving in the Indian Air Force, I would certainly have made a surgeon. This is not a flippant statement. I had elected for the appropriate subjects that would have equipped me to appear for the MBBS entrance examination, back in 1964. Medicine in general and surgery in particular were my fall back options. This is not to imply that I rated this qualification any lower than I did Military Aviation—fact was not that I loved Medicine less but, yes, I certainly loved flying more!

With this as the background, imagine my surprise when Dr. V. N. Shrikhande requested me to go through the book for my comments. I accepted his offer with pride tinged with some embarrassment and considered it a huge privilege to be invited to do so, as he is an accomplished professional and a wonderful human being at the same time.

It has been my good fortune to have known him outside of his medical practice and I have always marvelled at the man's varied interests and hunger for knowledge, despite having reached the pinnacle of his career. Basically, he is an explorer. He learns from all things that surround him. He is genuinely interested to know about other professions and the pulls and pressures that define the journey of other professionals in their various domains. He continues to educate himself in this manner, even to this day.

While going through this remarkable book, the reader will learn of real-life incidents that were faced by the author during his pursuit of excellence. These were incidents that either shaped his character or validated his beliefs such as: confidence in one's ability, sensitivity to other people's needs, personal integrity, ethical conduct, honesty, and humility.

There are some profound messages conveyed by the author in the pages of this remarkable book. It is replete with sage advice for fellow professionals, such as, "I told the students that if a patient does not respond to treatment, do not change the medication, change the diagnosis". There was an added dimension to his teaching — in his own words, "I did not teach only surgery, I taught them to become better human beings".

Chapter 10 is both heart wrenching and uplifting at the same time. It describes how we can work around the disappointment resulting from a poor hand dealt to us by a deck of cards called Life; how we must accept our infirmities without embarrassment and not attempt to keep it hidden under wraps.

The reader will accompany Dr. Shrikhande on a long, arduous, tension-filled, challenging, sometimes frustrating but, finally, a very satisfying and fulfilling journey. It chronicles the triumph of courage over adversity, of hope over despair, and indeed, of service over self! The reader will learn about 'serendipity' and how the Universe aligns itself to make our efforts bear fruit if the intention is to do good; about 'intuition', that it is "not a lottery or a wild guess. It comes from within, a product of deep thinking and experience".

Over the three decades that I have known and respected Dr. Shrikhande, I have observed some character traits that I believe have been instrumental in shaping his attitude and, in fact, have contributed towards his growth as an exceptional professional in his chosen field.

For example: when hurt by a personal slight, he uses the humiliating experience positively and vows never to be guilty of such behaviour himself. This is indicative of an evolved mind, secure in the knowledge of its own abilities and limitations. He attributes his success to Destiny and, in fact, feels a "keen sense of gratitude" at being blessed in this manner. Humility personified!

'Reflections of a Surgeon' is part AJ Cronin, part Grey's Anatomy and, interestingly, part philosophy, part Indian value education and part spiritualism! It is a humble account of a life that was well lived and explains in simple language, the advantage of remaining focussed, despite the 'noise' that surrounds our lives today.

I believe that ability, humility, compassion, and sensitivity are inter-related and often feed off each other in a synergistic fashion. Each of these attributes end up raising the level of the other! Dr. Shrikhande's story is an affirmation of that belief. I am sure that the reader will gain many an insight into how life can be well lived and how 'true' success should actually be measured.

It is all there in this book.

We must thank the author for 'baring' himself in a manner such that others may benefit from his life's remarkable journey thus far.

Dr. V. N. Shrikhande can rest assured that he has realised his father's dream. He has been an extraordinary surgeon for an ordinary man.

May his tribe increase.

Jai Hind!

Wg. Cdr. (Retd) Rakesh Sharma
Ashoka Chakra

Coonoor, The Nilgiris
April 27, 2015

(Rakesh Sharma, Test Pilot and the first (and the only) Indian in space, journeyed around the earth in a space station, Salyut 7, April 1984.)

Chapter 1

President's Operation

I had the unique honour of operating on the then President of India, Dr. Shankar Dayal Sharma, in 1994. I was on the medical specialists' panel that looked after the health of the Governor and other VIPs in the state. Dr. Sharma had a massive inguinal hernia; the operation done 20 years earlier had failed because of infection. He was scared of the prospects of another surgery and went on postponing it. However, the discomfort had reached a point where an operation could no longer be delayed.

I had operated on his brother—an internal medicine specialist from Bhopal—for gall bladder stones. The president was under the impression that I was an expert only in the field of gall bladder and pancreatic diseases, but not for hernia. His personal physician was Bombay Hospital's cardiologist, Dr. B.K. Goyal, my colleague of three decades. And so we were invited to New Delhi to finalise the treatment.

It was an early morning flight from Mumbai to New Delhi. There was a vehicle waiting in a special enclosure at the Delhi airport which drove us to Rashtrapati Bhavan, where we went past a row of saluting men in uniform before being escorted to the first floor. The President, the First Lady and some close relatives were waiting for us in the hall we were ushered into.

He was past 70, the hernia was massive, general anaesthesia was risky and epidural anaesthesia was not possible. *(Epidural anaesthesia meant numbing a limited area by injecting anaesthetic agents in the lower back.)*

I felt I could manage the case under local anaesthesia, a technique I had used throughout my career from 1955.

We decided the date and hospital for surgery after a detailed question–answer session.

I was given a suite in the residential wing, with a beautiful view of the lush green lawns outside the window. There was no sound or movement around except that of the armed security guards. I do not think that I could have found a better place to rest! I had performed an emergency operation the previous night and I thought I would sleep before catching the evening flight back to Bombay. However, I just could not sleep because my mind kept wandering back to my humble beginning in a small town, my personality as a shy and diffident student, the initial struggles without any professional, financial or infrastructural support. I remembered my father who wanted me to become an 'extraordinary surgeon for the ordinary man'. On this background, the present circumstances seemed strangely surreal. I had been chosen to treat the first citizen of the country. I felt a keen sense of gratitude to destiny.

The operation was fixed for April 4, 1994 and I reached New Delhi the day before. By then, the VIP treatment had already lost some of its novelty. Accompanying me was Dr. Kishor Adyanthyaya, a colleague in whom I had great confidence, Dr. B. S. Gharpure, Professor at the G. S. Medical College attached to KEM Hospital and my anaesthesist of three decades, and of course a set of familiar surgical instruments. Dr. Adyanthyaya is now Professor and Head, Dept. of General Surgery, at Bombay Hospital Institute of Medical Sciences.

When we met the President at the hospital the night before the surgery, he asked, "I have consulted several surgeons in the past and I was told that the operation is not possible under local. How is it that your advice is different from them?" The question was totally unexpected since it wasn't asked during our earlier consultations. All that I said was, "If experience is any guide, what we have planned for you is the correct decision."

A hunch or intuition has no logical explanation. Gut feeling has to be experienced to be believed. It develops in some individuals. Intuition cannot be reached by a rational path and cannot be taught or analysed. It is an ability to pick up and process subtle clues which are beyond explanation and analysis. I can offer no more explanation. Decision making is the final piece in the mosaic of experience, mistakes and observations.

Intuition is not a lottery or a wild guess. It comes from within, a product of deep thinking and experience.

I took the decision to operate under local anaesthesia, a technique I had followed for over thirty-five years. The hernia was so massive and long-standing that the problem was outside my experience, and the patient was the First Citizen of India. Many surgeons both from India and abroad, with sound reasons, had ruled out surgery under local anaesthesia. It was impossible for anyone to share my loneliness.

The night before was not without its jitters. I woke up with a feeling that something was touching a small mole at the back of my neck. After putting the light on, I saw a rodent escaping the room, but luckily there was no bleeding from the mole.

I had spent some nights in villages and in tents on open grounds while attending camps when the worst disturbances were mosquitoes and cockroaches, never rats, scorpions, or snakes. And to think that I had such an experience in the Presidential mansion of all places! I could not sleep.

I have never been a believer in good or bad omens, but that night in that place with probably one of the most important surgeries of my life the next day, I could not get rid of the doubts in my mind.

"Am I being warned not to go ahead with a difficult decision? What explanation can I offer if I decide not to operate? Am I going to make a fool of myself by running away from my decision and responsibility?" I thought.

The turmoil was disturbing and agonising. It was imperative that I had faith in my own intuition and abilities. I had to make this final decision on my own and stand by it no matter what. In the end I decided to go ahead with the operation. A mouse is considered as the vehicle of Lord Ganesh, the God of wisdom—that supreme deity in Hindu culture known to remove all obstacles, and I assumed this to be a good omen.

The way we look at the problem is more important than the problem!

The next day was not like other Mondays with a big operation list. I had only one operation but the patient was the President. The familiar (my anaesthetist, associate surgeon, instruments and confidence in my decision) was outweighed by the unfamiliar (the hospital, the operation theatre, and the nurses).

The operation had started (*in my mind*) three weeks earlier when the date was fixed. I went through every step of the operation in my mind as was my habit in my younger days when planning a major unfamiliar operation. I had even carried my delicate intestinal clamps which (*gently*) hold but do not crush the intestines, in case I was forced to handle the intestine. I was prepared for unforeseen situations. Surgeons are comfortable with their familiar instruments, just as Wimbledon champions bring their own rackets, musicians bring their own instruments, and authors prefer to write with familiar pens.

The moment of reckoning had arrived. I met the family members before the President was wheeled into the operating area and then followed the same standard routine I had used for many years. I entered the operation theatre with confidence that the operation would be successful. I took the patient's hand in mine when the sedative was being injected in his veins and reassured him of a cure. Moments later when I went to scrub, I overheard a senior surgeon passing a comment: "How can this operation ever be done under local anaesthesia? It is just impossible!"

The opinions of others did not displace my gut feeling. "Focus on the job at hand," I repeated to myself. I completely ignored

My parents Nageshrao and Kamalabai Shrikhande

Shrikhande-Nande-Khot family

Life Time Achievement Award by HPB Association, Coimbatore, February 15, 2013

Dr. Narayanswami (Mandya, Karnataka) felicitating me on my 75th birthday, 2006

Successful vas reunion operation in 1973
in Akola distict hospital

With President of India,
late Dr. Shankar Dayal Sharma, April 1994

With poet Kusumagraj, my sister and brother-in-law, Kolhatkar

With my wife and Jal Pardiwala

this untimely comment; my experience was my companion. Distracting negative thoughts are kept aside when I enter the operation theatre just like we remove our footwear before entering a temple. Surgery requires an uncluttered and intensely focussed mind.

The normal operating time for hernia repair is about an hour but it took three hours and twenty minutes because of technical difficulties. The entire area was scarred because of the previous surgery and infection and was akin to rebuilding a new structure in a bombed area. I can never fully explain the enormous sense of relief I experienced when I put in the last stitch after a marathon surgery.

The powerful realisation that I had achieved something that many others labelled impossible gave rise to a fierce rush of happiness—another defining moment in my life.

Over the whole duration, I had avoided any thoughts regarding the powerfully high status of my patient, and it is this attitude of emotional detachment that has to be nurtured with daily practice if you want to stand a chance of achieving your full potential as a surgeon.

If we can do what is difficult but possible, one day we can also do what is considered as impossible. The man who thinks it can be done, instinctively knows that risks are within control.

The anaesthetist there told me, "Sir, there was a lot of anxiety as to how such a hernia could even be tackled under local anaesthesia. We can't believe what we saw!"

Though I was showered with compliments from everyone present in the operating room and outside, the full impact of what I had just done did not sink in until I started seeing my name on national TV bulletins later in the evening. It was the moment of actual realisation of the onerous responsibility I had taken on in performing this surgery.

For the three days that followed, I stayed in a room adjacent to that of the President's. Next day there was a tap on my door, and to my great wonder…it was none other than the-then Prime Minister himself!

"I am Narasimha Rao."

I was left speechless. I fumbled around for words, "Sir, who does not know you?" We talked for a few minutes. He inquired about the President's health.

The next day we spent half an hour with the-then Vice-President, Shri K. Narayanan, having tea.

"I have been told that you have done the operation in an unusual way and that the surgery was very challenging. Could you explain?"

We explained it with the help of various diagrams, and at the end of it he congratulated the whole team.

After three days, we decided to shift the President back to Rashtrapati Bhavan. He was very particular to choose a time to ensure least inconvenience to the Delhi public.

This homecoming was a very happy moment for the family. After a cheerful send-off by the hospital staff, the motorcade left the hospital—our car just behind the one carrying the President. It was slow going, with crowds looking at us from both sides and the soldiers in uniform with their rifles, standing in attention with their backs towards the motorcade.

Under normal circumstances, we could have left Delhi after a day or two. However, when massive hernias are operated, the empty space in the scrotum gets filled up with serum, which may require aspiration.

Two days later, I had to deliver an oration at the annual function of a medical association, and so I flew back to Mumbai for a day. But as soon as I landed at Mumbai airport, we got the urgent message that the President had developed a mild fever. It was imperative that we returned to Delhi.

When I expressed my regrets to the medical association, I experienced a sense of *déjà-vu*. I had been invited for the same oration by the same medical association the year before, but it had to be cancelled because I had suffered a heart attack on the same day. Ironic was the word that first came to my mind. Needless to say, I was never invited for that oration again!

In the end I stayed with the President for a total of 18 days, because aspiration had to be done four times before the swelling completely subsided.

After making sure that his recovery was almost complete, I planned to go to the Halwara air force base, 320 km from Delhi, where my son-in-law was a fighter pilot. The transport had already been arranged and it was decided that I leave early the next morning by car. So when I got a message after dinner saying that the President wanted to meet me, I was a bit curious. It turned out that he was worried that I was leaving early in the morning.

The President called me to his room and said, "Please do not start so early. The Grand Trunk Road is dangerous at that hour. Many vehicles have no rear lights, there is no discipline on the roads, the cars coming from the opposite side dazzle your vision and the drivers are tired because of lack of sleep or unfit because of alcohol."

This was just the final confirmation of his attention to all possible details and his heartfelt concern for others. I was deeply touched.

I shared with him my experience of selecting a driver for my father after my return from England. The drivers were easily available but I was shocked to find that eight out of 10 drivers with a valid licence had no right to sit in the driver's seat. I asked them how they had obtained licences and the answer was that they had paid money to the agents.

India has the maximum number of vehicular accidents. The reasons are many; disregard for driving rules, bad roads, old vehicles, drivers who are either sleepy, incompetent, in a hurry or under the influence of alcohol.

These factors are interlinked in a chain of corruption and exploitation. Corruption in road building contracts, and exploitation of truck drivers who have to cover long distances as fast as possible to maximise profit. Unfortunately middlemen, bribes, delays and poor work ethics have infiltrated like cancer in all fields in India, but there are islands of hope in the sea of darkness around us. At least we have democracy and no fear of midnight knocks. That gives me hope that better days will come.

It all went off well in the end, but it was also a very lonely time for me. I had chosen the difficult path, full of uncertainties with no company but my own unshakeable belief in my decision. I was aware that it would have been a nightmare if I had failed. But though the operation was a challenging task, I never entertained the thought of failure.

No mountaineer starts his climb with negative thoughts. He has a plan to come back from the expedition.

Those who are afraid of failure are denied success. Those who are afraid of death are denied the joys of living. Accept the challenges so that you can experience the exhilaration of success.

I have seen that guidance comes to a man who believes that what is in his mind is the right solution and goes forward without a thought of failure. His trust in his intution makes the predictions of others irrelevant.

I wanted to know why the President had chosen to be operated in India when he had been strongly advised by all for a treatment abroad. His answer was simple. "If I had gone abroad for the operation, how could I have told the world that Indian doctors are second to none?"

When I was leaving England in 1961, I was asked why I was not settling down there. I gave two reasons in a light-hearted manner. "It seems that there is a new trend in high-class society that girls want to marry commoners, and I am not willing to take that risk!"

"What is the other reason?"

"If tomorrow, the Queen or the Prime Minister is to be operated on, I would not be selected, because I will be an outsider."

"As if you will be selected to operate on the President or Prime Minister of India!"

"Who knows!" was my reply.

All the talk was casual and in good humour.

A few months passed after the President's surgery. I was in Europe, when I got a call from the Rashtrapati Bhavan. I was asked whether it was possible for me to visit an ailing relative of the President in London. The First Lady told me, "We consider you as our family surgeon. If surgery is necessary, please do it in Mumbai or Delhi."

Once in London, a car was waiting at the airport for me. Luckily no operation was necessary.

I did four more operations (all for gall bladder stones causing frequent attacks of pain) for the family in the next two years.

Presidents going abroad for medical treatment is an expensive matter for the government and ultimately the taxpayer. The money saved by Dr. Sharma was used for improving the amenities for the President's staff.

It is my cherished hope that other representatives of the people and VIPs emulate his example. India has progressed a lot and I am happy that even the Prime Ministers are today opting for medical treatment in India.

I missed my father who was not present to see that I had gone beyond his expectations. Luckily my mother was alive to witness my achievements.

❑ ❑ ❑

Chapter 2

Childhood

I spent my childhood in Belgaum, a small town of 45,000 inhabitants, about 500 km south of Mumbai. Situated at 800 metres above sea level, the weather was cool even in summer and the place was known as a poor man's hill station.

There were so many mosquitoes that our hands would be stained with blood from swatting them! We slept under mosquito nets. Malaria was common and it was easy to spot those injected in their hips with quinine by their limp.

Our eight-roomed house was situated in a narrow lane. The streets were lined with open gutters. Houses had common walls and interaction with neighbours was easy. Roads were deserted in the evening. At night the silence was punctuated only by the barking of dogs. There were kerosene lamps and it was a daily routine to wipe the soot from the glass before use in the evening.

The toilet was located far away from the house and finding the way at night with the help of a lantern was a nightmare. It was an obstacle race on rainy days. The dark moving shadows on the wall would frighten me.

There was no drainage system; an open tanker swarming with flies and emitting a foul stench would make the rounds of the streets to collect the waste. The night soil was gathered in buckets by members of a particular caste designated for the purpose. They carried the buckets on their heads.

The sight and smell are still clear in my visual and olfactory memory. Our guests from Mumbai would look down upon us for our backwardness in following such unsanitary methods, which I had taken for granted as normal till I saw the bigger world.

Electricity was provided to only a part of the town. We spent eight years in a dark zone and looked forward to the day when we too would have electricity at home. Water had to be drawn from a nearby public well where we had to wait for our turn. We were encouraged by my parents to help our servant to draw water from the well. When the well dried up in summer, water was bought from the municipality tanker. Water scarcity is a common problem in India.

The town had a cantonment and a small air force base during British rule. It was fascinating to see planes perform aerial aerobatics from the windows of my house. The droning sound was a signal to keep all work aside, rush to the windows or to the street and to look at the sky. Fifteen years later came the jet age. The sound of the aircraft would be heard long after it had gone past. Years later, I found it difficult to explain to my crying children why no plane could be seen in the sky. They were too young to understand that the sound waves took some time to reach our ears, and by that time the fast moving planes were out of sight.

Our home was full of guests throughout the year. Interacting with them, I learnt at a very young age not to regard people, who did not know English, as uneducated or inferior.

I remember attending a wedding in my friend's family. The bride was from a rich Bombay family and her relatives were dressed in fine attire, had wrist watches and fountain pens that were symbols of affluence at that time. I felt absolutely backward.

In June 1939, my father took me to a high school, one of the oldest in our province, established in 1832. We entered the principal's room, the form was signed and the protocol for admission over. A peon took me to the class and I started my school education. The entire process was over in 10 minutes.

School did not interest me though some teachers were very good. I was an average student while my elder brother was a top ranker. He never made me feel inferior and I in turn felt no jealousy towards him. I was never compared with my brother at home. But in school, and among friends and relations, comparison was inevitable. Once a school teacher asked me,

"When the Almighty was distributing intelligence, were you in the toilet?" There was a ripple of laughter in the class.

This was in the 1930s when the concept of child psychology was unheard of; but my mother, who had only a few years of school education, and my father, knew the right way to bring up children with different abilities. My brother stood first in the matriculation examination and was felicitated in a public function in the city. I was proud of his achievement.

I was good at drawing and games like carrom, marbles, and could send a flat stone skimming over the surface of the water for long distances. I had a speech defect. I knew my limitations and therefore, had no ambitions.

Clothes were washed at home and dried in the sun. They were never ironed. Once during winter, a beggar came at our door with his naked child. I told my mother to give my newly-stitched shirt and shorts to that child and she gave them. Generosity is a divine gift which has to be nurtured from childhood.

The town had a library with a clock tower which was easily seen from the windows of my house. There was one alarm clock in the house; it woke us up with a sharp ring tone. Musical alarms that lull one back to sleep were not known.

Going to the library was a hobby. At times the waiting period to get books was several days. I read books recommended by friends.

During my medical college days in Bombay, searching for second-hand books sold on the footpath was a very enjoyable pastime. I found some very valuable books at a throwaway price. One was *Up from Slavery* by Booker T. Washington. My eclectic taste in books proved to be an advantage.

There were several playgrounds in Belgaum. We were fortunate that there were no tuition classes and we were out on the playground every evening. The day ended early.

The mode of transport was a horse-driven carriage called a *tonga*. There was also the *dhamani*, a closed carriage pulled by a pair of bullocks, a vehicle unique to Belgaum.

Bicycles were available for hire and the roads were safe. There was hardly any traffic on the roads. It was great fun riding a bike, and ringing the bell to caution the pedestrians gave us a feeling of authority. I would try to imitate the tricks the circus cyclists perform, especially riding down a slope with the hands off the bars. It was an intoxicating experience, something that I still remember. The scars on my legs remind me of my many childhood falls and I still have a distinct memory of the severe burning sensation caused by the tincture of iodine on wounds. I was never scolded at home for these falls nor prevented from cycling.

When I visit my hometown now, I feel sad to see that the playgrounds have disappeared and the cement-concrete jungle is spreading its tentacles. My cycling days came to an end when I went to Bombay; it was after a gap of fifty-eight years that I tried to ride one in Europe but failed! I was disappointed, but had to accept that age had crept up on me. Growing old is a 'losing' game. We lose hair, friends, memories, and also simple skills. I believed wrongly that cycling was one of those skills you could never forget once you had learnt it. We can no longer climb the staircase rapidly nor glide down the banisters! Playing and strolling in the rain can no longer be enjoyed for fear of falling.

There were a couple of newspapers reporting local events. Radios were played only in some cafes. We heard the cricket commentary standing outside the cafe near our home. My father bought a radio when I was 10. A ball point pen was gifted to my father by his cousin who had gone to the UK at a young age. Curiosity brought many to our home to see the pen in which one did not have to fill ink. Much later, in 1972, neighbours and friends crowded into our house in Mumbai to see a miracle called television.

My Mother

My mother was only 14 when she got married and had all three of us by the time she was twenty-two. She had only six years of schooling, but was gifted with a sound common sense and a zest for living. With extraordinary competence, she single-handedly managed the entire household, beautifully managing with my father's limited income.

I never saw her rest or waste time. When my father became a judge, she was required to attend some social functions. She learnt to play badminton, and picked up some English that helped during conversations. She had a fine sense of humour, and in her later years, would take rounds in my clinic to say hello to my patients. She had nurtured a big network of relatives which eventually faded after her death.

When I went to the UK, people could not believe that in India there was a system of arranged marriage, where the match was made by parents. My uncle got married to a young girl whom he had never seen. He was anxious to see her face during the marriage ceremony but because she was short, her head bowed and face covered with garlands, he could not. The marriage took place in the evening; there were no lights in the village and he saw her face only after daybreak. After marriage she stayed with her parents till she reached puberty. The couple had to wait three years to consummate their marriage. They had four children and a long, happy married life.

Today the incidence of divorce is on the rise despite long engagements during which the boy and girl get to know each other well. But do they really discover a lot about each other? The differences that crop up between the partners after a love marriage, are usually less tolerated, than if they do in an arranged marriage.

Early marriages were blessed with an advantage that children grew up when parents were still young. I have an elder brother and a younger sister. All of us had graduated while my mother was in her forties.

My mother came from a small village, Dombivli, about 30 miles from Bombay. My grandfather ran a dairy. There were many buffaloes near the house and the smell of their droppings was unpleasant. To go to the toilet, one had to cross the buffalo shed where the ground was slippery. I therefore preferred to use the open ground in isolated spots among the trees and bushes but there was also the constant fear of snakes and scorpions; I would carry a stick in my hand and avoided going alone. I clearly remember seeing big snakes on two occasions!

We were free to pluck mangoes from the trees behind the house. In the summer holidays our diet was mangoes for breakfast, lunch and dinner. My love for mangoes has not diminished a bit! I learnt that Pandit Jawaharlal Nehru, our former Prime Minister, regularly sent Alphonso mangoes as a gift to the Queen of England.

Sanitation continues to be a big problem in India. We have more cell phones than toilets! Rural women have to wait until dark to relieve themselves. They are exposed to the risk of snakes and scorpion bites. There are two Indias: one has shiny modern malls with branded goods, while the other lacks proper toilets. One of the big problems for tourists in India is the utter absence of clean public toilets.

The house in Dombivli was near the railway track. The sound of long-distance trains rushing across and local trains slowing down or speeding up gave me immense pleasure. The speeding trains, casting their powerful light, were a sight that thrilled me.

The names of railway lines had their own personality. GIP railway meant Great Indian Peninsula railway. MSM was Madras and Southern Maratha railway. BBCI was Bombay Baroda and Central India railway. Central, Western, Southern Railways and so on are prosaic and lack the charm of the earlier names.

We would sit on the railway bridge in the evening and see the trains thunder past beneath us. It was a great adventure to stand near the tracks and 'feel' the fast trains speed by, despite the elders' warning that the rush of air would blow us away.

The Deccan Queen between Bombay and Poona was a charming train. The colour was an elegant royal blue. We would wave at the passengers who would wave back. I longed to travel on the Deccan Queen.

The longing was fulfilled ten years later when I travelled from Bombay to Poona and that too, by the second class, when I was in medical college. I normally travelled by third class. Many people called it the Gandhi class because Mahatma Gandhi preferred it. We had toasts with tea in large white cups brought in a tray covered with a white towel that was served by uniformed waiters.

I felt great. I waved at people standing beside the tracks because I knew their feelings. As Poona approached, I became a little morose. I was the last to leave the compartment. I shot a last lingering look at the train before I exited the station.

I narrated the story to my friends several times. I thought they should share the unique experience of a Deccan Queen trip, that too in the second class! Years later, when I travelled by the bullet train in Japan, the experience did not match the feeling of that first trip by the Deccan Queen.

We were vegetarians. Milk was stressed upon as a healthy food for all ages. We kept a couple of buffaloes at home. My mother would go to the market to buy fodder and cotton seeds, milk the buffaloes and even supervise their deliveries! I tried my hand at milking a few times. It was a tricky job. They were kept in the small backyard overlooking the kitchen. A cowherd would come every day to take the buffaloes for grazing. My city cousins could not believe that buffaloes would calmly lumber across the house every morning to go out of the front door and return the same way in the evening.

The weather was cold, and the monsoons heavy, with breeding grounds for mosquitoes and flies rampant around the town. It was no wonder that diarrhoea, vomiting, malaria, pneumonia, TB and influenza were common. I lost some friends to common diseases. Three children in a neighbouring family died one morning because of influenza. A classmate attended school on Saturday, developed high fever in the evening and was dead the next day. A friend who visited me frequently had TB of the lungs. He often remained absent from school because of cough and fever. He continued to lose weight, stopped coming to meet us and one day I learnt that he had died. I missed him for some time. The phenomenon of the young dying was common.

Another friend died after two weeks of typhoid fever with bleeding from the intestines. When I now occasionally visit my hometown and walk along that street, I still remember his smiling face, curly hair, and his beautiful drawings. My father's clerk, a diabetic, passed away at the age of 50 and I remember someone remarking that he was fairly old! In the previous generation, many surgeons passed away in their sixties and now I am past eighty and still active. What a remarkable change in just a single generation!

During the holidays I would go to Kolhapur where my paternal grandparents lived. My grandfather would get up early in the morning. Though a leading advocate in the town, he did not miss his daily walk of five miles. He would go to bed early after a small meal. He led a very simple, active life and died in his 70s of pneumonia. Antibiotics had not arrived at that time.

Kolhapur was about seventy miles from Belgaum. The bus journey would take about five hours. It would stop at several places to pick up passengers on the way. In addition it would stop for tea or fruits. The roads were rough and narrow, but a bus was a great improvement over the bullock cart! I could not believe that one could be in Belgaum one morning and in Kolhapur the same evening! I relish these memories of my childhood sojourns. Now that highways have been built, it takes just over an hour to cover that distance. But I still have nostalgia for the old times when speed was not important because that made the journey interesting. There were no traffic lights, traffic jams, recorded music, TV or cell phones. Buses had open windows through which one could gaze at miles and miles of dense forest.

We would accompany our grandfather to buy crackers and sparklers for Diwali. When people saw my grandfather carrying the cane basket of crackers on his head, they were surprised that such a respected advocate did not hire a servant for this menial job. Someone asked, "Bapusaheb, why can't you employ a coolie?"

His answer: "Why should I shy away from doing some manual labour?"

My attitudes must have evolved through these experiences. Working with our hands and relying on oneself has a dignity. I enjoy the experience of preparing tea, washing clothes, polishing shoes and ironing. These become survival skills in old age!

Our neighbour in Kolhapur was a pious lady who spent many hours in prayers. She told me a story which I clearly remember. One day she saw a buffalo drowning in the marshy pool opposite our house. I was very disturbed imagining the terrible plight of the buffalo when the mud entered her mouth and nose. What agony that helpless animal must have suffered! Attempts to save her were futile. Her wails rent the air and the poor creature finally met a watery grave. What shocked me most was that our neighbour was narrating this episode with a smile. How was such a pious lady so insensitive to the suffering of the animal? I was seven years old at that time. My faith in religion and a man-made God probably began waning after hearing this story.

In 1942, we spent a month of the summer vacation in a village at Amba Ghat (*ghat* is a Marathi word for the winding mountain road) near Kolhapur with relatives and friends. The area belonged to scorpions and snakes, and we were the encroachers. On the very first day we saw a python moving sluggishly on the branch of a tree. I was eleven and the oldest among us was sixteen. We were instructed to carry sticks and strike the ground repeatedly, especially in areas where the grass could conceal snakes. We had heard stories of pythons swallowing animals after stifling them by winding around them. We were frightened, but a villager passing by assured us that though they were frequently seen, they were harmless. No wonder then that Indian gods are depicted in the company of snakes and wild animals!

We were about a dozen children and all of us would sleep on the floor in a big hall. I was scared of snakes slithering into our beds. I chose to sleep in the middle. Hernia belts were common in those days and were hung on a peg on the wall. The belt resembled a coiled cobra which only worsened my fears. There was a belief that if we recited a mantra—'Ram, Ram'—snakes would keep away. I recited it every night.

However, I would have enjoyed the holiday better if I'd had no anxiety over insects and reptiles. When I saw that the others were not as bothered, I was ashamed of my cowardice. Were the older children making a show of being brave? I did not know. I had heard of many stories of deaths from snake bites. An estimated 50,000 people die of snake bites in India every year even today. Anti-venom is now available in many health centres, but poor transport and ignorance become stumbling blocks in saving lives.

When I was about 10 or 12 years old, I had gone to Kolhapur and stayed in a landlord's huge house. The landlord was a kind, humane individual who treated everybody with courtesy unlike the typical rude and ruthless brutes depicted in the movies. One evening when I was in the veranda, his daughter sharply scolded a young servant girl. The landlord's mother, an old widow, told her granddaughter, "What makes you talk rudely with these poor unfortunate servants? This is a time for them to play and study but because of poverty they had to leave their homes to work for the rich. Thank god that you don't have the misfortune to be like them. Never hurt poor people."

That evening's episode is engraved in my mind. I have never been rude with those who are lower in status or class.

I fell ill on July 31, 1943. It was a Saturday morning. I came home with high fever and became so ill that I do not remember that I was shifted to the first floor along a very narrow staircase of the house. I had a relapse with the fever lasting for 47 days. The word antibiotic was not known. The only medicine was Coramine drops four times a day. I distinctly remember the small brown bottle and the bitter taste of the drops.

Cold sponging was done to control the high fever. No food was allowed, I was starved for fear of bleeding. However, I was encouraged to take plenty of glucose. Those round containers with their distinctive smell have been imprinted in my memory.

During my forty-seven days of illness, my blood was taken for investigation only once. I lost a lot of weight, felt extremely weak and took a long time to stand and walk, but I was alive.

When I went to Norway some years ago, I visited a graveyard. There were many tombstones in memory of children who had died of typhoid, pneumonia and other infections. The tragedy of premature death was common even in Europe not so long ago.

My Father

My father selected Belgaum to practise law. He had to struggle for a few years before he established his reputation for his competence and integrity and concern for poor clients. As a child during a visit to the barber's shop, I overheard customers discussing the lawyers in town.

My father's name was mentioned with respect because, in spite of his eminence, he accepted the briefs of poor clients and he charged reasonable fees. There was no way they knew that I was his son. Such experiences in childhood shape our character.

He was instrumental in establishing the first law college in Belgaum in North Karnataka. He was an excellent teacher and very popular with the students who frequently came to our house for advice. Mr. Nath Pai was one among them. Later on Pai became the President of the International Youth Federation in Geneva. Unfortunately he died when he was only 50 and India lost a respected parliamentarian, and a captivating orator who perhaps could have become a Prime Minister of India. (Pandit Jawaharlal Nehru admired Nath Pai and Atal Behari Vajpayee for their speeches in Parliament. He made it a point not to miss them. Forty years later, Atal Behari Vajpayee became Prime Minister of India).

I met Nath Pai's wife, Crystle, when I had gone to Vienna for a conference in the 1990s. She was very happy to hear that her husband had some connection with my family. Some of my father's students went on to become judges in the high court and Supreme Court.

When I was still in school I attended a case in a district court at Belgaum where a well-known attorney from Bombay, Bhulabhai Desai, had come to argue a case. My father was on the opposite side. The court was full of advocates and law students, and I had no place to stand. They were curious as to why this schoolboy in shorts was present in the court, but when I disclosed my identity I was treated with affection. My father was surprised to see me there, waved at me and smiled. I was thrilled. I still cherish that moment.

My father was my role model. I have clear memories of many incidents related to him. As a young boy of 12, I accompanied him by bus to a small town about 30 miles away from Belgaum. We went through a very narrow deserted street lined with houses and entered one through a partly opened door. There was a cobbled rectangular area in the centre with a basil or *tulsi* plant. The office was on the right side. My father bowed to an elderly gentleman sitting there with reverence and so did I. We sat on the floor on a thin white mattress. While the discussions were going on, the elderly gentleman was sipping tea, smoking *bidis* and spitting frequently in a bowl nearby. Opposite us, there was a shelf filled with law books and bottles of alcohol. I knew it was alcohol because there was a popular Marathi film showing around that time named *Brandichi Batli* (A bottle of brandy).

I wondered what was so great about this gentleman that my father respected him so much. My father was his polar opposite. He never smoked or touched alcohol. Soon after we left the house when we were in the street my father said, "Kishor, (*my nickname*) this gentleman is a great human being because he is very honest, prepares very well for every case, and argues on behalf of poor clients free of charge. He discourages his clients from going to the court when the case has no substance."

I now realise that the seeds of ethical behaviour were planted in my mind on such occasions.

Two years after India became independent, four advocates from the Bombay province were appointed as Sessions Court judges, a great honour at that time. My father was one among them. His first posting was at Karwar, a town on the western coast of India.

There were two bungalows as one entered the town, the one on top of the hill was for the collector and the one midway up the hill was the judge's bungalow. The place was fascinating, overlooking the sea, with a beautiful front garden and a dense jungle around it. Stories were heard of tigers visiting the hill and killing stray dogs.

There was no piped water, so the servants had to carry water up the hill on their shoulders. This sight would hurt my father. He would take his bath with only half a bucket of water and insisted on avoiding any wastage. A sessions court judge was a high ranking official and for him to be as considerate was uncommon. Upper class Indians often had a feudal attitude. When I was studying in school, I knew a junior engineer who would insist upon his servant following him carrying his hat to his house two miles away. He enjoyed the display of authority!

There had been two distinguished past occupants of our bungalow. One was Rabindranath Tagore's brother and the other Dennis Kincaid, an Englishman, who was born in India and unfortunately died in 1937 at a young age in a drowning accident near Karwar beach. He was in his mid-thirties and had already made a name as a good author. He had studied Maratha history with special reference to Shivaji, an outstanding visionary ruler of the 17th century.

(Shivaji is a remarkable figure in history of India. He had at a very early age a vision to rescue the country from the grip of oppressive rulers. The state of Maharashtra is blessed with mountain ranges. He found out problems of the harassed common man, collected people, especially farmers and those from the neglected strata of society, inspired them, built innumerable forts, established security along the coasts, developed guerrilla warfare, had a disciplined army which would move with a lightning speed on small statured horses, established a mint to have his own currency. He was fair to all communities, his army also had Muslims, and he spread his empire in large parts of India. He established a well

structured administration, even punished his own relatives for anti-social activities and thus established government for the people in a country which was feudal for centuries. No wonder he continues to be an inspiration for millions for over 350 years.)

My father was known for integrity. I wish to mention one episode. My maternal uncle who was a well-known writer in Marathi was operated for a recurrent dislocation of the knee cap when I was doing my residency in J. J. Hospital. He stayed at my father's bungalow because it was spacious enough for him to move around with the plastered limb. One day he filled his pen with ink from a bottle. My father told him that he should put the ink back in the bottle because it was to be used only for official purposes and not for personal work.

I was reminded of a story I had heard some years ago. A Chinese traveller Hiuen-Tsang visited India and was amazed to find peace, tranquility and respect for law in the country. He asked the emperor how this was achieved. He was told to see the Prime Minister Chanakya. The traveller went to him. He was busy reading with a lamp by his side. After working for some time he turned the lamp off, lighted another and only then started the interview. The visitor asked him for the reason behind his action.

"I was doing official work using an official lamp. Now your visit to me is a non-official one and so I will use my own lamp."

The visitor said, "You have answered all my questions by your action. When the prime minister of a country is so honest even in personal dealings, society will enjoy peace and prosperity."

Nine years later my father retired as a judge from Bombay Sessions Court. The day after he retired, as soon as my father entered the court, the peon came running to open the door of his car to pick up his attaché case. My father told him that he was no longer a judge and would carry his own papers as an advocate. My father left his official residence the day he retired. This however is not common in India where we see a sad spectacle of ministers, MPs and government officers keeping their residence for months and even years after retirement. In England, once he has relinquished office, the Prime Minister immediately moves from 10 Downing Street to his own private residence!

I remember the day my daughter's school-leaving examination results were declared. My father came hours before to my house and when the news came that she had stood first, we decided to celebrate the occasion with beer. He had never touched alcohol in his life, but he was very happy to join us in the toast with lemonade in a beer glass! Many a time, individuals who are austere and principled can be very rigid in their views. Fortunately for us, my father was very open and understanding.

He passed away in 1979, more than two decades after his retirement. There was reference to him in a specially convened meeting in the High Court. This was very unusual for a man who was never a judge of the Bombay High Court. The Chief Justice, Mr. B.N. Deshmukh, said in a packed court room, "The main quality of Mr. Shrikhande was that in spite of his growing age, he was as simple as a child. He was the purest possible man we could see around and if anything good was happening he would genuinely participate and reciprocate. Such a simple man was really difficult to find. He was extremely helpful to the juniors, and so far as his contribution to the Court is concerned, it was always possible for the Court to rely implicitly on any statement of fact and law made by Mr. Shrikhande. Temperamentally, he would not plead his case beyond the real worth that it contained. It was, therefore, safe to accept whatever he stated and that was another point for which he was liked equally by the Bar and the Bench. The greatness of Mr. Shrikhande is not confined to legal practice. Many people merely become successful lawyers and amass wealth.

In Bombay, after retiring from active practice, he decided to contribute something that could be useful. He was also an author. He studied the possibility of introducing Marathi as the medium of the judicial system in this state. Such a changeover always needs text books and Mr. Shrikhande wrote *The Mohammedan Law* in Marathi, and was the co-author of the Marathi book *Succession Act* with Mr Dabke. His manuscript on Torts was also complete and the finishing touches were being given when he passed away.

His interest was not confined to law alone. He was a lover of music and was the president of the Dadar–Matunga Music circle and president of the General Education Society, Dadar, which runs the Chhabildas High school. In this way, Mr. Shrikhande led a full life."

Raja Bhonsale, Advocate-General and President, Advocates' Association of Western India said:

"My Lords, on behalf of the members of the Bar, I wholeheartedly associate myself with the tribute paid by my Lord, the Chief Justice to late Shri N.S. Shrikhande who has passed away unexpectedly after a brief illness at the age of seventy-seven. In his death, the members of the Bar have lost a distinguished senior lawyer, a former Judge of the City Civil and Sessions Court, an eminent educationist, a connoisseur of Indian classical music and a warm-hearted human being."

He did not amass any property but what he left behind for us was invaluable. He was influenced by Mahatma Gandhi's spirit of simplicity and austerity. We received over 600 condolence letters and visits after his death. He remains my hero.

❑ ❑ ❑

Chapter 3

College Education

I completed my schooling in 1946 and decided to go to Pune, a city known for its excellent colleges, for higher studies.

Pune was 240 miles and ten hours away. As the train entered the station at Belgaum, my friends jumped in through the open windows (a common practice in those days) to 'catch' a comfortable seat for me. There was no reservation facility for the seats in the third class. They threw my luggage in through the window because there was a big crowd of people blocking the doors. Travel in India is always an adventure!

I assured them that I would keep in touch through letters. The guard blew the whistle, the train started. My friends must have seen my sad face through their tears, for they ran along with the moving train till the end of the platform. I looked through the window of the carriage to have a glimpse of the familiar sights which I would miss for six months. I was now alone for the first time in my life. Every minute, I was moving farther away from home.

Fergusson College had a big campus. I stayed in the hostel with students from different parts of India speaking different languages and with different food habits. Water was available at the turn of a tap, which was a novelty, but so was the sight of water being wasted.

One of the first things I did was to visit Jangali Maharaj road, which was also known as the eighty feet road. I wrote to my friends in Belgaum that what we had heard was true, there was no exaggeration; the road was indeed 80 feet wide. Things have now changed; a road that was considered wide then has now become a narrow one-way street. It is as if a towering personality had shrunk and become a pigmy.

This was my first exposure to cosmopolitan life. I felt quite shy and nervous. There were no fixed seats in the classroom; something that had given us a sense of security while at school. I did not open my mouth even once in the classroom, never went for any debates; took no part in sports. I now regret that I did not attend any lectures in diverse interesting topics for which Pune was well known.

I felt quite diffident in the presence of smartly-dressed boys and girls.

It was a notable event in my life when I bought my first fountain pen after a few months. My school friends came to see the imported Sheaffer fountain pen when I went back home during the holidays.

There were few girls and they always sat in the front row. I would admire the boys who could talk to them freely. I avoided the front rows to deflect questions from the professors. I never sat in the back rows, normally occupied by mischievous students who would shoot paper arrows at the girls or make noise during dull lectures. I felt neither intelligent, nor mischievous. I was amazed at the boldness displayed by girls playing tennis in shorts. I exercised regularly.

The winter was bitterly cold and I remember a few occasions when I took a cold water bath just to accustom my body to the extremes. I had read that too many comforts ruin the body's immunity to disease. I had brought my Raleigh cycle from Belgaum, but it was stolen from the cycle stand when I went to return a book in the library. I cannot describe how sad I felt. That was an era of bicycle thieves; now two-wheelers and cars are stolen.

Two important events took place during my stay in Pune. India became free on August 15, 1947, and I listened to Pandit Nehru give his famous 'Tryst With Destiny' speech.

I was one among a large crowd of people gathered at the iconic Shaniwar Wada, the palace of the Peshwas, when India won her freedom at the stroke of midnight.

The joy of the country becoming free was marred by communal riots during Partition. Mahatma Gandhi, who led the movement, was absent in Delhi because he was touring East Bengal, wiping the tears of hundreds and thousands who were victims of communal carnage.

Within a few months, on January 30, 1948, this messenger of peace was shot dead while going to a prayer meeting in New Delhi.

Bombay 1948

I passed inter-science and I had four career options: law, engineering, commerce, and medicine. Law was out of the question because of my speech defect. I did not like mathematics, physics, or commerce. I had realised how important a doctor's role was during my prolonged illness with typhoid fever in childhood. This must have aided my decision to be a doctor.

I came to Bombay to join Grant Medical College in 1948. I slept for a few nights in the open verandah of an apartment of a family friend in Girgaum, a crowded middle-class locality in the city. It was a common practice for the thousands who came to Bombay to stay with friends and relatives in their small apartments before finding a permanent residence. The concept of staying in hotels was non-existent.

Life in Bombay was hectic. The sight of trams on the roads was a new experience. Bombay with its local trains, double-decker buses, huge buildings and modern shops was a novel experience. Pune was full of bicycles and Bombay was full of imported cars. The city was cosmopolitan. I could even see some foreigners.

There were many cinema houses and people always seemed to be in a hurry. They wore clothes and wrist watches that made them look smart and modern. I would admire those who could catch a moving tram. I was worried that I would never adjust to life in Bombay. I remembered Belgaum where I had felt so secure. I did not miss Pune. Until I came to Bombay, I would sit on the floor for my meals so it was a change to eat at a table while in Bombay. I was introduced to non-vegetarian food without my knowledge by a close friend of mine who belonged to a strictly vegetarian sect. I was introduced to alcohol by my uncle in England who never drank. Life was interesting.

I used a telephone for the first time when I called my friend who was in the adjoining hostel. I talked loudly because I wanted my voice to be heard over the long distance! I still remember that moment.

I wanted to purchase a table fan for my hostel room, but it was not officially allowed. Belgaum weather was cool even in summer while Bombay would become hot and humid. The rector had even put up a notice that fans could be used by students only if they could produce their own electricity! Too many comforts are definitely not healthy for an individual's growth, but a fan during Bombay's heat was not exactly a luxury.

In the first two years, we had to dissect cadavers (unclaimed dead bodies) in the anatomy hall and experiment on frogs. The smell of dead shrunken bodies preserved in formalin and kept on marble tables for dissection still lingers on in my memory. We were given different parts for dissection—upper extremity, lower extremity, abdomen, head, etc. About eight students would work at a time on one body. There was plenty of light in the hall but the atmosphere was very depressing. Our bodies would become permeated with the obnoxious odour of the dissection hall and it would linger wherever we went. We had some outstanding teachers who taught us with passion. Nature's design of the human body amazed me.

The sight of the cadavers would trigger a chain of thoughts. Where was he born? How did he live? How did he die? They had died unheard, unsung, and unwept. What must have been the dreams of their parents? Did they go to school? How much did they suffer? Did anybody help them? What a tragedy to die with nobody to mourn for you. Very few students would think along this line but for me it was a natural, instinctive reaction.

Later in life, I occasionally saw patients dying with no one by their side. Death without a witness is a tragedy in itself. As I did dissections to demonstrate every structure shown in anatomy books, I felt grateful to those dead men and women whom I had never met. It is this sense of gratitude that is essential for us to become better individuals. Perhaps they must not have ever experienced this kind of concern while they were alive! The emotional aspect of human suffering is rarely touched upon in medical colleges.

I enjoyed the feel of the knife and I realised that I would be a surgeon. I was waiting for the time when I would move among patients as a qualified doctor. In those days medical students were always held in high esteem, awe and even envy.

In the past, medical education was very inexpensive. Now students have to pay lakhs of rupees for admission to a medical college. Medical training on the whole has now become an industry for profit. How can human values survive in this greedy society?

In physiology, we were studying muscular reflexes in unconscious frogs. When live frogs were caught by the laboratory assistants and the nerve fibres in their brains were cut to render them unconscious, it did not hurt me as much since the process involved marginal suffering. However, many years later I was shocked to read that frogs' legs, considered a delicacy, were taken off leaving the helpless frogs to die in agony. Man's capacity for cruelty is limitless.

I did badly during a part examination in the first year of medical college. I was told by the demonstrator, "You cannot utter a few sentences smoothly. How can you be a doctor? How can patients entrust their lives in your hands? Do not waste your father's money."

I was not discouraged by his comment, but I did feel sad. He saw my defects, but I knew my assets and that I would become a doctor. A surgeon should have a steady hand, a speaker, fluency of speech and a singer must have a melodious voice. Why should a speech defect prevent a keen medical student from becoming a surgeon?

Thirty years later, the same surgeon expressed a desire to observe me operate on a pancreatic tumour. He stood there for over five hours and showered me with praise, little knowing that in the past, he had thought me to be unfit to become a doctor! Later he sent his nephew to me for postgraduate studies in surgery. He is now a consultant surgeon abroad.

I wish I had known at that time that as a child Beethoven was told that he had no talent for music! I do not know the authenticity of this information but I enjoyed reading inspiring success stories of individuals who were regarded as average when they were young.

I was a slow reader but I read books on a variety of subjects including biography, philosophy, sociology and psychology. One book I particularly remember. It was *Uses and Abuses of Psychology* by Hans J. Eysenck, a German-born psychologist working in England. I came across his book by chance in 1955.

I think the book somehow put into my head that a good scholastic or academic career was no guarantee of success in life; the personality traits such as enthusiasm, hard work, empathy, concern, dedication, loyalty, capacity to take decisions, no fear of failure, open-mindedness, and inquisitiveness were more important. This notion became ingrained in my thinking and influenced my life.

There are gifted, intelligent students who do not make a mark in life. Reading adds wisdom to a man even if it does not necessarily improve his academic performance. I do not know how I happened to choose such interesting books that moulded my personality.

As medical students, we were constantly in contact with suffering and death. I particularly remember one instance when I was on casualty duty. A young man with stab wounds in his chest was wheeled in. He was dead, the body was still warm and his eyes open. Half an hour earlier he must not have had an inkling that he was so close to the end.

He was stabbed following an argument about the price of bananas. He had gone to see a film and while waiting for the bus he had felt like buying a banana from the fruit vendor.

Occasionally, we faced bigger calamities. A Royal Dutch Super Constellation plane crashed on a hill as the plane was approaching the runway at Mumbai airport. This was during the heavy rains in July 1949.

All the passengers perished in the tragedy. The dead bodies were brought to our hospital mortuary and placed in a row. Some were only a heap of flesh. The plane was carrying a group of journalists from the USA, one of whom was Hubert Knickerbocker. The incident brought home to me the fact that the very act of living was a risky affair.

For a few years after the incidents, when I travelled by plane, the visual memory of the victims of that crash would come to my mind. I felt comfortable only when the plane landed safely on the airstrip.

I was once on a flight from Chandigarh to Delhi. The weather was very stormy and both the plane and its passengers were shaking visibly. The captain of the flight knew me because I had operated on his brother. He readily agreed to allow me to enter the cockpit. He showed me how he was in complete command of the flight, manoeuvring the plane to avoid some bumpy air pockets like we avoid potholes on Indian roads while driving a car. His reassuring voice on the microphone while addressing the passengers was genuine. It made me feel very secure.

First Day in the OT

When I joined the surgical unit, I was eager to enter the operation theatre and observe the drama of surgery, the specialty which I had chosen in my career. This happened in 1950. The sister in the theatre gave us a cold, almost disdainful look. The residents working with big consultants displayed an air of superiority. The anaesthetist complained that we were in the way. In short we were not welcome in the operation theatre.

The surgeon, the main actor in the drama, was not polite to the young doctors and nurses. I could not see the operation clearly because I was short. I envied tall students.

I felt quite discouraged and on that day decided that I would treat everybody with courtesy when I became a surgeon. It was my regular practice when I became a surgeon to invite medical students to scrub and assist me in the operation. I know many students who became surgeons because of the exposure they had during their surgical term with me.

The first operation which I saw was a prostatectomy. The surgeon was full of arrogance; his behaviour was rough and he had a loud mouth. He removed the prostate gland and flung it aside! It was caught by an orderly who could have become a good fielder in cricket. Surgeons tend to be showmen!

The surgeon was shouting, "Quick, give me a sponge to pack the raw area, otherwise the patient will die of bleeding." The atmosphere in the operation theatre was quite tense and made us feel that disaster could only be averted by a competent surgeon with his skill and experience.

Nine years later in 1959, when I removed a prostate gland on my own, I saw that it was not a difficult operation.

A good teacher should make complicated things look simple and remove the psychological fear from the minds of students who wish to make a career in surgery.

I remember an eminent surgeon who was to perform an operation on the spine. He entered the operation theatre with a tin of cigarettes. He did not wear a mask. He was smoking during the operation, rolling the cigarette between his lips as deftly as he was working on the lumbar disc. He was addicted both to tobacco and to shouting. He would boast that ash was sterile and therefore cigarette smoking was not harmful in the theatre.

This was sixty years ago when there was no evidence to link tobacco with cancer, and the protocol for asepsis in the operation theatre was rudimentary. In the operation theatre, surgeons wore outside clothes covered with a sterile gown.

Masks were not common but caps were used perhaps out of habit. I have seen many hospitals where the operation theatres were used also as consulting rooms. I have been lucky to work in both eras and experience the mind-boggling changes in surgical procedures and in medicine. I have had an exceptional journey with experiences worth many lifetimes in just one.

Why I Became a Surgeon

When I was a student, a surgical career had adventure, prestige and even glamour. Many changed their minds when they came into the surgical wards and saw the stresses in a surgeon's life. I, however, found it attractive.

I was doing a casualty term in 1950 when a young man came in with a long lacerated wound following a bicycle accident. I thought it was an opportunity for me to test my surgical skill, but the CMO (Chief Medical Officer) who was only four years older than I was, thought that I was too raw for the job. I assured him that if I experienced any difficulty, I would rely on him to guide me.

That was enough to boost his ego. I took an hour and a half to stitch the wound and felt very thrilled that I could do what I wanted to do. It was like an artist who draws what is in his or her mind or a singer whose performance matches his or her desire. The orderly who assisted me commented, "I have been working here for 20 years, but I have never seen such a neat job. You will be a good surgeon one day."

I was thrilled because one more person apart from me felt that I had the potential to be a good surgeon.

❑ ❑ ❑

Chapter 4

Training in Surgery

I began my surgical career on January 1, 1954. I put on a white apron with a stethoscope in my pocket. As I walked to the hospital building, I decided that I would try to improve in some way every day of my life and be a good surgeon. I had no dreams of becoming a well-known surgeon.

When I realised that working with both hands would be an asset, I started brushing my teeth, shaving, putting on clothes, using scissors, and even writing, with my left hand.

I soon saw that ambidexterity made some steps easy during surgery. I was experiencing a new awareness of what my left hand could do. Some felt I was crazy!

I still recall my first operation. I was lucky to get an opportunity to operate independently on a patient with a hydrocele. *(Hydrocele is a collection of fluid around the testes, a common problem in India but very uncommon in the Western world.)*

The senior anaesthetist was very helpful with the novice surgeon. It was very exciting to see and feel the skin and the deeper layers separating with the swipe of my scalpel.

I enjoyed the experience and felt elated when I heard the nurse who had assisted me tell the matron that though I took time, the operation was so neatly done that it looked simple. I have heard similar comments many times in my career but the first one was special, which I will never forget.

When I was a junior, writing notes, doing dressings, starting IV glucose/saline, attending OPD, emergencies, preparing operation theatre lists and assisting in operations was a taxing routine with 40 indoor patients.

As senior surgical residents, we were allowed to do small operations, but any operation requiring general anaesthesia could be done only when a consultant surgeon was present in the operation theatre. This regulation was necessary because in the absence of a qualified surgeon, the hospital would be held responsible for negligence in case of a mishap. We were keen to do more and more operative work and grumbled that we had no chance. (The word commonly used is 'cutting' experience. I told my residents that surgeons operate, they do not cut! Personally, I never used that term.)

I was confident that I had the skills to do standard operations like hernia and hydrocele independently. At that time, I came across a book written by an Australian general surgeon on how to perform some standard operations under local anaesthesia. Serious complications like death were extremely rare under local anaesthesia with proper precautions. I realised that I had a window of opportunity to try this method and pursue my dream.

The technique was simple. The patient is given a sedative so that he is half asleep. The ears are plugged with cotton wool, and eyes covered with pads before taking the patient to the operation theatre. He does not see the masked men, bright lights, and instrument trolleys with knives and scissors. The part to be operated is made numb by giving a local injection of anaesthetic similar to the dentist making a small area in the mouth numb while working on the tooth. All are expected to speak softly and the surgeons have to be gentle with their hands. The operation takes time, but afterwards the patient has no vomiting and can pass urine without any difficulty. This method requires the full cooperation of the anaesthetist as well as the operation theatre staff. The presence of an anaesthetist is essential because in the rare event that something goes wrong, he is available for resuscitation.

I benefited immensely by this technique. I could even do many operations independently without a post-graduate degree. The junior consultant saw my operative skill and gave me opportunities to perform independent operations.

Three years later, when I was working in England, a patient admitted for a heart attack had a bout of severe cough, and the hernia in the groin suddenly became large and could not be reduced. General anaesthesia was out of the question, but I could do the operation under local anaesthesia and the patient survived. The next day my chief complimented me. The technique was known but very few practised it since it was time consuming and not easy.

As my confidence in performing independent operations grew and my consultant's trust in me increased, I also started operating on patients under general anaesthesia.

Volkmann's Contracture

In 1955, a young boy was admitted with a deformed forearm. It was the result of a tight plaster following a fracture. He had complained of pain following the plaster, but it had been ignored. The obstruction to the blood flow was not severe enough to cause gangrene, but was sufficient to destroy his muscles.

Believe a patient who complains of pain in a plastered limb—the golden fundamental rule taught in surgical training.

He was the eldest son and the poor family was waiting for him to complete his schooling and to take up a job. One mistake due to negligence had upset the plans. He required multiple operations and prolonged hospitalisation. This was very depressing and his family living in a distant town felt helpless and sad. I thought this boy should attend school during his prolonged stay in the hospital. Luckily the David Hume school was right next to the hospital and the patient was willing to study. The principal was surprised and happy to meet a doctor taking so much interest in a patient. The dean of the hospital would not give permission for the boy to leave the premises because of the hospital rules. I insisted and wrote a letter saying that I would take the responsibility if anything went wrong. As a result, for the first time in the 108-year history of Grant Medical College and J. J. Hospital, permission was granted to an in-patient to leave the hospital premises to attend school. The school did not charge any fees.

I have noted that when our concern is genuine, even reluctant people restricted by bureaucratic rules, do soften. The boy wrote to me many years later—*'I was a patient in Ward 24 where you were training in surgery. You took interest in a poor helpless person like me, in a large city like Bombay where I did not know anyone. You arranged for my education in a school and that changed our fortunes. I got a job in a cooperative bank. I have built a small house, raised a family and my children are going to school.'*

I was pleasantly surprised to meet this patient 20 years later when I went to Dhule, a district that is 500 km from Mumbai. He was working as an officer in a cooperative bank. His hand was still deformed, but he could manage his duties.

When I went to his house for tea, there was a large crowd of people waiting to see me. There were expressions of awe, gratitude, and tears in their eyes. I lived in a time when doctors were considered gods. Such experiences have enriched my life.

Life is a struggle for existence for millions in India who stay in slums and sleep on footpaths, work in subhuman conditions, to earn small amount of money which sustains their families living hundreds of miles away. They are doing productive work which is admired by many visitors from abroad, who came regularly to study life in the slums.

The awareness of their economic hardships and empathy for patients is vital in a doctor, but it is neither taught in medical colleges nor discussed in medical conferences. It was an era of complications and deaths after surgery. The patients who came to the teaching hospitals were poor and illiterate. A one-line consent was enough to proceed with the operation. Those who could not sign had to give a thumb impression!

Operations carried risk of infection and death. I had to convince patients about the dangerous consequences of refusing emergency life-saving operations. I used simple diagrams to gain the patients' confidence and most would agree for surgery. The family members of a youth admitted with acute appendicitis did not want surgery because in his earlier attack they believed that he had been cured with injections and saline.

"If he was cured, why did he get another attack?" was my question to which they had no answer. They agreed for surgery after my explanation, but the illiterate relatives imposed three conditions for giving the consent: the patient must not die, he must not suffer from intolerable agonies and he should not suffer from the same problem again! The normal approach was to take the refusal for the operation in writing from the patient. I did not view the patient's ignorance as an opportunity to avoid responsibilities and risk.

My colleague felt that we should not shoulder the responsibility of carrying on with an operation since the relatives appeared rather hostile! If they refused operations, it was their problem.

I however agreed to their conditions. I removed the gangrenous appendix and when the crowd waiting outside the theatre saw that the patient was alive, they distributed sweets. They were not interested in seeing the inflammed, swollen appendix! On the third day the patient's mother approached me with a request to examine her other son who had abdominal pain and said that if I so desired, I could remove his appendix!

Shirking responsibility is opting for security, but also an invitation to failure. Life is full of uncertainties and opportunities. I became aware of my abilities to comfort and convince the patients about the safety of operations, and as a result, I could get a lot of operative experience as compared to many of my colleagues. It was a wonderful era of excellent patient–doctor relationships with full autonomy given to doctors. They were accountable only to their conscience.

In the monsoon of 1956, Bombay experienced very heavy rains. A young girl in her twenties went to the terrace of her building to check the source of the water leaking into her flat, fell and landed on the shoulders of a young man who was walking on the footpath below. Unfortunately for him, but fortunately for her, he was there at that moment. She survived miraculously with a few bruises, but the young man sustained multiple fractures.

They were admitted in adjoining wards. She was screaming and grumbling and it was difficult to control her violent and irrational behaviour. In contrast, the young man was a picture of patience. He was very appreciative of our efforts and grateful to God and destiny that he had not died. The next day I took the girl to meet the victim of her fall who had accepted his injuries with such a stoic attitude.

It took several months of operations, immobilisation, pain and physiotherapy for the man to recover.

There are two types of people in this world—those who are grateful and those who are not. The former are a part of the solution while the latter are invariably a part of the problem. Ungrateful, self-centred individuals tend to be unhappy.

❑ ❑ ❑

Chapter 5

Departure for the UK

I couldn't sleep well on the night of September 8, 1957. In a few hours I would be leaving India to pursue my dream of obtaining a Fellowship of the Royal College of Surgeons (F.R.C.S.) in the United Kingdom and becoming a qualified surgeon.

I had completed three years of training as a surgical resident in Bombay, and the time had come to pursue my dream. Not many doctors went abroad at that time and air travel was rare. I booked myself on Lloyd's Triestino ASIA liner.

The era of readymade clothes had not arrived, and it was a time-consuming task to select material and get clothes stitched. Going to the travel agent, buying books, and writing letters to friends kept me so busy that there was no time to imagine the true impact of my decision. The day I was to leave, I woke up early and took my parents' blessings, all the while feeling uncomfortable in a suit, an outfit I hardly wore. As our car made its way to the docks, I looked hard at everything I passed as if to savour and seal them in my memory forever. Nervousness and fear seized me; it would be a while before I would see those scenes again. I experienced queasiness on the streets of Bombay, before the actual sea voyage began!

Sixty-eight of my friends and relatives actually entered the fully air-conditioned ship and examined the cabin in which I was going to live for the next two weeks. This was possible because one of my friends was a police officer, and security checks were almost absent in India then. Good connections, not necessarily important ones, make life simple. Today, every time I go abroad and pass through the increasing security checks at the airport, I remember the happy days gone by.

When the time for departure finally came, my friends and family left and I stood near the railings on the deck. The ship's horn sounded, the band started playing music, and I felt and saw us moving away from the docks. I could not stop the tears flowing from my eyes. One friend shouted, "Do not come back unless you get your F.R.C.S.!" I stood on that deck until the Indian shore had disappeared from my sight, with the sense that I had taken an irretrievable step.

Our first stop was Karachi. I was not an extravagant or bold individual. A few passengers went to see the town and came back in the evening with an air of bravado. A man approached me with a wad of Pakistani currency which he wanted to exchange for a few Indian rupees. I felt happy that our currency was more valuable than theirs!

Our next stop was Aden, where I visited a friend's home. We went by car and for the first time I saw the simple but wonderful innovation called 'cat's eyes', the reflective road markers. Some fellow-travellers purchased cameras but realised that they were fakes. The learning process had already begun!

We entered the Suez Canal, and I was wonder-struck by the engineering feat of joining two seas by creating an artificial canal. At Port Said, there was another halt. Many went to see the pyramids and belly-dancers, but I was constantly aware that I had no extra pounds to spare. (The same pyramids, that I missed back in 1957, I saw on my Egypt trip of 2006.)

Our next stop was Naples, my first exposure to a European country. We were looked at with curiosity. We appeared as different to them as they appeared to us. It was the first time I saw a television show in a restaurant by standing on the street, and the surprise and wonder in my expression as I gazed upon it drew attention from some of the locals.

Almost ten years later, I visited a village in Hyderabad for the inauguration of a family planning centre. There was only one chair in the hall for me as the chief guest, and outside was a big crowd peering in. I was curious to know why the crowd had assembled, since doctors couldn't possibly warrant the kind of attention reserved only for cricketers, actors, or politicians. I was told that the day before, the villagers had seen electricity for the first time in their lives. They still couldn't believe that one could light a bulb hanging high up on the ceiling by simply pressing a button. The expression on their faces reminded me of my own experience back in Naples.

I was aware that I was getting further away from my country with every passing moment. I felt restless at the thought of whether I had done the right thing in pursuing my higher education in England. I felt so small when I remembered revolutionaries like Madanlal Dhingra, who went to the gallows in England with a smiling face, Veer Savarkar, who plunged into the Mediterranean Sea near Marseilles and tried to escape into France while being transported by the British, and Vasudev Balwant Phadke, who died in an Aden prison.

Our generation was influenced by the patriotism and courage shown by these revolutionaries.

When the ship stopped at Naples, a waiter told us how anxious he was to meet his wife after a lapse of two months. After an overnight stay in Naples, our ship reached Genoa, the final destination. Again, the same waiter told us that he was very anxious to meet his wife waiting for him in Genoa. We laughed, remembering the saying that a sailor often has a wife in every port! From Genoa we took a train to Paris. Three things struck me:

I could not understand any of the European languages.

The train was very fast.

Beer was cheaper than water!

In Paris, we changed stations and then reached Calais. The boat for England was waiting for us. I suddenly felt at home when I heard the familiar English language and expressions. Soon we saw the white cliffs of Dover. The weather, however was grey and gloomy, and added to my increasing nervousness. I had finally arrived on English soil. It was the evening of September 23, 1957, and the moment I had been dreaming of was now a reality.

London: First Impressions

"Are you a doctor?", I was asked at the immigration.

"Yes."

"Welcome, sir."

White men who had previously ruled us, addressing us as 'sir' was an experience beyond belief. It was a good beginning to my stay in the United Kingdom. It was a time when doctors were encouraged to enter England. However, during my 1971 visit, I was grilled at the immigration precisely because I was a doctor.

"Have you come here to settle down?"

"No."

"How do we know that you will go back?"

"Ten years ago when I had a good job in the UK and the hospital wanted me to settle here, I took the risk of returning to India where I knew I would have a difficult time starting my career as a surgeon. I am doing well now and even if you want me to settle down here, I will not."

The previously stiff officer smiled, welcomed me and said, "We have to ask these questions owing to some unpleasant experiences with illegal immigrants."

On that first day in 1957, I took a train from Dover to King's Cross. The passengers did not look like the Englishmen who ruled us. They talked in English which was different from the language I had heard in English films.

I was an avid Sherlock Holmes fan, and the first thing I did the next morning was to visit 221 Baker Street. For long, I had imagined meeting a tall man with a bent back, a pipe in his mouth, hands stained with chemicals and ink, a prominent lower jaw giving the face a determined look, sharp eyes filled with intense concentration; a man indifferent to the life surrounding him. And with him would be Dr. Watson, trained in the art of observation by his teacher in Edinburgh, a city I was going to visit shortly. The charm of reading Sherlock Holmes continues. No wonder that Sir Arthur Conan Doyle had to bring him back after his disappearance in a deep ravine in Europe!

I was surprised to experience cleanliness, courtesy, discipline, footpaths devoid of hawkers, cars moving without honking, nice parks, respect for old people, and concern for children and the handicapped. I was reminded of the contrasting conditions in India at every step. Even fifty years later, Indians' conduct in public life is often depressing to see.

Edinburgh

I took a train from London to Edinburgh. I marvelled at the difference in the scenario: unoccupied seats, noiseless railway platforms, clear instructions for passengers, and absolute cleanliness. There were no crowds to give friends and relatives a send-off, no garlands for departing passengers and no people running alongside moving trains to bid adieu. The English countryside was very pleasant. I saw small towns and villages, healthy, well-fed cows grazing along the lush green fields, and general calm and greenery throughout my journey.

However I missed the *batata vada* (a savoury potato snack very popular in India), and hot tea and coffee served during train journeys back home. I reached Edinburgh on September 29, 1957, a Sunday evening.

My college friend, who had arranged for my stay, came to pick me up at Waverly station. The only thing that appeared familiar to me was the typical English taxi, made familiar through the movies. As we drove away from the station, I found a city of deserted streets, old buildings, and an overcast gloomy sky above.

My impression of Edinburgh was based on pictures of the famous Princes Street on greeting cards. The house was at 6 Lauriston Garden Road, a cobbled street. (I remembered Lauriston Gardens from a Sherlock Holmes story.) We opened a creaking door at the entrance and went up a narrow winding staircase, with my friend lugging my suitcase. I had an eerie feeling of suspense and intrigue, and was reminded of Alfred Hitchcock's *Psycho* which I had seen before leaving Bombay.

An old lady opened the door. The room where I was going to spend a few days was so small that the narrow bed almost totally filled it. My friend left after half an hour, having instructed me where to meet him the next day. The landlady asked me whether I would like to eat something. It was only 6.30 in the evening and I presumed that she was offering me tea. In India offering tea to guests is a custom whatever the time. As I had already had tea in the train, I declined the offer. I was looking forward to having my dinner later. I unpacked my suitcase and settled down in the room.

Later, I went to the dining room to find it silent and empty. The landlady had retired for the night. I was taken aback. In India guests were never allowed to go to bed without a meal. I did not know what to do.

There was a disturbing silence around me—no movements inside the house, no sounds coming through the closed windows, and not a leaf moving—but there was a raging storm within me. The comforting sounds of car honking, the conversations across buildings and the barking of stray dogs were missing. Whether all the travelling was worth the trouble, I wondered.

It was now too late for second thoughts. I decided that I would not allow the feeling of depression to touch me. The only remedy was to work, work, and work. I knew my family was waiting for me to return after my training as a surgeon. I remembered my friend shouting from the docks as the steamer had started to move, '*Do not come back without your F.R.C.S.*' I had given him a thumbs-up indicating that I had accepted the challenge. I arranged the books, and started studying.

I was alone, far away from anyone I knew. I opened the books before going to sleep in that lifeless room. There is a saying in ancient Sanskrit literature that unless you cross the seas, your education is incomplete. I went to sleep on an empty stomach for the first time in my life. However, that night in Edinburgh was not wasted! I did not break down, my resolve to work hard was strengthened, and I could sleep. I had made a good start.

First Day in Edinburgh

As I entered the college building known as the Surgeon's Hall the next day, a tall elderly Englishman with grey hair entered the building and held the entrance door open for a cleaning lady to get in. I was the next to enter. He accepted my thanks with a smile and a graceful nod of the head.

It was only later that I discovered that he was the Dean of the Institute and an internationally-renowned pathologist who had been knighted by the Queen. Apparently politeness was ingrained in the English. That the head of an institute could be so courteous towards a cleaning lady was incomprehensible to me. I knew such a thing would rarely happen in India.

The Surgeon's Hall was full of students; a majority of them from outside the UK. The common topics of conversation were the tough exams, the scores of failed attempts, the tasteless food, the depressing darkness during the day, the biting cold, and the longing for home.

I met two of my college friends from Bombay. The first comment was, "So you too have come here to join the mess we are in. We have failed three times and intend to write to our friends in India that they should not come here."

This was a cold welcome on that grey morning. My reply was prompt, "I have come here because someone must pass at the first attempt." In this discouraging environment, I had to constantly believe in my successful performance.

We were sitting in the lecture hall waiting for the professor. A man came in and we thought he was our professor. All the Indian students, including me, stood up only to realise that he was an attendant who had come to clean the board! For us, anyone white was superior. Indian advertisements show men and women with fair complexions. When a child is born, invariably two questions are asked, 'Boy or girl? Fair or dark?'

When I left the Surgeon's Hall in the evening, at the bus stop, I saw a boy and a girl kissing passionately, oblivious to the world around them. They looked so natural, I envied them. It was not a culture shock for me. What upset me more was the sight of a drunken girl lying on the floor at a hospital party some months later. I believe that such scenes are now common in India too.

After a few days, I shifted to another place. I was happy to share a big room with a student from my medical college in Bombay. The oppressive feeling of loneliness was gone.

I preferred to walk the two miles to reach the Surgeon's Hall in the cold wind, an unpleasant but stimulating experience. I had to wear so many layers of clothing that I perhaps resembled an Eskimo.

I had occasionally taken cold baths in the bitter winter during my hostel days in Pune. Doing something different from the usual increases determination and confidence.

I saved three shillings on the bus fare and used the money to turn on the gas heater in the bedroom while reading at night. Central heating was not available. The bed was warmed by hot water bags. I had to curl up in bed to maintain warmth; even the slightest movement and contact with the icy mattress was a terrible experience. It was after a few days that I realised my mistake in choosing a big room for a winter stay.

We envied our married colleagues, but later I learnt that most of the women, who were only housewives, were stressed and unhappy. They were missing the warm weather and the luxury of servants in India. My decision to come to England while still a bachelor, was the right one.

My new life was shaken up by the murders in the Edinburgh-Glasgow region. A young girl of sixteen who went for a dance never came back. Her dead body was found in a garden. Within a few days, a man, his wife and son were murdered in a house near Glasgow.

A girl was assaulted in broad daylight in a park near our home, and the sensational news in the press made me hesitant to walk on the deserted streets, especially in the dark (in winter, it would get dark by noon). The image of a beautiful Edinburgh that I had imagined from pictures of the famous Princes Street/gardens, got blurred. Such things do happen all over the world, but with these sporadic incidents, my expectations of a safe life in the UK took a beating.

First Christmas

A few months later, the landlady invited me for my first Christmas party. One Indian girl from East Africa and I were the only two foreigners among a gathering of about ten other guests. She commented, "We were very happy when you were ruling us. Our leaders have made all the mess." Many in England believed that the British had gone to India to civilise a backward race. I felt very embarrassed and kept quiet. However, when the landlady asked me my opinion, I said, "How can any country rule another in the kingdom of God?"

I knew that my landlady and the guests were a church-going group and here was my chance to deflate the uncomfortable situation. She came and hugged me, telling the group that she had always felt that the Indian doctor was very intelligent, and a well-read man. I had not told her that I did not believe in God created by man. The general belief in those days was that India would not survive, democracy would not take root, there would be civil war, scarcity of food, and the country would disintegrate. The British rule brought many good things to India. Indian civilisation had its glorious chapter, but we had become feudal and insensitive in our attitudes. Undoubtedly, Western civilisation introduced us to the concepts of freedom, equality, and rule of law, but it also exploited and looted our wealth. The rulers did not come to India just to reform us.

The fellowship course was over in the last week of December. The winter was severe; I had no job and was left with only ten pounds. I remembered a friend who had said that he could arrange a job in his hospital for me because many doctors had gone on vacation. It was a source of great relief to enter a centrally-heated place after three months of the bitter Edinburgh cold. The food was free, I could move about with a light layer of clothing and my only expenses were for a haircut and airmail postage to India once a month.

The Christmas mood was in full swing by this time. I did not take any part in the fun and festivities because I was shy. I did not know how to dance; I did not relish wine and did not know anyone. However, I spent a fruitful one month in the children's hospital where I learnt a very important lesson that children were not to be treated as small adults. There is a very small margin for making errors; a small amount of blood loss can prove fatal and that children should be handled like delicate flowers.

My chief, Andrew Laird, was a man of few words. When I went to say goodbye to him on the last day, he surprised me by inviting me for lunch. I had never visited such an exclusive restaurant during my stay in the UK. As soon as I entered the foyer, someone promptly helped me to remove my overcoat. The waiters were better dressed than I was. When the chief asked for my choice of wine, I did not feel shy to tell him that I had not tasted wine and that he should choose for me. The waiter came with a lighted candle, poured a small amount of wine in a glass. My chief rolled it near his nose before taking a sip. He approved with a nod and then our glasses were filled with wine. I was reminded of scenes in Hollywood films and felt completely out of my depth. I quietly assessed the bill which was more than my expenses for two weeks. After that he took me home. They lived on top of a hill and his wife was waiting for us at the entrance.

"Are you the doctor from Bombay? My husband speaks so highly about you that I was keen to meet you."

The couple took me around the beautiful countryside for two hours. In the evening, he introduced me to his children and later, he and his wife dropped me back to the hospital at night. It was an uncommonly warm gesture from a consultant who was known to be a reserved individual and I am delighted to recall that our association was a turning point in my life. After my examination, he offered me the post of a senior registrar and I kept in touch with him. His recommendation helped me to get a senior post after six months that transformed me into a confident surgeon capable of performing major operations independently.

There is an interesting little recollection linked to this story. Twenty years later, one of my patients was to go to Glasgow on deputation for his office work. I suddenly remembered Andrew Laird and sent him a letter and a small gift. Laird had retired many years earlier and though my patient could not meet him, he succeeded in sending the parcel. This letter arrived a few weeks later.

31st July 1980

Dear Mr. Pednekar

Your letter about the unforgettable Dr. V. N. Shrikhande has come as a most pleasant surprise and it has given me a great uplift to think that he remembers me in this way. Very often I think of him, as in discussing past assistants with other surgical colleagues. I instance him as being the most talented of the residents and registrars who came to my unit at Royal Hospital for Sick Children in Glasgow.

I only had his help for one month, a matter of great regret to me, but in that time he picked up every detail in operative surgery which I tried to impart to him. His operative skill was outstanding and it demonstrated what I have just written: that he had not missed a detail of what I had shown him.

I am somewhat overwhelmed by Dr. Shrikhande's kindness in sending me a present and I am grateful to you for your efforts to contact me. I live hundred miles away from Glasgow to which I make very infrequent visits.

Perhaps you will be good enough to give me his address. You can send him this letter, as it will show that I have not forgotten him nor has my wife. You can inform him, in the meantime, that I am fit and well and enjoying life to full.

With many thanks and with highest regards,

Andrew Laird

Three years later when I visited the UK, I spent a weekend with Mr and Mrs Laird at their beautiful home. That evening I went with him to the village pub and met his friends. He introduced me by telling them how his assessment about me becoming an outstanding surgeon had been proved right. He was proud of me and I was honoured and touched beyond words.

At the entrance of the pub was a nice quotation:

'This bar is dedicated to those excellent gentlemen who make drinking a pleasure, who reach contentment before capacity and who whatever they drink can take it, hold it and still remain a Gentleman. We request our customers not to stand near the bar when it is in motion.'

Words cannot describe my elation during that visit. Even without much alcohol, I was enjoying this moving experience! Once again I was grateful to destiny. I had met Laird by chance, because I had no money left in my pocket in December 1958.

Few years later, when I started my work in India, a paediatrician met me. He had a case of a baby born with pyloric stenosis.

(Normally food passes from the stomach into the first part of small intestine (duodenum) through a valve called the pylorus. In pyloric stenosis the muscles are so thick that it prevents the stomach contents from entering the small intestine. The baby vomits after every feed; the vomiting is forceful and the infant is so hungry that it wants a feed again. It loses weight. During the operation the thick muscle is divided without opening the lumen. Patients recover quickly and feeds started a few hours after the operation are retained.)

Administering general anaesthesia to a debilitated baby is highly risky. Many babies have died because of anaesthetic complications and not from the operation. I had learnt during my one-month stint in Glasgow that these babies can be easily operated under local anaesthesia through a small incision. This was something new in India. I did the operation under local anaesthesia and the infant could be breast fed successfully after three hours. The paediatrician attended the operation to see something he had not seen before. A baby was saved because I had got the opportunity to work in a children's hospital abroad though only for a month. That child now would be a man celebrating his 50th birthday!

'Sometimes when I consider
What tremendous consequences
Come from little things
I am tempted to think
That there are no little things.'

— Bruce Barton

Saving a life was a wonderful achievement!

I passed my F.R.C.S. at the first attempt. I could now return to India any time. I was very happy, but more than that I was surprised because some teachers had made us believe that getting an F.R.C.S. qualification without at least one failure was possible only for a few talented students. My examiner was Sir John Bruce who was very pleased with the way I discussed a case of cancer of the rectum. I learnt that only two out of nine students passed on that day. Nobody had accused me of brilliance. Many times afterwards I would wake up with dreams that my results were wrong and I had actually failed.

When I walked to my room that February evening in 1959 in Edinburgh, I was alone and there was no one to share my joy or celebrate the occasion with. The streets were deserted and dark. Edinburgh was gloomy, but I was happy. The envelope which contained the result was my most precious possession. Cold winds were piercing my clothes, but I knew that I would spend the remainder of my stay in England in hospitals with central heating. My life was no longer filled with the terror of examinations and staying in cold rooms. I also realised another important fact of life. The joy of success lasts for a short time but the pain of failure lasts till you succeed. Three of my colleagues were not lucky and I could see their dejected faces when I met them the next day.

I took up a hospital job as a surgical registrar and decided to try for F.R.C.S. in London. The fear of failure was irrelevant and for the first time I gave an examination without any additional preparation or anxiety. Three months later I passed, an event that was nothing short of a miracle for me. I heard that the son of a well-known surgeon connected with the Royal College had failed for the third time. Had this happened in India, it would have been breaking news. I revelled in the extreme sense of fair play in daily living that I experienced in England.

In the evening, successful candidates were invited to meet the examiners. I shook hands with eminent surgeons whose names were familiar to me from my college days. That experience is engraved in my memory. The chief examiner was Prof. Charles Rob, the famous vascular surgeon of St. Mary's hospital in London, co-author of the book on operative surgery by Rob and Smith. He had a very impressive personality.

He asked me, "Where were you educated?"

"Grant Medical College, Bombay", I replied.

"Bombay Univeristy must have an excellent standard. You have done well!"

He was so impressed by my performance that he asked me to meet him if I was interested in further training. I do not know what would have happened had I agreed. As I savoured my success that night, I could not help remembering a teacher at my medical college in India who told me that a medical career would not suit me.

I boarded a train the next day to return to my hospital in Manchester. I stood near the open door as was my usual practice when the train departed from the station.

Even today I enjoy the scenes on a railway platform: people waving goodbye, hugging each other, wiping their tears and waving their handkerchiefs. I heard the whistle and as the train was about to leave, an Indian youth came running and boarded the train. I helped him with his baggage as he boarded the train. We were both surprised; we were friends from the same school in Belgaum and had met most unexpectedly in a distant land after a gap of sixteen years. There was so much to talk about during the three hours of travel that I did not realise that the train had reached Manchester. He showered me with gifts to celebrate the unexpected meeting of two friends in a London train.

My friend Damu (Damodar) came from a poor family in a small village. It was a practice in those days for poor children to visit people's homes, sing some hymns and in return receive food. This was not regarded as charity but as appreciation for the struggle they were going through to complete their education.

Damu was one such boy. And then one day he disappeared. Our next meeting was in a train departing a platform in London! His story was one of struggle and success. He went to Bombay in search of a job, worked as a coolie, slept on the footpaths and railway platforms, got a job as a labourer in docks, and one day joined the merchant navy. Being a very intelligent, hardworking man, he progressed and became an officer. He had gone all over the world (barring China) by ship. I was very happy with the way our destinies had taken us to unexpected achievements, but reunited us here all these years later. We parted company with a resolve to keep in touch which we did.

We met in Bombay on two occasions. He fell in love with a girl, married her and got a job in Canada. I could not attend his wedding. He built a house in Canada, sent me the photograph and invited me to spend my holidays at his home. However, life is unpredictable. One Christmas day, some years later, he was returning home after some shopping, when a big log of wood from a truck in front of him rolled down and killed my friend instantly. What a destiny!

His entire life, that was built on struggle, was over. When he finally had an opportunity to relax, everything had ended in the blink of an eye. The story of struggle and success had ended with tragedy.

An Indian doctor, whom I knew, drove 120 miles to meet me on a Saturday evening for dinner. His family friend in India was in search of a marriageable boy for their daughter. The girl was well-educated, and armed with an MA from a well-known university in India. The gentleman had brought her photograph. She looked nice. In most of the photographs the bridegroom-to-be looks handsome and the girl beautiful. If I consented, a bungalow, car, hospital, and a dowry of Rs. 2 lakh (which was negotiable) would be made available! I could settle down in England or America after marriage if I wanted. It almost appeared as though they wished to buy a son-in-law! I told him that my father, who married in 1926, had taken a dowry but returned the money after a few years. To accept a mistake and reform was a feature of my father's character. My friend understood what my answer was but nevertheless we remained friends. The dowry system is not dead. Education has become very expensive in India. In some families this money is recovered from the bride's family.

I was now looking for surgical posts to gain operative experience. I had several calls for interviews and had no doubt that with my qualification, my chances of getting selected were excellent wherever I went. I contacted one of my friends, Dr. P. M. Madhok from Grant Medical College, who was in England. He gave me some sound advice.

"If you have a plan to settle in England, go to a teaching hospital," he said. "If your plan is to return to India, work in a district hospital with a heavy load of work and if you want to have fun, dance, and go to parties, you should choose a hospital in seaside resort areas."

My choice was clear. There were 24 applicants for one job.

In the interview I was asked:

"What is your operative experience?"

"I have done standard operations such as appendix, obstructed hernias, intestinal perforations."

"But have you done major operations on stomach, gall bladder, kidney stones, thyroid etc.?"

"No."

"How is it that you have passed your F.R.C.S. exam and still not done major operations?"

"Experience in operative work is not a condition for passing F.R.C.S."

"Our hospital handles a lot of major operations. Will you be able to manage the work?"

"I will not fail you if given a chance."

The interview was over.

I knew I would not get the job.

I came out and stood near the office window where the interview candidates were paid railway fare and other allowances for the return journey. The standard practice was to invite the selected candidate, while the others were told, "Each one of you is qualified for the vacancy, but unfortunately there is only one post."

One name was announced. It was mine. It was surreal.

I was again asked, "Are you sure you will be able to handle the job?"

"Yes."

"Doctor, we have sixteen residents in the hospital. You have to manage them."

"I do not think it will be a challenge for me to manage people."

"Any more questions?"

"Will I be able to get major operative work? I am very keen to get operative experience."

The surgeon winked at me. "Please join us. We hope you will not complain about the heavy duties which will soon be your responsibility."

All through the months I worked there I wondered why I was selected. Several months later, I met the secretary as he was entering the hospital building. I summoned the courage to ask him how my selection was made.

He told me to accompany him to the office and showed me a letter of recommendation given by my chief in Glasgow. It read, "Though he worked with me for a short time, he was one of the best in the last twenty years. I hope he will join my unit as a senior surgical registrar after he finishes his post."

The other thing that helped the committee finalise the selection was my honesty. "You were the only candidate who was frank enough to admit that you had no experience of doing any major operations and that you wanted the post only to garner experience. We felt you were transparent and genuine."

I joined the hospital on June 12, 1959. It was a Friday. I took my luggage from the taxi, kept it in the foyer near the entrance and went to see my consultant in outpatient department. We had tea. What he told me next was like a shock treatment.

"There is a lady waiting for surgery to remove gall stones; operate on her tomorrow. I am going to London now and the Chief (head of our surgery department) is in Greece on a holiday. There will be no other surgeon in the hospital except you."

He winked at me and smiled.

"You wanted (operative) work and this is the best way to welcome you to the new job."

I had never done a gall bladder operation before but showed no anxiety and replied, "Of course, yes."

While leaving he took me aside and said, "Do what you want but do not cut the bile duct or clamp the artery supplying the liver. You know what happened to Sir Anthony." Sir Anthony Eden was Winston Churchill's son-in-law and the English foreign secretary and later the Prime Minister. He died of complications of gall bladder surgery which was performed by a leading surgeon in London.

(The bile duct is a duct that collects bile from the liver and transports it to the small intestine to help in the process of digestion of food. The duct is likely to get damaged during the operation, a most dreaded accident that every surgeon fears and faces at least once in his or her lifetime.)

I visited the ward and saw the patient whom I was going to operate on the next morning. She said, "I am so lucky to be operated by you tomorrow. I am told that you are a highly qualified surgeon and have gained a double fellowship at the first attempt. I am safe in your hands."

I did not display my anxiety. That night I went through the operative surgical book and visualised every step I was going to take the next morning. This was like an actor who goes through rehearsals before appearing on the stage. I was unable to sleep. A new hospital, not a single familiar face, a new operation theatre and a surgeon who had not done a single gall bladder operation. But the patient had faith in me and I held onto that.

I went to the operation theatre at 8 am and introduced myself to the staff. I had to play the role of a confident surgeon. What I felt once the operation was over was beyond words. The theatre staff was surprised when I told them that I had never done gall bladder surgery before. I was under tremendous stress, but the stress motivated me to do my best.

I knew I would do the operation without any complication. In every activity some risk is involved but one must decide where to draw a line before the danger zone. At a personal level I feel that if we do not take risks in life, we have to pay a heavy price in lost opportunities. Every opportunity has a shelf life. Nowadays surgical training is much better organised and a situation in which a novice is called upon to do major surgery, thankfully does not occur.

This episode took place 50 years ago. It was not the best way to learn, but the only one available for me. Had I told my chief that I would prefer to do the operation when someone was around, I would have made a wrong start. I knew that I would succeed.

My schedule was: five operation sessions a week, emergency every day, alternate weekends off. Fortunately for me, during the 1950s, the 48-hour week had not arrived. This experience drastically changed my surgical career for the better. Legislations have been made about working hours for resident surgeons abroad because tired doctors can make mistakes and harm patients. The other side of the coin is that frequent interruptions are not conducive for a doctor in training to appreciate the course of a disease.

A resident who sees the patient, attends the operation and takes care after the operation is more likely to develop better all-round perspective of the disease. I was trained in that era.

We were told that a young surgeon had to spend ten thousand hours before he could practice independently. The waiting period is long and restricted hours of work make it longer.

June 13, 1959 was thus a great turning point in my life. At the age of twenty-eight, I conducted my first gall bladder operation in a foreign country when no other surgeon was present in the hospital. I had seen only two gall bladder operations in India during my residency in the 1950's. One patient died of sepsis. Gall stone disease was not common and the operations were considered major. I remembered this patient at every important milestone in my professional career. I feel grateful to those patients who entrusted their lives in my hands and gave a meaning to my existence as a surgeon.

(When the bile duct is damaged bile leaks out and gets collected in the abdomen. Infection sets in with disastrous complications. The bile has to be drained out through the tubes to fight infection. The repair of the divided duct is a very complicated job. The duct is hardly ten mm in diameter and it has to be joined to a loop of intestine so that the bile will enter the intestines. Very few surgeons are trained to carry out this operation.)

Dr. Richard Catell of Lahey Clinic was a known authority on treating bile duct injuries. Winston Churchill invited him to operate in London but Catell preferred to do the operation in his own setup. Sir Anthony was flown to Lahey Clinic, Boston for his operation. A long-lasting cure was not possible, further operations followed, and he ultimately passed away following complications that set in later.

Dr. Richard Catell made a profound statement, "There are two groups of surgeons; those who have divided the bile duct and those who are going to divide it in future."

I have done more than 3500 gall bladder operations and divided the bile duct twice. The first time was thirty-four years after the first operation in 1959. Both cases were difficult. I was very cautious, but things did go wrong. Even the most experienced pilots can meet with fatal accidents. Not because they take chance or are careless. They have experience of facing difficult situations and coming through them successfully, but occasionally they fail. In my two cases, I recognised the accident on the operation table and could do a successful repair. The patients were informed about the accident after the surgery and their smooth post-operative recovery was a great relief for me.

I have taught my residents the wisdom of experienced surgeons. Complications are more common when the surgeon is very confident and the operation appears simple. Car accidents are common when the driver is confident, the car powerful and road superb. It is easy to be complacent and we need to guard against this. In short, bile duct injuries can occur both in the hands of inexperienced and experienced surgeons, but in different situations. No operation is without risk.

After the operation on the first day in England, I went to the male ward. The sister-in-charge of the ward was busy writing the patients' register. I introduced myself to her. With only a momentary glance at me, she asked me to wait. In India, the sisters instantly get up from their chair when the surgeon enters the ward. This was a new experience for me.

After some time she got up and shook hands with me, called a nurse and gave me detailed information about every patient in the ward. I didn't have to ask any questions while we went around the ward of 20 patients. I admired her competence and authority and told her so when we had tea after the round.

"Sister, I have learnt a lot from you. We have made a good start and I am sure we will get along well."

Though at first appearance she seemed a serious person, I found her to be a sensitive and kind individual with a subtle sense of humour—typical of the English. We got along extremely well. In spite of the heavy workload, I was lucky that the indoor patients were efficiently managed.

I will never forget the story she told me of a flamboyant surgeon with whom she had worked as an operation theatre sister. He was in the habit of shouting and losing his temper. On one occasion, he threw an instrument on the floor. She removed her gloves, stood away from the operation table and looked directly into the surgeon's eyes. There was complete silence in the theatre and the tension mounted.

Ultimately, the surgeon realised that what he had done was wrong. He apologised to her but while putting the gloves back on, she said in a clear voice, "This is the last time you have behaved like this. If you repeat such tantrums, I will leave the theatre and you will have to answer the consequences." He never lost his temper again.

One night I had a phone call from the night sister that a patient with abdominal pain had been admitted to the emergency ward. My resident had instructions to keep him under observation but according to the night sister, the patient had a perforation of the ulcer. She requested me not to mention that she had called me.

I went to the ward, confirmed the sister's diagnosis and saved the patient's life with an emergency operation. This was not an isolated example. Experienced non-medical staff can be very reliable in their assessment and even guidance. I have learnt plastering from ward boys in orthopaedic wards.

Nurses can make a doctor's life miserable. A recently appointed casualty medical officer scolded the on-duty night shift nurse, in everyone's presence, when she told that a patient with a small cut on the head had been sent home after putting in three sutures and was told to report later in the day.

"Are you a doctor? Do you know that a head injury can be serious and the patients need close observation?"

He did not know that sisters with experience were given night duties and were to be trusted for their decisions. She felt slighted. The casualty department staff knew how to teach the arrogant novice a lesson. There was a continuous stream of patients going to the casualty for small problems and the new doctor now started getting night calls for every case. He soon realised his mistake and offered his apologies. Common sense demands that a newcomer should not try to change an established system as soon as he takes charge.

A frail old lady had a fall when she was shopping. She had some pain in her hip but could walk up to the ambulance without much difficulty. An X-ray showed a crack in the thigh bone. All that she required was to rest in bed for a few weeks. I told her how lucky she was to get a fracture that did not require an operation or even a hospital stay. She looked very disturbed and said, "I stay alone."

I asked her, "Do you have any relatives in town?"

"I have a brother who holds a senior position in Rolls Royce."

"I will phone him."

"Doctor, please don't."

"Let me try."

Her brother came and hugged her saying, "Hello dear."

He asked me, "What can I do for you?"

"Can you please keep your sister at home? She will be quite independent except for needing help to go to the toilet."

"Doctor, I wish I could. But tomorrow, I am going with my wife to south of France for a vacation for ten days."

I saw him leaving the hospital in a chauffeur-driven Rolls Royce car. The patient could not hold back her tears. I felt that the brother could have cancelled his vacation and was surprised that he didn't. Old age without family support is a tragedy.

Soon after I joined the hospital, I found an odd practice. One day in the week was reserved for performing circumcisions on children. Two young residents were entrusted with this work; one would give the anaesthesia and the other would operate.

Circumcision is a simple operation but giving anaesthesia to a young child is risky. When I expressed my reservation to the Chief he said, "But this is the way things are done here and nothing has gone wrong." He added, "Unless we throw responsibilities at them, how are our young residents going to learn? It is not possible to provide an anaesthetist in our set up."

Some weeks later I had an urgent call from the casualty department informing me that a child had suffered a cardiac arrest during circumcision. I rushed to give a cardiac massage, but it was too late. The heartbeat was restored, but there was permanent brain damage. Ten hours later, the child died.

I still remember the grieving father holding the dazed mother. Their world had been completely shattered in a matter of hours. He was their only child, born many years after marriage. I prayed that the couple would have another child though I knew it was unlikely in view of their advanced age. The tragedy would cast a lifelong shadow on their lives.

The circumcision was done not because it was absolutely required, but because it was a routine practice there before a boy started school. Soon after this episode, an anaesthetist was officially appointed. Every operation carries some risk and there is nothing like a minor operation.

My American friend's grand-daughter died during a minor operation on her face in a day-care centre in San Diego. For a good pilot, no flight is minor and for a good surgeon, no operation.

Bevan's Death

I was at a party when Aneurin Bevan's death was announced on TV. Tears rolled down my cheeks, something that surprised my English friends. I had a reason which I alone knew. I had heard his talk when I was a student at the Grant Medical College, Bombay, sometime in the early 1950s.

In his introduction, the Dean told us that Mr. Bevan was the son of a miner from Wales who established the N.H.S. (National Health Service) in the UK to serve the poor, neglected population. I have always found such examples of upward mobility in society inspiring.

Mr. Bevan had a speech defect, but it didn't stop him from becoming a powerful speaker. This interested me because I, too, had one and my greatest desire was to become a competent orator. I had heard him interviewing Somerset Maugham who also had a terrible speech impediment. So men could succeed in spite of stammering, a thought I never let myself forget. I felt like writing a letter to him after I heard the interview but I did not have the courage to do so. I've been writing it in my mind ever since.

My dear Aneurin Bevan,

I first saw you in my medical college in the early 50s. You had worn a cream-coloured suit and your face was red because of the Bombay heat. The anatomy hall was packed and I was impressed by your enthusiasm and wit. You said nice things about Gandhi. I saw you walking briskly after the talk. I was alongside you, though a bit further away.

Five years later, I came to England and learnt about your contributions to the NHS. I heard you interviewing Somerset Maugham and realised the common trait the three of us shared. We were all stammerers. Maugham qualified as a doctor but never practised medicine. I have chosen surgery for my career. I have no interest in politics and no interest in writing.

You chose the NHS hospital for treatment of your stomach cancer. In India the ministers and the elite either go abroad or to expensive private hospitals and the expenses are borne by the taxpayer. They do not go to government hospitals! I hope they follow your example one day.

Warm regards,

Dr. Vinayak N. Shrikhande

As usual the day had started at 7 am and it was past midnight after an emergency operation on a girl of 8 for a perforated appendix. I thanked every member of the operation theatre, met the anxious family, showed them the inflamed, swollen burst appendix I had removed and assured them that their child was out of danger.

After returning to my room, I threw the apron on a chair and was so physically exhausted that I drifted off to sleep in my hospital clothes. I was woken up by the telephone and the agitated voice of the operation theatre sister informing me that a towel clip was missing. Every surgeon fears such a call. I rushed over and the atmosphere was very tense because even a thorough search had not located the missing clip.

The one unusual event during that night had been power failure during the operation. I had covered the wound with a sponge. The power was restored in a short time. I wondered whether a towel clip lying loosely over a sponge had slipped inside the abdomen. The operation theatre staff had never experienced a single episode of power failure. Unusual events are bound to occur in unusual circumstances and an X-ray of the abdomen would detect the clip but what explanation could I give to the patient's family for needing an X-ray in the middle of the night after a successful operation? And what if the clip was not found after the X-ray?

Was there any other unusual factor apart from the power failure? I asked the sister whether any new member had joined the staff team. I saw a ray of hope when I learnt that a new trainee had joined the same day. She was called from the nurse's quarters to the operation theatre.

We asked her whether she had seen a towel clip anywhere. She quietly said that there was a clip lying on the floor which she cleaned and put back in the cupboard. She did not feel it was necessary to inform the sister about it because she did exactly the same thing at home when she saw a spoon or fork falling down! Over a dozen people assembled in the OT area heaved a sigh of relief.

I was asked what I would have done if the clip had remained untraceable. The answer was clear: I would have taken the X-ray and if the clip was inside the abdomen, I would have taken it out after coming clean with the patient's family and faced the consequences. Missing a sponge or an instrument is a part of our professional risk. The different articles left inside the body would frighten patients and surprise surgeons. I have seen an X-ray showing a glass bottle left inside the abdomen after a surgery in a New York Hospital!

If an unusual situation arises, think of a new factor in the usual set up; in this case a new nurse in the operation theatre.

Breast Cancer

While taking a ward round, I saw a young woman with breast cancer who was admitted for an operation the next day.

She asked, "Sir, are you Mr. Wilson?" (Doctors after F.R.C.S. are called Mr!)

"I am Mr. Shrikhande."

I knew she wanted Mr. Wilson to operate on her.

I said, "Mr. Wilson is not in town but he will do your operation when he returns after two days."

The staff nurse who was taking the round with me told her that though I was a junior, I did all the operations in the hospital when the two seniors were on leave. She pointed out several of my patients in the ward on whom I had carried out major surgeries. I signalled to the nurse to keep quiet, because I saw the woman's embarrassment.

"Doctor, please do not misunderstand me. I was told by my family physician that my disease is serious and that Mr. Wilson would operate on me."

I understood her anxiety and fears. I did not feel hurt. With my small stature and young age, I did not fit the image of a senior surgeon in whose hands she could entrust her life. After the ward round, I told the staff nurse that the patient had advanced cancer and the outlook was poor. When the disease would recur, she would feel that had she been operated on by a senior person, she would have done well.

I explained this episode to my Chief after he returned from London. He met her. The patient was again embarrassed.

“I had no intention of hurting the young doctor, but I was told that you would operate on me.”

‘You have not hurt him, you have hurt me. How could I ever entrust the lives of so many patients to a person who is not competent? If I have to undergo an operation, I would choose him. Don’t worry; both of us will do your operation.”

I was enjoying my progress. Such experiences were repeated small victories, far more important than occasionally performing a major spectacular operation. This has been my experience throughout my life.

One day during an emergency operation for colon cancer in a sick old patient, the staff nurse assisting me proved very incompetent. There was a delay at every step. I was annoyed but I did not want to lose my temper because I had decided at the very beginning of my career to remain calm during surgeries. After the operation I went to the surgeon’s room for coffee.

I was so upset that I phoned the matron.

“Matron, I normally never grumble about the staff, but today’s experience of poor assistance can endanger a patient’s life. Is it possible to avoid such situations in the future?”

In a cold voice, she answered, “Doctor, we have to work with untrained surgeons at times, but do we ever complain?”

The Matron was not well-liked in the hospital. Nobody had seen her smile and she kept a keen eye on which nurse went out with whom. However, in her reply she conveyed a lot of wisdom. That was one more turning point in my life. I can’t choose a team. I must manage with whatever is given to me.

One particular patient who has left a deep impact on my mind was a young patient with cancer of the urinary bladder. Everything was tried, but the disease could not be controlled. He was put on deep sedation to control his pain. When I went for a ward round one evening, he greeted me with a smile. “Doc, how are you?”

Shrikhande Clinic

From L to R: With brother Nilkanth, son Shailesh
and nephews Rajeev and Ravindra

With Justice M. S. Menon, Munnar, Kerala

With Pandurang Shastri Athavale, at Shrikhande Clinic

With Prof. Y. G. Bhojraj

With Prof. Andrew Laird, UK

From L to R: Dr. Bhopatkar, Alex,
Dr. Ankola and Singh, Edinburgh, 1958

At Khardung La Pass (18380 feet), at age of 77,
with Major V. P. Singh, 2007

Four hours later I was called to write his death certificate. I could not believe that this was the dead but still warm body of the young man who had greeted me with a smile! He was only forty and tragedy struck him for no fault but the unseen and unknown hand of destiny.

The extraordinary behaviour of ordinary individuals has left a lasting impression on my mind. These instances which are common in a surgeon's life would serve to make anyone a philosopher and better human being.

We are accustomed to hearing stories of courage shown in combat, during natural disasters such as earthquakes and floods or of people who braved a burning building to evacuate the trapped victims. We remember patriots fighting for freedom, sent to the gallows or giving their lives defending India's security. However, they were dying for a cause. How can we explain the quiet acceptance of death by a young man with cancer of the urinary bladder? Reading such real-life stories from a surgeon will hopefully have a positive impact on some individuals who start the day with complaints, go to bed confused and spend a restless night in spite of sleeping pills. It is the courage of ordinary individuals in the face of death that I find inspiring.

Could this stoicism be a part of British character? I remember an incident in the casualty department when a young girl of about ten came with a knife injury to her hand. She was frightened by the sight of blood and was crying in pain. Her mother though consoling her, was repeatedly saying, "I hate to see tears in your eyes; wipe your eyes." And when the girl continued to cry, she said, "I am ashamed of you." I do not remember having such experiences in India.

Colleague from East Africa

Dr. Kirti, one of my colleagues in England, was from East Africa. We were on a similar wavelength when it came to thinking about life around us. One day we were discussing the future of people of Indian origin in his country. His forefathers had been settled in Africa for more than two generations, but it was clear that they were soon approaching the time when they would have to leave the country. Even the whites would have to quit, but he was certain that Indians would be driven out first. The reason was that there was a difference in the way the Indians and white people treated the local population.

"Those who work with Europeans get a uniform, have fixed hours of work, yearly holidays and are given travel expenses. The whites have built schools, hospitals and churches for the local population and many Africans have become Christians."

He further added, "We treat them in a different way. There are no fixed hours of work, the servants get no uniforms and are looked down upon as inferior humans. At the same time, we are extra polite and courteous to the whites. We have built places of worship, but our money goes to London and Switzerland. "

The feudal attitude is still seen in those in power. At a surgeons' conference, the guest of honour was the chief minister of the state. As usual, he was late and to avoid further delay the president of the association started his talk. Ten minutes later the chief minister walked in and the president stopped his lecture.

The inauguration ceremony began, the lamp was lit, the prayer recited and many adjectives used in the praise of the chief guest. He did not express regret for the delay even once. He constantly looked at his watch and delivered the usual speech advising doctors to serve the rural poor. It was a sad sight to see people exiting the hall immediately after he left.

Things are now changing and politicians are rarely invited to academic conferences.

Oath in Court

I had to attend a law court to give evidence in a case of post-operative death of a cancer patient.

I was asked the following questions:

"What is your religion?"

"Hindu."

"What is your holy book?"

"We have none!"

The judge looked puzzled

I asked, "Can I explain?"

"Yes"

"Hinduism is a culture and not a religion. We have no central authority. We have no holy book. Hinduism is a way of life with a liberal code. You may not believe in God and you can still be a Hindu. You can pray or not. You can be vegetarian or non-vegetarian. I need not take the help of the religion to speak the truth."

"Do you have any book that guides you on how to live?"

"The Bhagwad Gita. Many great leaders who guided the destiny of my country were inspired by reading this book."

The court was adjourned so that a copy could be found. The main library in that town did not have a copy of the Bhagwad Gita. When I told them that I was willing to take an oath on the Bible, the judge was confused but accepted my offer.

The judge called me to his chamber and said he was curious to know about what I had said in the court. He was surprised when I told him that we had millions of gods. I said, "We can even make our own god by taking a stone, painting it red, placing a flower and starting to pray! We have no central authority that dictates what to eat and what not to eat, whether contraceptives should be used or they are prohibited, whether to pray or not. No one can order us to go to temples, what dress to wear. We may not believe in God and still remain a Hindu. We do not believe in conversions, we have never carried out crusades, we have never tortured non-believers. Whenever we see a sunrise, a lake, a river, a place of worship or we switch on the light, our hands automatically come together for thanking the supreme.

Gandhi was a devout Hindu, but he read scriptures of all religions and his successor Jawaharlal Nehru was an agnostic.

This acceptance of different beliefs and their contradictions is deeply-rooted in Indian culture. I am fortunate that I am accountable to my conscience and not to any authority.

Our poets and philosophers have even advocated physical pleasures, but at the same time not forgetting the universal ideals of gratitude, forgiveness and enlightened purpose in life. They have stated that God is not in the temple, but everywhere around us and also within us, that there is no place where there is no touch of divinity.

Our only curse is the caste system, poverty and illiteracy. But luckily we have a secular constitution and democracy." Finally, I told him that my father did not believe in God created by man, but my mother prayed for two hours a day and they got along well. We had a very interesting discussion over a cup of tea.

Death on a Motorbike

It was late at night and the usual rush in Casualty was almost over. I was going to have a cup of coffee in the doctor's room when an ambulance arrived and a patient was rushed in on a trolley. It was a young man who had met with a motorcycle accident. The pulse was very fast and weak. He was unconscious. There were no marks of injury. We started treatment immediately but he continued to sink and died within a few minutes.

He was a well-built young man with long black hair and a clean-shaven face. Several thoughts crossed my mind. Where was this boy going? When did he leave his home? Was he married or a bachelor or in love with a girl? If he was married, did he have a child? What would be the fate of his young widow, his family, father and mother? I was making notes, but I couldn't stop thinking. He did not know that it was the last day in his life: his last lunch, last breakfast, last bath, that he would not return home.

I stood up when his father came in with a dazed look on his face. He identified his son, then removed his hat and cupped his son's face. I put my arm around his shoulders. Human touch can convey a lot when words are helpless to lighten the sorrow. He sat down on a stool, tears running down his face. After a while he got up, wiped his tears, placed his hand over the body and said, 'May God bless you.' He thanked me and left the casualty, a broken man. My eyes were moist but as surgeons we train ourselves not to show emotions—we have to wear a mask even outside the operation theatre.

The Gift of Life

I was about to leave for my lunch when I suddenly heard the increased activity typical of an emergency ambulance arriving at the casualty entrance. A strapped patient was being wheeled on a trolley by the ambulance and police personnel. She was shouting, "Let me go, I want to die."

She had met with a car accident. There were bruises on her face and all over the body. The clothes were bloodstained and torn in several places. She was not in a mood to calm down. Her pulse was steady and a quick examination did not show any evidence of serious injury. She continued shouting, "Doctor, let me go, I want to die."

I put my hand on her shoulder and I looked into her eyes. "My job is to save lives," I said. It turned out that she had tried to commit suicide by driving her car into a tree.

In spite of the abrasions, cuts and blood and torn clothes, the striking feature was her remakable beauty. It was difficult to control her. I said, "I am very curious to know why a beautiful girl like you wants to end her life." And I added, "Thank God, you are a lady driver and so you missed your target." A lady driver, like the mother-in-law, is a universal topic for humour. A smile broke out on her face and she calmed down.

"Doctor, I will speak only when the police and ambulance staff go out."

I was alone in the examination room with a nurse by my side. The story that she told me was something I never expected. She said, "You called me beautiful but you should have seen me fifteen years ago when I won a local beauty pageant. My life changed. I got invitations for events from many parts of England. I was surrounded by admiring men. I did not know where to stop. I was drunk with success. Soon the excitement dwindled. I felt bored and lost. That was the time I met a man who understood me. We married and I settled down. We have two nice children but I have ruined their lives."

She continued, "Both my children are not keeping good health. They often get coughs, fever, vomiting. One son has not been able to put on weight and this is because my blood is poisoned. My children are paying for my past misdeeds."

I explained to her that these problems were common in many children, even of healthy parents. I assured her that a simple test would verify whether she had contracted a disease and even if the tests showed positive, excellent medicines were available to cure the disease. I wanted to know whether there was any discord with the husband, driving her to commit suicide.

"Not at all. He knows everything about my past life and I would in fact feel very happy if he would physically thrash me. But he is such a good soul and that is why I feel guiltier that he married a spoilt girl like me. I really wanted to end my life so that he could marry a nice girl and lead a new life. He is a very well-placed man and would find a match in no time." I knew she was serious.

I said that he could have a good wife, but could he also find a real mother for her two children? She broke down. I said, "You are a mother, there is only one mother in one's life and while trying to absolve your sense of guilt you have no right to ruin the lives of your children whom you brought into this world." I took a Parker pen from the pocket of my apron.

"This pen which I can buy for a couple of pounds is very precious to me because it is a gift from grateful parents for saving their child who was operated by me for a burst appendix. The most valuable gift is the gift of life. I can never understand anybody who wants to throw away that gift."

I had touched an inner chord. Within 20 minutes I witnessed a remarkable transformation—an irritable, shouting, mentally-disturbed patient now had a serene smiling face. She shook my hands and assured me that she would never do such a stupid thing again. Two months later the family came to meet me with a bottle of wine and a thank you card.

"It was our luck that we met a doctor like you. We will always remember you." She was looking beautiful in a smart blue dress with her handsome husband and two children. The main problem in this patient was not her injuries, but something deeper that was bothering her. A small talk with interest, compassion and assurance had magically calmed a hidden volcano in her mind.

Doctors should carry smiles, hope, enthusiasm, common sense, humour and the human touch wherever they go.

Scotland Yard

A retired Scotland Yard officer was admitted to the hospital. I never lose a chance to interact with patients or their relatives so as to enrich myself through their experiences.

I was curious to know how Scotland Yard had maintained such a high reputation all over the world. He told me that integrity and fairness were the two values mentioned at all levels every day.

I asked him, "Is there any example of an innocent man harmed?"

"Rather uncommon because the British judiciary is fair and it demands clear evidence to prove someone guilty. We cannot afford to be lax in our investigations. But we are not infallible and judges are not gods."

He suggested that I should read the book, *10 Rillington Place,* that narrated the true story of a series of mistaken assumptions that sent an innocent man to the gallows. When the real evidence was released, the home minister, in whose time the execution was carried out, took a leading part in exhuming the body to give the corpse a Christian burial.

That made no difference to the man who was killed by hanging but the authorities showed decency in accepting their guilt. If we decide that a man is guilty, we can always collect evidence to prove that the assumption is right.

Scotland Yard is no exception. But this is in sharp contrast to some totalitarian regimes where the inconvenient are first punished and evidence is collected later. Many people have disappeared after a midnight knock.

I often hear the statement, "Let a hundred criminals be set free, but not a single innocent man get punished."

Unfortunately many jails are filled with individuals who have committed minor crimes while the big fish are experts in avoiding the nets of the law. The work done by Kiran Bedi in Tihar jail, the largest jail in Asia, was an eye opener for many.

Mystery of the Missing Gauze and Denture

Sunday morning was a day of comparative leisure. I was reading *The Times* while sipping tea. The telephone rang and I heard the upset voice of the operation theatre sister informing me that two gauze pieces had remained in the patient's abdomen during the previous day's prostate operation.

"How do you know?" I asked her.

"Last evening, when I went home after work, I could not sleep. This was unusual because normally when I touch the bed, sleep overpowers me. My husband suggested that I visualise in detail everything I had done from the morning and throughout the whole day until I went home. I went through the mental drill in minute detail. Nothing had gone wrong at home."

"I drove to the hospital and remembered every step of the operations performed that day. Being a Saturday, the operation list was small and suddenly I remembered that two ribbon gauze tapes that were used to pack the side of the prostate had not been taken out. I got up and my husband drove me to the hospital at midnight. I went through the disposal bag and two gauze tapes were indeed missing."

No further questions were necessary.

I called the chief. Three hours later the patient was wheeled to the operation theatre to check the wound and the pieces were removed.

The sister offered her resignation which was not accepted by the hospital board because of her fine record for more than twenty years. It is through small incidents like these that taught me important things. The subconscious mind records everything. If anything goes wrong, it remains recorded. The messages from the subconscious mind leads to restlessness and a conscientious person will discover the cause. She was wise to accept her husband's advice when she could have easily taken a cocktail or a sleeping pill, a common instant remedy.

I remember an incident about a surgeon. An emergency operation for a ruptured appendix was performed on a judge. Everything went well and the surgeon was very happy about his diagnosis and the timely intervention. As he was removing the gloves, he heard the anaesthetist asking whether the patient had come to the operation theatre with or without dentures.

The surgeon was alarmed. The anaesthetist had noticed that two upper teeth were missing and the patient obviously had a denture. He had not inspected the teeth when he started the anaesthesia before passing a tube through the mouth into the windpipe.

There were two possibilities. Either the patient was brought to the theatre without a denture or the denture had slipped into the food passage or the lungs during anaesthesia. The operation theatre floor was inspected and all the receptacles were thoroughly checked but no denture was found. No one had the courage to ask the family members waiting outside whether the judge had kept the denture at home. It would have caused great alarm.

The anaesthetist could not remove the tracheal tube supplying oxygen to the lungs, but if the denture was in the lungs it could kill the patient. The tension was rising. An X-ray showed no denture and there was a sigh of relief. Enquiries made later on revealed that the judge himself had left the dentures at home. Such stories are exchanged among surgeons and anaesthetists while taking coffee in between operations! All this tension could have been avoided by following a strict check-list before wheeling the patient into operation theatre.

Learning to Cope with Death

I had just removed the lung of a patient with advanced cancer. During the operation it was found that the cancer was also spreading to the other lung. This happened 50 years ago when tools for investigation were limited and surprise findings on the operation table were common. The outlook for this patient was very poor. The chief felt that the patient would not be able to go home.

After the operation, when we were having coffee in the adjoining surgeons' room, the sister came running to tell us that the patient was bleeding from the tube which we had placed in the chest cavity. The chest was opened. A ligature placed on a large blood vessel had come loose and he had massive blood loss. Though the bleeding was controlled with the fingers, we could not save the patient.

I felt terrible. The patient whom we had reassured only two hours earlier was now only a body to be transferred to a mortuary. The theatre sister, who was very strict and cold, now appeared understanding and supportive. Her cold appearance was just a mask to maintain discipline and be able to do justice to the serious nature of her work. She told me that such things do occasionally happen, even in the hands of seniors.

My chief who was a well-known surgeon in the UK told me that a surgeon tied thousands of ligatures during his lifetime, and on rare occasions the knots could become loose. That explanation, though rational, did not remove the sense of guilt and incompetence I felt at that time.

I had to go out to tell the patient's wife about the mishap. It was a great burden on my mind but his wife took my hand and said, "I know it is not good news. But he is now relieved of his agonies. I was prepared for this."

I was instructed to take the evening off and spend time with a girlfriend or go to the pub with friends. I did nothing. I could not have dissolved my terrible feelings in anybody's pleasant company. I had to face the tragedy and suffer in the solitude of dejection and frustration. There was no 'band-aid' remedy possible with medicine or alcohol. I had to suffer alone; this is a surgeon's life. I was restless for the whole evening. I wondered whether I had chosen the correct career. Was it worth it to carry such stress throughout my life? I could not sleep that night; I felt depressed and guilty. I was remembering the patient's smiling face before he underwent anaesthesia; he had held my hand and kept it close to his chest. His dead body and his wife's tears were making my night intolerable.

The next day was also an operation day. We had another case of lung cancer and my chief made me do the operation on my own. It went off smoothly and I did not experience such a complication again in my career of over fifty years. I really admired my Chief and the theatre staff who instead of criticising me gave me words of encouragement. I cannot imagine what would have been my state of mind if they had shown doubts about my surgical competence.

A week later, the pathology report of the patient who had died on the operating table, showed that the highly malignant growth had already spread to the opposite lung and adjacent organs. This was decades before CT Scan and MRI and it was impossible to judge the spread of the disease during surgery. In this case, even if the operation had gone smoothly, he would not have lived for more than a couple of months, and that too, in a miserable state because of breathlessness. That my mistake saved the patient a few weeks of agony was the only flimsy consolation.

This single episode made me very cautious about tying ligatures. Engineering students are taught that the strength of any engineering structure depends upon the strength of its weakest link; in surgery, a single defective knot or stitch can kill a patient. I have quoted my experience to generations of surgical residents and observers—it is good to be cautious and prevent a calamity than be flashy for exhibiting one's skill. It is known that:

We must work if we want to learn.
If we work, mistakes do occur.
Learn from your mistakes and mistakes done by others.
Avoid them and then you become an authority.

In one of the hospitals where I worked, the chief of the kitchen was Margaret. She would openly say, "Dr. Shrikhande is the only doctor who never complains about the food." She would make Indian dishes for me to express her appreciation. I told her that I owed this to my training at home.

As a child I did not like certain vegetables, but my grandfather made me eat whatever was cooked at home without criticism. Food wastage was not allowed. This attitude paid good dividends, even in England where I did not like the food.

I went for a ten-day holiday to Europe with my friends during my final months of stay in England. Not knowing the language was a big handicap; I really felt like a foreigner. The big problem was to choose dishes from the menu card which we could not understand. We would choose the item by reading the price of the dish! Sandwiches and beer at roadside cafes was an enjoyable experience.

We visited Paris where everybody looked like a tourist. In Germany, there were the remnants of World War II destruction at many places and I could hear the echoes of tramping boots, the Nazi soldiers barging into the homes of people whose only crime was that they were Jews. I had no courage to visit the sites of former concentration camps. Even religious leaders were silent when God's children were being massacred. This is one more reason why I do not believe in the rituals of religion. I returned and the familiar sounds of English made me feel at home.

Alfred Gregory

During my stay in England, I had an opportunity to meet Alfred Gregory who was a world-renowned mountaineer, professional photographer, and explorer. He was a member of the first successful Mount Everest expedition. He reached 28,000 feet on May 28, 1953 to place the equipments which were to be used by Hillary and Tenzing for their successful ascent the next day. His daughter happened to be a nurse in our operation theatre. I had no experience in mountain climbing but had read two books on mountaineering before we met so I could initiate some conversation with this celebrity.

Mountaineering books give one the clear message that a good mountaineer is one who never crosses the point of no return. He is not a careless man who rushes into rash adventures. He calculates his every step and plans how and when to return. I found that the principles of mountain climbing were applicable in surgery as well.

One evening I met him and his wife for dinner at a seaside restaurant in Blackpool. As we were sipping wine I asked him, "What were your thoughts when you reached the peak?" With a gentle smile he said, "How to come back home and be with my wife."

He put his arm around her waist and his beautiful French wife blushed. He added, "Whatever newspapers write, mountains are never conquered. We just reach the peak and plan the return, which is more risky than the ascent.

Many expert climbers have lost their lives not while going to the top, but during the descent. No climb is successful unless the climber returns to the base camp."

What I learnt from a great mountaineer, photographer and philosopher in one evening during a dinner conversation could not have been possible by reading books. My passion for meeting people from different fields has enriched my life and I am ever grateful to my profession for making this possible. I never wanted to know what my IQ was but my CI (curiosity index) has remained quite high.

New Surgical Technique

Never cross a point of no return, a message of caution to mountaineers, made me change my technique in gall bladder operation.

The removal of a gall bladder has been a well-established operation for almost a century. Damage to important structures can occur even in experienced hands. We were taught a technique called 'Hilum first cholecystectomy'.

The dissection starts deep inside the abdomen where there is maximum risk of damage. I felt it would be safer to do the exact opposite: go from the superficial to the deep part and in case of difficulties, stop the operation and back out so that no harm is done. We thus avoid crossing a point of no return.

I practised and advocated this technique called 'Fundus first cholecystectomy' in every surgical meeting and operative demonstration. It was more than a decade before many surgeons were convinced about the safety of the technique.

This method of operation was known but not practised by the majority.

My Impressions of the UK

I wanted to buy a blood pressure measuring apparatus before leaving England. The shopkeeper showed me one and when I asked him whether it was the best available, he said, "The best one I would recommend is unfortunately made in Germany and it is even two pounds cheaper than the English one we have here." He added, "I do not know what is happening to my country, but we are losing our supremacy."

When I told him that I would be leaving the country within two days, he requested me to finish my other shopping and come back after two hours. He had kept it ready when I returned. He could have very well sold me the one he had and charged more knowing that I was in a hurry and there was no possibility of my coming back even if I had any complaints. Such integrity in daily affairs was not my experience in India at that time.

However, things are changing for the better now. After my return, I recommended that shop to colleagues and students who wished to purchase surgical instruments.

I had always wondered before going to England, how such a small nation could establish a global empire. How did Englishmen manage to rule and live in India, African countries, and Burma where the weather was so different from their home country? I had some answers after staying there for a few years.

Everyone did his or her job with integrity. There was no favouritism based on contacts, caste, or colour in everyday life. There was a sense of impartiality. There were no VIPs with beacons on their cars who had privilege of movement. There was tolerance in the atmosphere. They were good listeners. Many had interesting hobbies and a spirit of adventure. They went all over the world; Mount Everest, the South Pole, the Amazon and Africa when communications were primitive. They enjoyed sports, and adventure. They had excellent traditions in education and research work. One institute, Cavendish Laboratary, Cambridge had over a dozen Nobel Laureates!

There was also a democratic atmosphere. The surgeons would tell me, "You do what you think is best, but I would do the operation this way." I saw that nurses, in the OR (Operating Rooms), wards and even casualty, were authoritative. In India, women who could not find other jobs took to nursing. We had no Florence Nightingales there, and nurses were treated as inferior individuals. However, the negative attitude towards women's education and their important role in the workforce has changed in India today.

The British had a sense of humour; they did not argue much. Politics was hardly mentioned. Football was far more popular than cricket. The expression, "Really? Very interesting!" usually meant, "I do not agree, I am not interested in what you are saying. Let us please change the topic."

Religion was a personal affair. Hospital campuses had churches. Many churches in the UK wore a deserted appearance, and the church courtyard was a place for lovers to meet and old folk to visit.

Speaking loudly, asking personal questions, and not allowing a person to complete a sentence were considered bad manners. Their "How are you? How is life?" were like our 'Namaste'. It was not an opening for you to recite all your complaints. Indian restaurants were frequented only by Indians. (Things have now changed beyond belief. The Englishman has developed a liking for Indian food.)

English, Indian and African boys and girls moving about in pairs was a common sight. I wondered what would have happened had we seen a white girl and an Indian man or vice-versa in the India of my youth.

I was the best man when my Indian colleague married an English girl. The wedding ceremony was simple, short and only 30 guests were invited for lunch. The wedding was at 9 am and the couple drove away for their honeymoon at 4 pm. The waste of money and food, and the show of wealth at Indian weddings disturbs me.

I was never made aware of my speech defect even once. All doctors kept a diary to note down the jobs they had to do and they normally kept their word. No one picked up a phone without a pen and paper handy. There were never any questions asked about my colour, nationality or religion.

I hope that one day school children in India would not have to state their caste/faith in the admission forms when they join a school. The identification of individuals by a caste is a curse for India.

They had respect for time and privacy of others. There were no class distinctions at work; even a ward boy would not tolerate uncivil language from doctors. Doctors would refer to nurses by their names.

Discussions in academic meetings were egalitarian. A young doctor was free to ask questions of a senior consultant. You entered the shop or a pub, and were welcomed with a smile.

Police and people were good at giving instructions on how to locate a particular place. When two people came together in a shop, they would form a queue. It was a common practice to maintain eye contact while talking.

During my first job in an English hospital, I remarked that men wore pants and bush shirts in India. Everybody laughed loudly. That day I learnt that in England, pants did not mean trousers. I was also under the impression that golf was the sport of the elite, until our hospital ambulance driver invited me to play golf one weekend!

Everything from weddings to funerals had a design and order. Christmas was the only time when there was a festive atmosphere. Alcoholic drinks were served even in the wards and with a mistletoe twig in hand, a boy could kiss any girl. Some colleagues felt that mistletoe should be at hand all round the year!

I spent four years in England where I felt safe and respected. I enjoyed my stay and work. I did not sacrifice anything in returning to India. I returned because I did not belong there. I was missing my home and people. I have frequently gone back to England since. I am nostalgic for the Burton shops for suits, the ABC restaurants for inexpensive snacks, the subtle humour and the old pubs. I feel sad that many of the pubs have closed down; they were so quintessentially British!

Return Journey

I had arrived in London on September 23, 1957, and was now leaving from Heathrow on September 23, 1961. Memories of my experiences in the UK flooded my mind. I made notes on a rough piece of paper while waiting for the plane at the airport. Heathrow was so small 50 years ago.

I had driven a car in India for four years but failed my driving test in England. Incidentally, I had operated on a relative of the inspector (the man who took my driving test) a few months before the test. He told me why I had failed; I had not checked the side mirror before starting the car. In India I would have got a license even without the test; it would have been unimaginable in India for a driving inspector to fail a surgeon who had saved a life of his relative! Personal associations can bypass the hassles of rules and regulations in everyday living. I could have got the license delivered at home without the test!

An announcement for boarding the Air India flight to Bombay was heard. I joined the queue and entered the plane. I was thrilled as that was my first flight, and that too for a long distance travel on a plane. The air hostess welcoming me with a smile, her look at my boarding pass and the courtesy with which she directed me to my seat was a novel experience. She helped me to put the hand baggage in the over head space and offered me a soft drink.

Instructions were given to fasten the seat belt. The engines started and the plane taxied towards the take off area. My eyes were focussed on the ground when the plane gathered speed. As it took off, I had a last glimpse of London. Tears rolled down my cheeks because I did not know whether I would see it again. I was anxious to reach India while was also sad to depart from England. We passed through the clouds and suddenly there was brilliant sunshine, while London disappeared below the thick blanket of clouds.

I gathered that the passenger next to me must have been a veteran traveller because he seemed to know every crew member in the plane; even the commander came to greet him. I started the conversation.

"“You seem to travel frequently.”

“Yes.”

“Where do you come from?”

“Bombay.”

“What brings you to England so often?”

“My sports activities.”

“Which sport?”

“Cricket.”

“May I know your name?”

"Vinoo Mankad."

I felt so embarassed because I could not recognise one of the outstanding cricketers of our days. I told him that as a young boy I had heard his name on the radio commentary by Bobby Talyarkhan, standing outside a coffee shop at Belgaum. Though I was in London for four years, I never attended any cricket match. My schedule of activities was so tight that I was either busy in libraries studying for my examinations or in hospitals working day and night.

He said, "Neither do I know you, though you are a highly qualified surgeon."

But I had yet to start my career in India and nobody knew me.

He was a decent man, and his fame had not ignited his ego. Rarely do we see famous people who have remained so unaffected and down-to-earth. Our first halt was in Geneva where he treated me to beer. We parted company at the Bombay Airport and decided to keep in touch.

I had mixed feelings. I was sad to leave England which had helped me to become a confident surgeon. I felt lucky that I could spend four years in a country whose people were endowed with many sterling qualities. I would miss the hospital work, innumerable gardens and excellent pubs.

But I was happy to return to India and be among my people. Not once had I talked to anyone from home during my four years away. The era of computers and cell phones was decades ahead. STD was a new term; the subscriber trunk dialling service meant one talked directly without the aid of the operator. The Queen of England who was in Bristol in 1958, directly phoned the Mayor of Edinburgh 300 miles away. It was the greatest distance a call could be made at that time.

I was returning to an India where some of those who had come to see me off at the Bombay docks had passed away. When I went by ship, my trunks were full of books and some bones for anatomy studies. The words security, screening, and frisking were unknown! When I first returned from England, my suitcase was full of surgical instruments. The inspector at the customs could not believe his eyes when he did not see any luxury goods, such as a Grundig spool tape recorder, camera and whisky bottles in the luggage of a passenger who was returning after a long stay abroad.

He asked me, “When are you going back to England?”

“I am not going back.”

“Really? Why have you come back?”

“I did not feel like settling down in England.”

“I believe that life in England is very good. Many go abroad for permanent settlement.”

“But this is my country.”

“What is the value of these surgical instruments?”

“About four thousand rupees.”

“So much?”

“Yes.”

“We are proud and happy that you have come back to India to look after the sick people. Just pay a nominal tax for the imported goods.”

I had a warm welcome from the customs at the airport. This was unexpected for passengers who had no personal contacts with immigration officers. My first experience coming back to India was positive- perhaps a good omen for my future career. There are pockets of goodness even in a corrupt society. On that day I decided that I would create such pockets; I would light lamps in the darkness.

In September 2014, I went to the UK with three friends on a nostalgia trip by car. I visited places where I had stayed in Edinburgh, went to hospitals where I had worked. Everything had changed, but not my memories. We travelled on new motorways. M1 was being built during my time over 50 years. I did not see a single accident on the way, there were no damaged cars and no ambulances carrying the injured to the hospitals. Pedestrians are safe and drivers respect the traffic lights. The UK had not changed with regards to traffic discipline.

I met many of my students who are now consultants in hospitals all over the UK. Their pay scales are up and they have fixed hours of work. In my times we were generals among surgeons and at present they are specialists in narrow areas! They know more and more about less and less. This is inevitable in this era of high specialisation. They have however lost their autonomy. Managers rule them. Our dining room table was always stocked with fruits, bread, cheese and milk. In that hospital one had to now buy a cup of coffee.

There is a hanging sword of medico-legal complaints—the American culture has now infiltrated hospitals in the UK. I was fortunate that I worked in the UK 50 years back in the golden era of trust between patients, doctors and hospital administration.

London still has enviable parks for people to walk, children to play, lovers to meet, elderly people to read newspapers or just relax. These parks are London's lungs. There are libraries, monuments, museums, exhibitions; no wonder more than sixteen million tourists visit London every year.

❑ ❑ ❑

Chapter 6

Waiting Period

I returned to India after a four-year stay in the UK. Many were surprised that I was not wearing a tie, my accent did not sound foreign and I could speak fluently in my mother tongue. The English rulers had left the country, but the English language had taken a strong grip over the youngsters. I started my practice in a small rented consultation room and experienced the agony of waiting for patients for a long time.

I was addicted to round-the-clock work, patients queuing up, long operation lists and daily emergencies. I did not know what to do with my time and my surgical expertise. There was no urgent need to earn money because we were staying in a joint family with my parents, my brother and his family; eight of us in a small apartment.

I knew that I would have to wait because I had chosen to settle down in Bombay, a city of more than four million where I hardly knew anybody. I met some senior surgeons for guidance and they all asked the same question, "Why have you returned to India instead of settling down in the UK or USA? Why should patients consult you, an unknown outsider, when the city has well-established surgeons of national repute?"

There was a difference between what I imagined and what I experienced. The picture that emerged was disheartening. A young surgeon without any medical and financial background, and without influential social and political connections had to overcome many obstacles.

I was told that there was fierce competition and it was almost impossible to get work done without giving kickbacks. I did not believe that following an ethical path meant failure. I have always been an optimist. I am now nearing journey's end, happy with the path I chose.

Patients choose surgeons with good reputations. The question of how one could earn a reputation without work was daunting. But knowing that even eminent surgeons had to wait for success at the beginning of their careers was reassuring. Dr. V. N. Shirodkar, internationally-renowned gynaecologist, told me that he did not see a single case for many months after starting practice in the 1930s. I remember his comment, "One day we seniors will die and if you have worked well you will take our place."

(Dr. Shirodkar had invented an ingenious technique for treatment of women who suffered from repeated miscarriages because the muscles which surround the opening of the uterus were weak. They conceived but miscarried in early pregnancy. He invented a suture that went around the opening of the uterus and was cut once a full term was reached. His one stitch blessed many women with motherhood. Dr. Shirodkar's obituary had the heading: 'Motherhood orphaned'. I had heard from a senior gynaecologist that he was flown by a private jet to Rome to operate on Sophia Loren, the famous Italian actress. The operation was successful and she was blessed with motherhood. She offered to establish a foundation for his work in USA. No wonder that in Edinburgh's surgeons' hall a professor asked, "How many of you are from Bombay?" A few hands went up including mine. He said, "I know there is a genius in Bombay whom I know personally, Prof. Shirodkar!" I cherish that moment.

Twenty years later I operated on Dr. Shirodkar's wife for gall bladder stones. I was told by his daughter that she was invited to the birthday party of Loren's child and she felt proud when the actress introduced her to the crowd as the daughter of the gynaecologist from Bombay who had blessed her with motherhood.)

Musicians, actors, advocates, politicians, and sportsmen can become famous at a very young age, but a surgeon who starts his career late and works in the secluded atmosphere of the operation theatre cannot.

A surgeon's reputation is built up very slowly; every satisfactory interaction with the patient, every good operation, has a cumulative effect.

In Bombay, I travelled by bus and local train. It was difficult to travel in overcrowded trains and stand for long periods at bus stops especially during rains and in oppressive humid heat. Soiled shoes and body odour are not expected from a consultant surgeon. I reminded myself from time to time that it was just a passing phase.

But a surgeon outside the operation theatre is like fish out of water!

I had a chance to become a full-time surgeon in a government hospital. There were few trained surgeons in the districts and I could have established myself easily in a short time. However, I had made a firm decision not to accept a full-time government job. There were frequent transfers, a lot of administrative work and interference from government officials, political parties, and vested interests. I would have had to retire at the age of 58.

Bombay had a special position in the country. If I was considered competent in England there was no reason why I should not do well in Bombay. When there was no work I would observe the work of eminent surgeons. I saw that they had the following traits in common: they were committed to their work and had good surgical skills. I knew that I had both these qualities.

I was busy with work in a government hospital where I was getting an honorarium of Rs.150 per month for petrol expenses. I hardly had any private practice. The waiting room for patients would remain empty and the consulting room was my waiting room. Apart from me there was a cardiologist, a paediatrician and a psychiatrist; in the consulting room complex. All were attached to teaching hospitals in Bombay as junior consultants. As none of us had work, we started visiting an Iranian restaurant very close to our consulting rooms for tea with instructions to the consulting room attendant to call us in case a patient came. We hardly had any calls.

One Saturday evening, as we came out of the restaurant, we met a very senior and respected family physician. He was obviously upset at our spending time in a restaurant when we should have been in our consulting rooms. When we told him that we had no work, he candidly advised us that if we wished society to look at us as consultants, we should conduct ourselves as professional men, spend time reading medical journals rather than enjoying tea in a restaurant. That was the last good advice he gave us because the next evening while giving a lecture to felicitate Dr. R.V. Sathe, the new vice-chancellor of Bombay University, he collapsed and died of a massive heart attack. Since that time, I have never visited a restaurant when I was supposed to be at work.

My appointment to a teaching hospital was another turning point in my life. My patients, the medical students, residents, and hospital staff spread my name all over the state. Eighteen years after I began practising, I was invited to the prestigious Bombay Hospital as an honorary surgeon which made me known all over the country.

Whenever I had to operate in a private hospital, I would carry my own instruments, boil them, and arrange the trolley myself. These small nursing homes with 20 or 30 beds were run by family physicians with minimal facilities. On many occasions I have myself shaved the patient and performed the operation with only one untrained nurse. I would instruct her how to wear the mask, cover the head with a cap, how to wash her hands, and put the gloves on.

Even a simple hernia operation would take a whole morning, but it suited me because at that point in my career, my problem was not lack of time, but too much time on my hands! I would feel happy that in this big metropolis one patient had chosen me for his operation. This would boost my optimism. Later, when I operated from 8 am to 11 pm with a team of five or six qualified young surgeons in one of the finest hospitals in the country, I realised what an interesting journey I had had.

I had to wait for years to settle down in private practice. One day, a patient came to my consulting room. I asked, "Tell me, what is wrong with you?"

"Nothing."

"Why have you come here?"

"I want to have a certificate for leave on medical grounds."

"When nothing is wrong with your health, why have you come?"

"I am employed abroad where an F.R.C.S. is a highly valued degree. If I produce a certificate with your qualifications, no questions would be asked."

He had come for a visit to India, but because of unexpected work he wanted to extend his leave period. He showed his passport to prove his credentials and assured me that nobody would know. I would have earned more than a week's income by writing a few lines but I declined. I felt stronger because I knew that no one could buy me.

It was by chance I got involved with the Family Planning Program in India.

I met a senior surgeon, Dr. G. M. Phadke, who was involved with the family planning movement in India. He was internationally known for his work on the rejoining of the vas deferens in men who had undergone vasectomy, but wanted fertility to be restored because of death of children or wife. He suggested that I should visit the family planning centre for doing vasectomies. That solved my problem of work, though for only one day in the week. Unfortunately, before I came to know him well, he passed away.

I started going to his hospital for my general surgical operations. There was a big void after Dr. Phadke's death. Patients came for getting reunion surgery done, but there was no surgeon interested in this work. Dr. Phadke's resident, Dr. Vinayak Shinde, an ayurvedic diploma holder and the theatre assistant, Sakharam, an illiterate man from a rural area, volunteered to teach me the operation of reunion of vas. The operative technique was simple but demanded gentleness that gave excellent results. I used eye instruments for taking fine sutures through the thin vas. The results were good.

I gave lectures in surgical conferences, and made a film which was a difficult undertaking fifty years back. I demonstrated the operations in many parts of the country. Both the State Government and Central Government appointed me as an Honorary Surgeon and Technical Advisor in the Family Planning Program.

Patients were poor and operations were free, but the feeling that my surgical expertise was giving excellent results and that I was rendering important service to society boosted my confidence.

The Director of Health of the State Government issued letters to all hospitals stating that I would be willing to demonstrate the operative technique and also train surgeons. Newspapers gave publicity to this programme of reunion of vas. I got busy at a time when I had hardly any work as a surgeon. Surgeons were not interested in this minor, non-challenging, non-paying work. This proved to be my opportunity.

There was an international conference on family planning at a hall close to my hospital. A well known professor of economics gave a lecture and concluded that unless the birth rate came down, the economy would not improve. When the time came for discussion I went to the podium and said. "The learned professor's talk was very convincing, but I feel confused because next time I may hear an expert presenting equally convincing data to prove that unless the economy improves, the birthrate will not come down."

I heard a prolonged applause. A WHO expert met me during the coffee break and within a few months I was chosen to conduct a conference for experts in implementation of the Family Planning Program in the east.

I was appointed as a WHO consultant to conduct a conference in Dhaka for experts in Southeast Asian region. I was invited to give a lecture at an international conference on family planning in Geneva.

(Vas deferens is a tube that transports sperms from testicles. In a vasectomy, the tube is divided and the cut ends are ligated. The pathway for sperm transport is thus blocked. It was believed that the capacity to produce sperms disappears after vasectomy. But nature is remarkable, since testes continue to produce sperms, and successful reunion is possible years after vasectomy.)

The belief that vasectomy was not reversible was changed by Dr. Phadke's work. The family planning work, lectures, operations, demonstrations and the travels all over the country kept me busy and this work fitted my social commitments.

The Government of India wanted me to take a delegation of surgeons to Korea to see similar work, but I suggested that we should invite the surgeons from Korea to India. A two-day workshop was organised and attended by surgeons from all over the state. I was very happy that a trip abroad was cancelled.

It is my conviction that we have no right to fritter away scarce foreign exchange. India must find Indian solutions and create our own model, whenever it is possible. It is known that many delegations sent by government and municipal corporations under the pretext of study tours, are sightseeing tours at the citizens' cost.

My work of reunion of vas brought many visitors from different parts of the world. Malcolm Potts, President of International Planned Parenthood Federation, arranged my lecture in Cambridge. His wife had come for training to Mumbai. I also demonstrated the operation of vaso epididymal anastomosis for male infertility in London.

IPPF (International Planned Parenthood Federation) medical bulletin in their August issue of 1977 published my work on reversible vasectomy in which I had stated, "Vasectomy if properly performed is a reversible operation in a great majority of cases." That was a time when reversibility was not considered reliable.

I received a letter from Bangalore, "Your slides on vasectomy were excellent and gave us an insight in the new way of recanalisation of vas. It was a great education for us all; the evaluation forms are a testimony to what we learnt from you."

I was still not known as a surgeon in Bombay, but was known in many parts of India for my work on recanalisation of vas. I was happy that I had something useful to do.

When I went to England, BBC invited me for an interview. I was to talk for about seven minutes, but the interview lasted for eighteen minutes. I was told by the BBC anchor that this was the longest time given for an interview in this category. When we were taking tea, the interviewer felt that I should be appointed as an ambassador of the reversible vasectomy program.

I do not recall correctly, but I think I received twenty pounds. I came out and in a nearby shop I saw a beautiful blue typewriter. I purchased it for eighteen pounds. Electric typewriters were a novelty and I enjoyed working with it for many years.

Every man requiring reunion operation had experienced tragedy due to deaths from influenza, meningitis, car accidents, falling in wells, burns, snake bites and even poisoning and murders for property. How fortunate I was that I could bring sunshine in so many homes.

A doctor couple had one son and a daughter. Unfortunately the son died of a short illness, but the husband had got vasectomy done. The operation of reunion of vas was successful and one year later he wrote to me that his wife had delivered a son who was a replica of the son they had lost.

Six years later, I was visiting southern India to give an oration. As our car was going through the town I suddenly remembered that the doctor was from the same town. I did not have his address nor did I remember his name. I went to a chemist's shop and wanted to see whether he could be of any help.

As I described the doctor, he said, "Sir please wait. I know whom you want." He phoned him and within ten minutes the doctor came with his son with tears in his eyes. He was so much overcome with emotions that he could not speak.

He took us to his home and there was a great celebration. My photo was placed in his prayer room. This is India.

The son is now an Associate Professor of Medicine and another daughter born later is now the Chief of an Intensive Care Unit in California!

On my 75th birthday there was a well-attended public function to felicitate me. This doctor had specially come and after his talk he decorated me with traditional robes and head-gear from South India.

He later wrote to me, "I was overcome by emotion on seeing the number of persons whose respect you have earned through your values. Our present generation has to see how a person could earn love and affection from the society by following the path expected of our noble profession. I am happy to note that your children are also in the same groove. I pray almighty to give you all, abundant health, wealth and wisdom."

Once we had a conference in Bombay where I gave a talk on reunion of vas. Everybody in India was bombarded with the constant theme that India's population was about to explode and that birth control was the need of the hour. As people did not like the term birth control, it was replaced by 'Family Welfare Planning Program' which included birth control. Specialists from many parts of the world had gathered in Mumbai.

I demonstrated how a divided vas could be joined again. A surgeon from abroad, trained in England, met me after watching the operation. He said, "The technique of reunion is so superb that I want to get my vasectomy operation done by you." It was done.

He wrote to me on 27th January 1975 after the operation that he worked till 11 pm. The next day too he was busy with a conference and on the third day he went to Madras to demonstrate a gastrectomy, took a ward round, gave a lecture to postgraduates and the next day left for his country.

He added, "I think my mobility is a testimony to the skill and the gentleness with which you did the operation and the lack of complications is a tribute to your technique. Please quote me at any time if you wish."

A consultant pathologist from an African country lost his only son in a car accident and unfortunately he had to do his post-mortem. Every day when he went to the hospital, he would open the register and read his son's post-mortem report. The family could no longer stand this terrible tragedy and decided to leave the country. His brother-in-law was a surgeon in the USA who had heard about my work in the reunion of vas and that is how the unfortunate couple consulted me in a state of depression. I later received a letter.

"We are extremely happy to inform you that we were blessed with a male child on 16.2.1981. It is our fortune and God's grace and we are always grateful to you for restoring the peace of mind to us. We are greatly indebted to you."

I had a very interesting letter from a patient involved in activities with scientific background -

"You performed the recanalisation operation in May 1967. It was my mistake I did not send you the semen report because I wanted things to go in a natural way. I know I was illogical but that's how I felt.

I am glad to intimate to you that my wife is two months pregnant. As a matter of scientific interest I may tell some special circumstances that occurred. During August my wife came across a pornography book and we talked of the various details described in the book. The result was a lot of sexual excitement and repeated intercourse for a week and that was the time my wife conceived.

Apologies for not sending the report and thanks again for your great services and your great human qualities.

I will write to you again after her delivery."

The letter never came!

I once conducted reunion operations in Dhule district hospital when 16 cases were operated during the weekend. In

14, the semen test was positive, two never replied. With great efforts and by involving the health services and social workers, I got photographs of seven couples with their newly-born children. Most of the patients were rural poor. This shows how follow-up records are almost impossible in India.

I was asked a question at an international conference in Geneva in 1973 as to how we knew that the child was born from the male operated for reunion of vas. My answer was simple. I said, "a man undergoes vasectomy operation, he wants a reunion, his semen contains no sperm, I do the operation, sperms reappear in semen and the spouse remains pregnant and that is enough for me and the society to believe that the child belongs to the couple." Scientific medicine will not accept this explanation.

I had performed more than 200 operations and every successful patient was a walking advertisement that vasectomy was reversible. Though there was small mention of my work in scientific literature, the information that vasectomy was reversible had reached all over the country.

My aim was not to get academic approval, or add to my CV, but to convey to a large number of Indians that vasectomy was a reversible operation.

I was invited to give a talk in Delhi on the role of a surgeon in family planning. The Secretary of Health and Family Planning in his inaugural talk had stated that if the family planning program failed, he would hold doctors responsible. In my talk I said, "We are professional men who should never go in search of patients. In fact a person who should undergo vasectomy is a healthy man and not a patient."

I added that the political parties, social workers and religious leaders who could influence masses should motivate people and we doctors would operate on them, but it is wrong to expect doctors to collect patients. Normally I receive an appreciative response, sometimes a standing ovation after my talk, but on that day there was profound silence in the hall. The secretary was visibly angry and before leaving the lecture hall he repeated the threat to doctors.

In the end the president of the organisation with the usual show of sycophancy, profusely thanked the chief guest for sparing valuable time guiding the delegates. After the VIP left in a motorcade of cars flashing red lights, I was surrounded by the organisers who complimented me for my outspoken talk but wondered how I did not fear talking against the government policy during the Emergency. The same individuals who thanked the health secretary, complimented me for my talk.

This is a typical Indian attitude. We were ruled by foreigners for over 800 years and I wonder whether during this time the genes had been programmed to praise the masters. But there are indications already that things are changing. India is waking up with confidence.

It requires courage to speak.
It requires patience and courage to listen.
This is the soul of democracy.

My work in reunion of vas brought cases of male sterlity and with them cases of sexual problems in men. I had to do a lot of counselling, a field in which I was a novice. I was surprised when one day I received a letter addressed to 'Dr. Shrikhande, Sex Surgeon, Bombay!'

That was proof of postal efficiency in India! In a city of 5 million, the letter came to me without any address! I wanted my name to be known as a surgeon away from the limited field of reunion of vas, male sterility and sexual problems!

How Patients came for Consultations

The owner of a well-known chemist shop consulted me for a parotid swelling. What was the reason? I prescribed very few antibiotics. He concluded that a surgeon who uses minimal antibiotics must be a competant surgeon. I refused to prescribe tonics, vitamins and enzymes just to make patients happy. My prescriptions were short but I spent a long time talking with the patients.

(Parotid gland is a large salivary gland over the lower jaw under the ear lobe and secretes saliva which moistens the food for mastication and swallowing. Majority of parotid swellings are not malignant but need surgical removal. The facial nerve which traverses through the gland supplies the facial muscles and damage even to one branch of the nerve leads to facial paralysis a tragedy for the patient and bad advertisement for a surgeon. These patients now a days go to ear, nose and throat (ENT) specialists and plastic surgeons but I was in an era of general surgeons who were considered generals among surgeons!)

I had never done this operation in the past. I had seen one surgeon doing it. I was fascinated by the delicate dissection of every nerve fibre that was necessary for surgery. I thought I would be able to do this operation. I went to the anatomy museum of the Grant Medical College and spent good deal of time on grasping the details. A week later I did the operation and dissected every nerve fibre. Patient was happy that the swelling over the cheek had disappeared and I was delighted to see patient smiling without any facial distortion. Slowly, references of parotid tumours started increasing and I felt happy when my ENT surgical colleague got his young niece operated by me for a parotid tumour. I was enjoying the good things happening in my career. I was asked a question in an interview if I was not worried that the patient would sue me in case I damaged the facial nerve. I was not gambling, I knew that I could do the operation safely. Instinctively I knew how far to go.

I remember another interesting episode at the beginning of my career. A young girl was brought to me for operation of a hyperactive thyroid gland which had failed to respond to medicines. The casualty medical officer had watched me operating on thyroid and was impressed by my technique. I was wondering why the anti-thyroid medicines were proving ineffective in this young girl. Was the diagnosis wrong?

I decided that I must examine the patient carefully. She refused examination of the chest because she felt too shy. I never once experienced this situation during my stay abroad. In India, even men feel embarrassed to remove their clothes in front of the doctor!

The doctor accompanying her informed me that the family was conservative and already two doctors had examined her and advised operation for thyroid and was it really necessary for me to auscultate the chest? When I declined to treat her unless I was allowed to examine her the way I wanted, she agreed. It was a surprise to all including me that she had a defective heart valve. This happened about 50 years ago. Luckily I had done a post in thoracic surgery and so the diagnosis was not difficult. I had avoided a fatality in the operation theatre.

I was trained in the era of the clinical approach which has now rapidly disappeared. Clinical medicine had many deficiencies but technological medicine also has great limitations. The doctors are losing touch with their patients; thinking doctors have been replaced by doctors who treat on the basis of reports. Technology has made some surgeons technicians.

Everything old is not gold and all things recent are not a blessing. I taught medical students that they must learn to ask questions. I would give the example of the famous Sherlock Holmes story *Silver Blaze* by Conan Doyle. Why did the dog not bark when the horse was stolen before the Derby race? I asked why the antithyroid drugs did not act in a young girl.

A family physician who was well known in our area was so impressed that he referred hundreds of patients to me during the next 30 years. Such opportunities arrive without prior intimation. One bad case in the beginning of one's practice may also ruin careers.

Many years ago, I was called to operate on a doctor's relative in his nursing home. I was elated because in this vast city, a doctor had selected me from among hundreds of surgeons. I went to his office where I was served tea.

I wanted to see the operation theatre and was told that I was already sitting in it! What I thought was an examination table was the operating table and the doctor's room was in fact his operation theatre. I did not have the courage to refuse because it was a well-known place. Antibiotics were used liberally and they defeated the terrible germs hovering in that part-time operation theatre. I made up my mind that it would not happen again.

Soon after I started working in the teaching hospital, residents from other units came to observe my surgeries. My chief who was 30 years senior to me was allergic to anything new and started creating problems. He felt threatened; my operating list was slashed and I got only leftovers, meant for the residents.

I learnt a very important lesson that if I have to survive I had to see that my seniors felt comfortably superior.

I had to maintain a low profile, I utilised the time to teach residents and students.

No one could stop this. I could make a name as a good teacher. I had my chance to operate on emergency cases; he would not attend midnight emergencies because he stayed far away from the hospital. We must always try to look for windows of opportunities when the other doors are closed. Lucky are those few who get a senior who appreciates a junior's good work.

I travelled once a week by a suburban train to a charitable hospital 60 km away from Bombay. I conducted outdoor patient examinations and performed routine operations which did not require much post-operative care. I was paid a small sum of Rs. 150 a month. I did this for seven years and developed many contacts. Patients requiring major operation would come to me in Bombay.

I also visited a town 200 km from Bombay on three weekends in a month for a year. The train would leave Bombay in the evening on Saturday and reach Nashik city late at night. I would work the whole of Sunday and return home in the evening. One weekend in a month, I was on emergency call in Bombay.

There was no qualified surgeon with my degrees in Nashik. I could earn more making three visits to this town than what I earned during the rest of the month in Bombay. There is now a medical college and many super-specialty hospitals in Nashik.

One day when I went on a ward round, I found my resident and ward sister agitated because the relative of a patient dying of stomach cancer told them that I had taken money for his admission to the ward. They assured the relatives that it was impossible that I would do anything of this kind.

Unfortunately, there were a few among the doctors who would collect money for admission and operation in hospitals where the poor were treated free.

I went to the relative and asked him who he believed had given me money. He told me that the man who got him admitted to the hospital had collected the money on my behalf. I took him through the ward and he was convinced that not a single patient had to give money for admission.

The roots of corruption are deep and wide and it is safe and wise to keep on an ethical path away from temptation. One should vow to be a part of the solution and not of the problem.

Giving and receiving bribes has become an accepted practice in many fields and the medical profession is no exception. But doctors have a responsibility to set examples of ethical practice. A good surgeon may not amass wealth, but can lead a comfortable life in the twilight of his career.

"If wrong you do and false you play,
in summer amongst flowers,
You must atone,
You shall pay in winter
amongst showers."

— Longfellow

Longfellow's poem is the truth which some realise late in life. Ethical individuals must succeed in life and successful individuals should remain ethical in life otherwise future generations may get a message that honesty does not pay.

Though I was not connected with any network of power, privileges or social circles, I could become a role model for two generations of surgeons. I feel very satisfied that many surgeons whom I trained have a reputation of being good surgeons following ethical practices. I know that some have trodden the wrong path. Nevertheless, even if a handful choose the right path, our job is done. There is a law of wastage in any human activity!

Doctors are often castigated for their selfishness, cheating, and exploitation but I have frequently seen the other side of the coin—rich patients exploiting the doctors. They take admission to the general ward and occupy the bed that is meant for those who cannot afford the expensive one. They cheat the hospitals and also the doctors.

Education in human values will have to be included in the medical curriculum so that at least some will look after India's poor. Unless we sow, we cannot reap. I continue to be an optimist because in spite of this depressing picture there are doctors, nurses, and hospitals who are doing excellent work against odds, something that I have personally experienced throughout my career.

❑ ❑ ❑

Chapter 7

Visit to Districts

I was working in a teaching hospital in Mumbai where the facilities were very inadequate and it attracted patients from the rural areas. I suggested to the administration that teaching hospitals should be linked with district hospitals for mutual exchange of experiences; that surgeons from Mumbai should go to districts and district surgeons should visit Mumbai.

When I broached the topic to my colleagues, the common response was: "What purpose would we serve by visiting hospitals with inadequate facilities?" They did not agree with my view that unless we experienced the problems of district surgeons, we could never contribute to improve the services in rural India. Their suggestion was to let the district doctors come to Bombay and see our work.

I remember an instance where a well-known surgeon from the USA came to Bombay under the technological transfer scheme. Many delegates attended the conference. The suture material got over in the morning session itself! Surgeons from abroad do not know the ground realities in India and city surgeons are ignorant about how surgeons work in the interiors. That was the picture forty years ago.

I was brought up in small towns and knew the quality of services in local hospitals. Unless experienced surgeons went to districts and worked with doctors in their set-up, things would not improve. Deficiency in infrastructure can prove to be a stimulus for creativity. I have demonstrated major operations in the district hospital set-ups and felt very happy to see some surgeons motivated to do better work in their set-up rather than blaming their poor facilities.

I remember an episode during my second visit to UK in 1971 when I visited some centres in England to observe the operative techniques of surgeons of repute.

Dr. Norman Tanner of London was a very well-known surgeon for stomach ulcers. Luckily on the day I visited the hospital, no assistant was available and he requested me to assist him for two operations. It was a great opportunity to see the master at work. He later gave me a lift in his expensive chauffeur-driven car. While getting down from the car, I said, "Sir, I had heard about your contribution to gastric surgery ever since I was a medical student in 1951 and today I had the great fortune to assist you. Wherever there is a reference to gastrectomy, your name will appear in golden letters."

With a twinkle in his eyes, he put his hand on my shoulder and said, "Anyone can do good surgery in London, but I think to remove an acutely inflamed appendix in a small town in India would be a more difficult and a more gratifying operation."

I narrate this instance whenever some colleagues who have trained abroad complain about the inadequate facilities in India. I tell them to go to the interior, observe how work is done there and show them how they can improve the quality of surgery.

We should train surgeons to do the best they can with whatever facilities they have and that is progress.

In 1974, I went to Dhule, a district town 400 km from Mumbai, for demonstrating common operations in the government hospital. Eight cases were selected by the local surgeons and the operative demonstrations done with the equipment available in the hospital.

I demonstrated operations for recurrent hernia, thyroid, anal fistula, etc. I must make a special mention of a patient with undiagnosed severe abdominal pain for several months. Only one X-ray was taken with barium meal on a crude X-ray machine by a technician. Endoscopes were not known. I decided that the patient needed an exploration, in medical terms, a laparotomy. It means opening up the abdomen and tackling the disease. No disease could be identified on preliminary assessment. Everybody expected it to be a negative laparotomy, and in such a situation, the normally adopted practice is to remove the appendix and hope for relief from the symptoms.

Experienced surgeons make it a point to inspect the back of the stomach which is difficult to feel. It requires additional dissection. When I lifted the stomach, the hidden culprit came to light to everybody's surprise and my relief: There was a deep ulcer on the posterior wall of the stomach which had perforated into the pancreas, the most inaccessible part in the abdomen.

I removed a major part of the stomach, and the next day when we went for a ward round, the patient on his own told us that he had not experienced any of the pain which had made his life miserable. This was the first time that an operation of this kind had been done in that hospital. The trip was highly successful. There was a feeling among the surgeons that it was possible to do more work with the facilities available to them. My demonstration in various parts of the country were met with a similar response.

One surgeon who attended the camp at Dhule was Dr. Ravindranath Tongaonkar. Three years later he informed me that he had a chance to go to Oxford for training for a few months and wanted my recommendation. I told him that in case he was not selected, he should come to Bombay with his anaesthetist wife for some time, and we would show them enough operative work to transform his performance. One day, the couple arrived and stayed for two weeks to see my work. What he wrote to me on his return to Dhule is very interesting.

Sunday 17th Aug 1975

"I have already started using your teachings, such as not worrying about every bleeding point, using minimum instruments, doing sharp dissection, etc. The most important outcome of my visit was that I could perform a vagotomy gastro jejunostomy for a case of duodenal ulcer. This was my first vagotomy but I could do it with confidence as I had assisted you in a very small hospital in a

suburb of Bombay when you had demonstrated it to us beautifully. This was the first time I did not use a single artery forceps while opening the abdomen.

I could cut the triangular ligament without holding it with the artery forceps which I would have otherwise done for fear of bleeding. I could do good mobilisation of oesophagus, identify both vagal nerves and sent sections of both to the pathologist.

Of course I must admit that I did not dare to do the Finney's gastro duodenostomy as you have advised especially because the ulcer was just at the site of anastomosis. So I did the usual gastro jejunostomy with which I was well versed.

I am certain I would not have dared to undertake vagotomy if I hadn't seen you doing this operation so methodically, cleanly, and most simply, without using blood which was the practice when I was a student.

I wanted to go to the UK but you have rightly guided me to come down to Bombay where good work will be seen in a friendly set-up.

Now a stage has come when I can use new techniques in surgery just by observing them. I must also thank you for introducing my wife to various good and competent anaesthetists so that for the first time we could use long-acting muscle relaxants in our hospital.

The relaxation anaesthesia will open a new chapter in my surgical practice. I know how often you have stated that good surgery is possible only with a good anaesthetist. I know very few people with such a helping nature as you.

A word about your instruments. I have started using your forceps. It is working excellently. I used it for the intestines as well as for the skin. I have stopped using Allis for the first time for holding the skin. I realised how post-operative pain can be minimised by paying attention to small details.

I was very impressed to see how you express your gratitude to others for their assistance in surgery.

Thank you for sending me the book 'Up from Slavery' by Booker T. Washington.

I have never looked down upon manual labour, how so ever menial it may be. In school, college, and right until the time I passed my M.S. exam, I cleaned the tables at my uncle's restaurant during the festive season.

I never gave my clothes to a laundry for washing. In the early days at our hospital, my wife and I cleaned the floors and toilets ourselves. Even today, I take the lead at household or social functions (Rotary Club events for example) when it comes to cleaning or collecting chairs or mats, and others generally follow. I found the same values emphasised in Washington's book."

Dr. Tongaonkar completed his medical education at Pune University, standing first in every examination. He could have settled down in Pune and earned greater financial rewards, but his father was a Gandhian, which influenced him to start a small hospital in a remote rural area. It has now become a well-known surgical centre in our state.

It is interesting to see how Gandhiji's influence continues to work long after his death. Dr. Tongaonkar became the President of the Rural Surgeons' Association of India and last year (2014) has been elected the President of International Federation of Rural Surgeons. It is a great joy to see students trained by me becoming role models for the younger generation.

Dr. N.M. Prabhu, President of Karnataka State Chapter of Association Surgeons of India, Hubli, wrote to me on Dec 27, 1984, "*The trouble you took to demonstrate the basic aspects of gastroscopy and biliary surgery are truly commendable. I fail to find the right words to express my gratitude for the same. I now realise why you have reached such a high position as a respected surgeon. The noble qualities of your heart coupled with remarkable surgical skill have led you to that well-deserved position.*"

Many professionals from law and medicine go to smaller towns to find more work, but my purpose was to establish good services near the patient's home.

❑ ❑ ❑

Chapter 8

Ward Rounds

I was lucky to work in a teaching hospital where the outpatient department, ward rounds and operation theatres were the real classrooms that taught the medical students and surgical residents by personal example.

Apart from being academic, the ward rounds should also be comforting, encouraging and prescribing hope to the patients. For me, it was a natural instinct to hold a patient's hand, pat his shoulder and talk with him even about non-medical matters. Human touch is crucial in comforting anxious minds and has great value in a patients' recovery. Faith is a powerful force which cannot be measured in a laboratory.

I remember an episode in a hospital in the UK. The consultant was a methodical, sincere man, excellent in his technique, but unfortunately had little understanding of the patients' mental state.

He had a grave expression and no one ever saw him smile. A patient was to be operated on at 2 pm. The conversation at 10 in the morning was:

He had the case paper in his hand. "You are Mr. So and So, right?"

"Yes, doctor."

"How long have you been not well?"

"How much improvement have you felt with medication?"

"Is the discomfort really so bad that you have opted for surgery?"

"You know surgery will be a great help, but there are some side-effects about which I am sure you are aware?"

I could see the patient becoming upset. As soon as we left the ward, I got a message from the ward sister to come to the ward as soon as I was free. I found that the patient had changed his clothes and was waiting for the discharge. He said, "I have seen the doctor on four occasions, and everything was discussed. What business did he have to ask the questions again when I was worked up and tense about the operation? I refuse to be operated by him. I will come again, but only when he goes on a vacation."

Some doctors generate hope when making a ward round and others leave behind devastated minds.

Nurses were considered inferior in status-conscious Indian society. How did I convey that this attitude was wrong? On entering the ward I would first greet the ward sister with, "How are you? Shall we start the round?"

One day the ward sister complained that students took the foot-stools from near the patient's beds during clinics and never placed them back in their original places. (The wards were crowded with patients; there was no adjacent room for teaching the students. There were foot-stools by the side of patient's bed for relations to sit.)

When she had asked them to keep the foot-stools back in their proper places, they had rudely retorted that she had no business to give the order.

I explained to the students that just as mothers had the responsibility of maintaining discipline at home, likewise sisters had authority in the ward. In England we had to take permission from the sister even to enter the ward. We had to follow the norms that the sister had laid down. The problem did not crop up again.

Patients were referred to by their names and not by cot numbers or diseases. Screens were used to maintain the dignity of patients during examinations; poor patients in my ward who were from the villages or staying in slums or on the footpaths were treated with dignity and empathy. Their expressions of gratitude were an unending joy for me throughout my career.

I was shocked to see as an examiner during postgraduate examinations in a city in the South India that breast examinations and inspection of private parts were done in the wards without the use of screens. When I showed my annoyance, I was told that the patients did not mind! They did not know that silence was the only expression of the poor and neglected. When I asked them whether they would like to be treated in this shabby way, their mute reply was of an embarrassed expression!

I mentioned this episode when I gave a talk the same evening to medical students. I told them that it had been my experience that if doctors regarded the poor and illiterate as human beings, they regarded us as gods.

One day when a new batch of undergraduate students came to the ward, nobody was wearing an apron, some boys had not shaved and a few girls were dressed as if they were going to a party after work. No one had stethoscopes because they felt that surgeons did not need them.

I thought about how to make them understand the way they should conduct themselves in the ward. In our times the ward sister would check whether we had a torch to examine the throat and eyes, a stethoscope, and an apron. Students had no courage to question the teachers, but times had changed.

A few months earlier, a consultant surgeon, trained in the 1950s like me, was annoyed to see a student wearing saffron clothes with chappals in the hospital compound.

He asked, "Why are you wearing these clothes?"

"They are my clothes."

"You are not supposed to wear such clothes in a medical college."

"Who told you so? Who are you to advise me?"

"Come to the Dean's office with me just now."

"Why should I come? He has not called me. If you have a problem, you go. I have no complaints."

We could never talk with our seniors in this way when we were students only two decades earlier.

I remembered this episode on that day. How should I handle this?

Finally I said, "How are nurses recognised in films?"

"By their uniform."

"How do you identify a doctor?"

"They wear white aprons."

"Do they carry a stethoscope?"

"Yes."

"Is a surgeon ever seen unshaven?"

"No."

"Will a patient trust a surgeon who has a shabby appearance?"

"No."

"Do we ever see a judge with jeans, chappals and T-shirt?"

"No."

I told them that we had to play our roles in the drama of life. Men carry their badges for identification in the place of work. Patients should identify you as the doctors of tomorrow.

The next day everybody turned up with aprons and stethoscopes.

One day I saw students narrating jokes and laughing in the ward. Not many patients understand English and they might have felt that the laughter was at their expense. They would feel hurt because of lack of concern for their suffering. One needs to maintain decorum in courts, temples, and churches, and that is also true of hospitals.

Whenever I meet my past students, they have something to say of the way I taught them. I met some doctors who were carrying a lasting impression of my one comment, "Whenever I enter a ward, 60 eyes look at me with hope and I must therefore conduct myself with enthusiasm, smile, empathy and reassuring touch."

I would go to every patient and ask simple questions.

- How are you? Same, better or not so good as compared to yesterday?
- How much improvement have you experienced... how many paise in a rupee? This question even the most illiterate patient could answer. In England, the question was: How many shillings in a pound? (This style of questions was very unusual but appreciated even in England.)
- Did you sleep?
- Have you passed urine?
- Have you passed gas, had a motion?
- What you have eaten?
- Are you moving your legs, walking ... how much?

I would always look into their eyes, pat them, and their grateful expressions were a tonic for me. These days a patient's condition is discussed in a low voice with attention focussed on the daily charts, CT scans, and blood reports. They treat the results of the investigations and not the patient.

Patients feel that they are in impending danger from some health problem. The doctor's team moves on rapidly to the next case. The human touch is missing and patients remain dissatisfied. Here is another example of man distancing himself from man.

My American surgeon friend from San Diego Dr. Olgard Dabbert M.D. wrote to me, *"It is more difficult to look at ourselves in the mirror and reflect on the changes that have occurred in just one generation.*

While the science of medicine has advanced, the listening, the empathy, the compassion, the availability and the BOND between the doctor and the patient have all been relegated to an uncomfortable corner, waiting to be rediscovered."

There are two diseases that make patients untouchables. One is leucoderma which disfigures the patient, but is not contagious. The other one, leprosy, was a curse on the human race. Patients developed deformities in their hands and face, and festering wounds. They became untouchables and outcasts.

The story of Paul Brand, an English orthopaedic surgeon who did pioneering work in Christian Medical College in Vellore in South India, is worth mentioning. It appeared in the *Journal of American Medical Association* in March 1959, "*A young leper came to his crowded clinic one day and presented his crippled hands. When the digital joints and muscles had been carefully tested he was told that something could be done to restore power and usefulness to his wasted and anaesthetic fingers and he was passed on to the staff to be admitted for operation.*

On the way, he suddenly halted and broke down in a storm of tears. To the nurse who sought to comfort him, he explained that his emotional outburst was due to overwhelming happiness, not because the surgeon had told him his case could be remedied but because instead of shrinking from contact with him as he had expected, the surgeon had taken his two deformed hands gently in his own and in so doing had done what even the members of the lad's own family had always been afraid to do, and when finally the surgeon had patted him on the shoulder and looked at him with a friendly smile, the load of bitter resentment at his lot which had been piling up in his heart for years suddenly vanished. He had heard the first kind word spoken to him in all the time he had been a leper."

Human touch is as basic a need as food/clothing/shelter. My final farewell to my uncle who died with his head in my lap was that I held his hand when he was gasping—a very intimate and powerful communication. He was at peace in the end.

I am not a Facebook fan, but one day I received many phone calls that made me check the Internet and this is what I read:

June 5, 2013

"It was 7:30 am on a Wednesday nearly 31 years ago at GT Hospital near Crawford market, VT, Mumbai. The young house surgeon was very happy that day. His reason for happiness was the surgical reward he got from his seniors and teachers. There was an unwritten rule in the game of surgical learning. The measure of your success was the number of appendixes, hernias and hydroceles operated upon and the number of abdomens opened and closed. Patients were identified by their cot numbers and illnesses rather than by their names, and they were considered as bodies with damaged parts. The young doctor was picking up the skills of his seniors and acting as a demigod for the poor and needy patients.

As I said, I was very happy that day. Though the junior-most, I was part of a prestigious surgical unit in the Sir J.J. Group of Hospitals headed by the renowned surgeon, Dr. V. N. Shrikhande. That day I was going to assist Shrikhande sir in a hemicolectomy, i.e. removal of a large intestinal tumour on the right side along with the adjoining bowel. Shrikhande sir was expected to enter the main O.T. precisely at 8 am. The O.T. sister was arranging instruments on the trolley. The anaesthetist had just started setting up a fresh IV line, when a group of 7-8 third-year MBBS students entered the O.T. A smart-looking girl came forward and started asking me about the case. I told them about the large, palpable colonic mass in the right side of the abdomen and how interesting this case was. As the students gathered around the table and took turns to palpate the abdomen, Dr. Shrikhande entered the operation theatre. Sir saw the scene and asked me, "Upadhye, what's this?" I said, "Good morning, sir. He is a 45-year-old male patient, a labourer from Byculla. His chief complaints are abdominal pain, vomiting, and loss of appetite..."

"Upadhye, I know that. Tell me, when did these students join our unit?"

"One month ago, sir."

"When was the patient admitted?"

"Ten days back, sir...."

"So they had time to examine this patient in the ward."

"We got him investigated...."

Sir interrupted me and asked me the next question,

"Upadhye, what does he do?"

I said, "Sir, he's a labourer, he pulls a cart from VT to Crawford Market."

"So, he's poor."

"Yes sir, very poor."

" Upadhye, tell me...."

"The next two questions he asked me changed my life. It changed my attitude. It gave me an altogether different vision."

"Sir asked me in Marathi, "Upadhye, tyala tension yet nahi ka?" (Upadhye, isn't he anxious and tense?) "Upadhye, tyala man naahi ka?" (Doesn't he have a mind and emotions?)"

"It took me a little time, but I understood what he was trying to say. I hung my head in shame. I was struck dumb. These two questions opened my eyes. It started transforming my robotic mind into a human one. I have been taught surgery by many teachers, seniors, and my friends during my time at the Sir J. J. Group of Hospitals. I also learnt surgical skills from many experts at conferences and workshops."

"Dr. V. N. Shrikhande taught me surgery, yes. I consider myself very lucky to have a guru like him with a heart of gold, a sharp surgical mind, and the skills of an artist. I am honoured to be the student of a respected surgeon and an easily approachable human being."

"When I look back, I am satisfied with my life. I did not become a great surgeon. I did not have extraordinary surgical skills. I did not give lectures in conferences or demonstrate my surgical expertise in workshops, nor did I present outstanding papers. I am satisfied that I understood the trauma my patients were going through and this was taught to me by Dr. Shrikhande. I always tried to be a

good human being, a rare quality that Dr. Vinayak Shrikhande had in full measure."

Such a feedback from a student energises me even at this age!

I must quote one anecdote. I was making a round in Bombay Hospital when a lady stopped me and said, "Sir, do you remember me? I was your student 30 years ago."

"No, I don't recall you. Where are you now?"

"I am a surgeon settled in USA and for that I owe a great deal to you."

"How come?"

"I went to the USA, but did not get admission into any programme. I did only locum jobs and was feeling rather frustrated. One night a patient was admitted for retention of urine. The two doctors on call could not pass the catheter. I asked them to give me a chance because I saw that their technique was incorrect. I remembered your clinic when you had stressed: Comfort the patient, reassure him that there will be no pain. Urethra is seven inches long, only lubricating the tip of the catheter is not adequate. Lubricate the urethra and not the catheter.' I did that and the catheter slid in smoothly. I remembered the humourous way you had said, that we should not treat the catheter like the long spoon misers use to take a few drops of *ghee* (clarified butter) from a jar!"

The patient was related to the trustee of the hospital management committee. Within a fortnight, I got a regular job; and since then I have not looked back."

(Male urethra is a single tube about 7-inches long and has different segments through its course namely penis, perineum and prostrate. When a patient is in pain and tense, passing a catheter may pose a problem. There was a time when the practice was to lubricate the tip of the catheter and introduce into the urethra till it enters the distended urinary bladder. The practice has changed. Disposable catheters have come and the lubricant jelly is pushed in the urethra to lubricate the entire length. ...Sounds very simple, but not practised 40 years back!)

One clinic had changed a young doctor's future. I did not burden students with data and statistics. I taught them some common procedures every doctor must know well, like passing a stomach tube through the nose in cases of intestinal obstruction and passing a catheter when patients are unable to urinate.

I taught my residents how to write letters to referring physicians and write discharge notes, a neglected activity in hospitals in India. One or two residents always accompanied me for my lectures. I taught them how to take photographs and prepare the presentations for lectures. The era of power point presentation, cut and paste technique had not arrived.

The operation theatre is a place that demands the dignity of a place of worship and everyone was treated with courtesy. I remembered my experience as a student in 1950. I had now an opportunity to practise what I had planned.

Our focus of attention was the patient. Fear of the unknown is a nightmare. Patients are wheeled into the operation theatre in an anxious state. He sees everyone wearing a mask, he does not know anyone there. He knows only the surgeon who has advised the operation. Throughout my career, I never operated without talking to the patient and letting him see me before he was given an anaesthetic because my presence, my touch, gave them confidence. On occasions, the theatre staff got restless, but the patient's interest was uppermost in my mind. Patients were also never disrobed before anaesthesia. It was a common sight to remove patients' clothes like removing wrapping paper around gifts.

The normal practice is to inform the team to start the operation so that no time is wasted. The use of an operation theatre is charged by the hour. Many times I have met patients who never saw the surgeon who operated on them, because after the operation, the patient is shifted to the ICU, and when he is better the juniors see him till he is discharged. The system works well for efficient working but not for human relationship.

I had made it a routine to talk with anxious relatives before starting the operation. Sometimes when the operation was lengthy, I would send a word through the nurse to inform the relatives that the patient was fine and that they shouldn't worry. The resident would show them the diseased part which had been removed during surgery.

I taught the residents and even the nurses how to put on caps, masks, and scrub the hands. The water wastage while scrubbing hands before surgery would hurt me. Not many were aware that even modern hospitals in Mumbai have to buy water from tankers. I would remind them that men, women and children have to walk for miles to fetch water, a common distressing sight in India.

Assistants and sisters were shown the important steps of the operation. One or two medical students were encouraged to assist in the operation. I remember a surgeon who said, "On the first operation day, I assisted in gall bladder surgery and decided to become a surgeon."

A patient with post-operative complications was sent to me by a past resident. The patient suspected negligence and though the problem was not serious, he had a grudge against the surgeon. I drained the pus and explained how and why infections occur even in modern reputed hospitals.

I sent him back to the same surgeon for a follow-up. The doctor-patient relationship must not be disturbed on flimsy grounds and there was no negligence on the part of the surgeon. I received a letter from my resident: 'I continue to learn from you how to help juniors and guide patients'.

Books can inspire, educate, and even change individuals. I have therefore given books as gifts to my students. *Up from Slavery* by Booker T. Washington was a book given to me in 1956 by a friend who bought it for a rupee from a footpath vendor near Churchgate station, Bombay.

That book was a reaffirmation of what I had learnt from my parents, that hard work, constant improvement, dedication, integrity, gratitude, and simplicity are the greatest assets in life.

Washington was a slave born on a farm in southern USA. He experienced humiliation and a harsh life. He attended a one-room school, did menial jobs in a household and struggled hard to escape from poverty.

He succeeded and founded the Tuskegee Institute. He held the view that a black man's salvation lay in hard work, education, simple living, and self-reliance. His was a success story of upward mobility and has a universal message for all time. He led the blacks in America in the struggle to improve their lot.

This message from his book is ingrained in my mind:

"I beg you to remember that whenever our life touches yours, we help or hinder. Whenever your life touches ours, you make us stronger or weaker. There is no escape. Man drags man down or man lifts man up..."

— Booker T. Washington

The book was not available in India. When I went to London I learnt that the book was available at Foyle's. The salesman was surprised when I told him that I wanted to buy fifty copies. He sent for the manager who asked, "Why do you want so many copies?"

"I read this book when I was an undergraduate student in Bombay and it had a big impact on my mind. Good literature can change or mould attitudes. Unless we sow, we cannot grow."

"What do you do in Bombay?"

"I am a professor of surgery and it is my practice to give inspiring books as presents to my residents."

"I am happy to meet a surgeon and book-lover like you and it is my privilege to give you a concession in the price."

I have still kept the copy of the book given to me sixty years back along with a few other gifts that I consider priceless treasures.

I have preserved an envelope containing Rs. 11 given to me by a Parsi gentleman on October 19, 1961 when I started my practice in Bombay. He said, "Please keep it; it will bring you good luck." I still remember his kind, smiling face. These are the true mementos. Grateful minds are happy.

A student wrote, "Sir, I am very happy to inform you that I recently got married and took no dowry. I come from a very orthodox family and in our community, expecting and demanding dowry is the usual practice at weddings. There was a great deal of opposition from my family; even my in-laws felt a bit hurt that I was not accepting a dowry from them which they could easily afford. But sir, working with you for six weeks as an undergraduate student completely changed my thinking. I was lucky. Two of my friends have also decided not to accept dowry."

Any attitude which is insulting to women must be opposed. Respect for women should be inculcated in the young in schools and colleges and one should set a good example by one's behaviour. I did not teach only surgery, I taught them to become better human beings.

❑ ❑ ❑

Chapter 9

Shrikhande Clinic

In 1977, I started Shrikhande Clinic, my small surgical set-up, in Hindu Colony, a quiet residential locality in central Mumbai. It had been my dream to create a centre of excellence. By then I had gained sufficient experience and confidence to make this a reality.

Shrikhande Clinic represents a philosophy, one that I desired would continue long after my tenure. Public hospitals have served poor patients for many years, while private hospitals were few, catering to only a small section of society. Nursing homes (as they are commonly referred to in India) serve large populations who do not want to go to public hospitals nor can afford the bigger private ones.

I had minutely observed many hospital theatres before designing my own. I was no architect, but I had a clear vision of how I wanted my clinic to be built. A vision that was brought to life by my engineer brother and an architect friend. I made unconventional choices - be it the use of space, the colours used in the operating room or the presence of soothing music during surgeries. It was not an easy path. I remember an especially difficult time when the construction work had stalled for over two weeks as I was unable to pay the contractor a sum of Rs. 10, 000. No bank would grant me a loan. Many of my friends lent me the funds, and I paid interest until I could repay them. Now when I receive frequent phone calls from banks, offering me loans, I am tempted to tell them that they are 40 years late!

My two close friends, Dr. Vinayak Shinde, who assisted me for over two decades, Mr Ravi Desai, my school friend, and my wife, Dr. Suhas, were my support system from the start.

Mrs. Bharati Joshi-Gore has managed the operation theatre with great efficiency from day one. She joined three months before the start, and in fact stayed with us at home, with the family. The credit for our introduction goes to my student from Grant Medical College, Dr. Sunil Vaze. I appointed her even before meeting her, merely from the way she spoke to me over the phone.

I must also remember with gratitude, our staff of 16, most of who have been with the clinic since the beginning, and my driver, Shetty, who has been with me since 1977. All of these people have helped me establish this modest hospital of repute.

My wife, Suhas, not only fully supported my decision to start this venture, but she also regularly assisted me during surgeries in the initial years until unexpected domestic responsibilities took up all her time. My son-in-law, Dr. Anand, has been a constant since 1982. It is rare to come across individuals who can share your vision and values and seamlessly fit in. He has added the specialities of therapeutic endoscopy and laparoscopic surgery to the general and G.I. surgical work, and continues the traditions of our noble profession. My daughter, Dr. Anjana, has been looking after the administrative and financial management of Shrikhande Clinic, including caring for the staff, with great maturity and competence, since the untimely death of Dr. Shinde in 1993. My younger daughter, Vasanti, has always contributed in different capacities over the years as and when needed. Before joining Tata Memorial Hospital, my son, Dr. Shailesh, took active part in the clinic. Dr. Rasika Sandu has been associated with the clinic since 1995. Over the years, she has been an invaluable help as a clinical and surgical assistant. I can proudly say that my entire family has lived my dream!

More than 8000 procedures, including a large number of major gastrointestinal operations, have been performed since its inception 38 years ago. Over 40 residents, who had completed their MS (Master of Surgery), have been trained at Shrikhande

Clinic. More than 350 surgeons from India and a few from abroad have attended surgeries as observers. A small hospital has proved to be a good training centre.

We never ask for deposits. Professional fees are adjustable, some are free. I am often asked how we can sustain without taking a deposit from the patients; what if the patient never paid? My answer is simple – "The proportion of grateful, honest patients far outweighs that of those who aren't." I believe in the inherent goodness of people, and asking for a deposit from a patient who entrusts his life to me, does not suit me. Times are changing fast. Insurance cover was not common in the earlier times, as it is now. However I firmly believe that small nursing homes like Shrikhande Clinic will continue to be relevant because of the ethical practice, reasonable fees and the personal attention to the patients.

❑ ❑ ❑

Chapter 10

Overcoming a Stammer

I was born with a speech defect. Stammering haunts me; it is like a shadow that never deserts me except during sleep. Many inadquacies can be compensated for, but how does one keep a speech defect a secret?

I was perhaps the only student with a stammer in my school. A stammerer is always on top of the mimicry hit list. Oral examinations were a nightmare, the telephone was a terror, and introducing myself would make me nervous. Stammering is like driving a car which frequently stalls in heavy traffic. Other car drivers honk and you are subjected to their odd expressions.

I did not have to travel by bus in Pune or Belgaum, so the problem first surfaced when I came to Bombay. I was filled with anxiety when buying a ticket in a bus or at the railway station. I have, on occasion, written my destination down on a piece of paper, such as 'Dombivli return', because I would stammer on the word 'return'. The person issuing the ticket would look at me with pity, assuming I was mute.

Speaking on the phone still poses difficulties. The person on the other side gets impatient on getting no response. I have at times bought a ticket to Kalyan when I just wanted to go to Byculla by paying four times more! Nobody can appreciate the torture a person with a speech defect goes through. I was also scared of interviews and of introducing myself, even in small gatherings. Unfortunately, medical science has found no cure for this hindrance. For reasons not known this defect is much lesser in females.

When you are stuck on certain words, it is a humiliating experience to have someone else complete your sentence.

As it is, it is hard when others display impatience or indicate with hand gestures that you should slow down. Overweight people are always aware of their excess weight. I am supremely conscious of the heavy tongue on which I have no control at most times. In fact, when I try to control it, it fails even more miserably.

Any jokes centred on a person's physical defects make me sad. I remember an episode thirty years ago in Pune. We had gone for lunch and as we were coming out of the restaurant, a family got out of a Mercedes Benz car (a status symbol in an era when India produced only two car models). The boy laughed at my son's appearance—he had a kidney problem at that time and was treated with medication that made him very fat. His face was swollen like a football. I wanted to slap the boy. That was the only time I have felt like physically hurting anyone. His parents, instead of chiding their son, followed suit.

Culture and wealth do not often go hand in hand.

Many remedies were suggested for my stammer in childhood. "Speak slowly", "do not be in a hurry", "utter every word carefully", "practise reciting of Sanskrit shlokas", "put marbles in your mouth and shout". These suggestions were as simplistic as telling a disturbed man to relax and remove all thoughts from his mind! Even that in itself is a thought! Armchair advice is easy to dispense.

Ever conscious of my speech defect, it became my habit to take inspiration from individuals who had overcome handicaps and succeeded in life.

I knew that Somerset Maugham, whose books I read with relish in college, had a severe speech defect. When I was reading *Of Human Bondage*, I could empathise with the miseries suffered by Philip because of his club foot. My stammering was like a club foot that one cannot hide and that makes one miserable.

Somerset Maugham wrote of fellow-author Arnold Bennett, who also stammered, in his book of essays, *The Vagrant Mood:* "Few knew the distressing sense it gave rise to, to bar complete contact with other men. It may be that except for the stammer which forced him to introspection, he would never have been a writer..."

I was in search of someone who was a powerful speaker in spite of his stammer.

And the opportunity came in 1951 when I heard Aneurin Bevan, the British Health Minister, giving a powerful talk in spite of his speech impediment in the packed Anatomy Hall of the Grant Medical College in Bombay. I still remember Mr. Bevan in a cream suit, his face red because of the heat, talking to students before he left. I was fascinated.

A handicapped person finds ways and means of using other faculties. I became a good listener. I listened to my patients with full interest, patience, and concentration. A gentle touch with my hands, a reassuring expression and a smiling face worked wonders. My stint as a resident doctor was an important turning point. My patients ignored my speech defect and trusted me; my enthusiasm, concern, my touch, and my smile were my assets, both in India and England. My ward rounds were full of hope and enthusiasm. Individuals can convey their empathy and concern through a kind of energy that others can experience but cannot describe.

I have regularly experienced that when you are really keen to achieve something, everything falls in place. I happened to attend a symposium in 1963-64 where some promising young medical consultants were speaking about their way to the top. The Chairman was the late Dr. A.V. Baliga who was the foremost surgeon in the country known for his popular clinics in medical colleges, his exceptional clinical acumen and skilful surgery. At the end of all the speeches, Dr. Baliga rose to give the concluding comments. He spoke for hardly ten minutes, but his talk was so outstanding that the others faded in comparison. On that day I realised that an ability to talk from the podium is a very important asset for a surgeon to succeed. I decided that I had to do something to manage my speech defect. And within a few weeks, things started moving.

On a Saturday morning not soon after, I heard my colleague speaking confidently in a weekly clinical meeting in our hospital. After the meeting he gave me a lift in his car. When I appreciated his skills in speaking he said, "What is so great about that? Anyone can talk."

"But I have a speech defect."

"So what? Anyone can talk."

"Can you guide me?"

At that particular time our car was going past an institute where he had taken lessons in public speaking. He took me there. The dean of the institute, Professor Cawasji, after a conversation with me, felt that I was a well-read person and there was no reason why I could not become a good speaker. I thought that he was encouraging me just as doctors give hope to patients who are losing their battle with life.

I was impatient. I wanted to learn public speaking and I joined the class. I however left it halfway because I could grasp the essence of the art. I realised that without jumping into the water, swimming cannot be learnt. I wanted to stand behind a microphone and face the audience. I gave the first talk of my life at the age of thirty-four before an audience of fifteen doctors. I was drenched with sweat, but I could talk.

My first stab at public speaking was an utter surprise to me. After the next ten lectures, I knew I could hold an audience's interest. I was making rapid progress. I have never looked back.

I visited an exhibition of the work of foot-and-mouth artists where I saw this poster:

'They said I could not paint because I do not have any hands. I have proved them wrong. Have you ever wondered what it would be like to live the rest of your life without the use of your hands? We unfortunately have to. Since we can't use our hands we create paintings with the brush held in our mouth or between our toes.'

A handicap can inspire some individuals to excel and reach unusual heights. I have given hundreds of lectures at national- and state-level medical conferences as well as at social functions. However, even now I feel some tension before I start a talk, and at the same time, a sense of achievement when I get a good response. Every conversation, every speech, still continues to be an obstacle race.

Many people, including doctors, have approached me to guide them on how to manage stammering. I tell them that I do not know. There are two things which are beyond my understanding.

My stammering disappeared after an attack of typhoid in 1943. Unfortunately, it resurfaced after a few weeks and has remained with me since. I also cannot explain why once I stand on a rostrum, my speech suddenly improves. Normally, it is exactly the opposite.

I have been fortunate to be invited to give lectures at different events. I was the chief guest for a prize distribution ceremony in a prestigious school in Mumbai in the 1970s. Two days later, I had a telephone call from a lady who told me that her daughter aged ten had kept the members of the family spellbound by giving a talk based on all the points she had noted from my talk. I invited the parents to bring the child to my consulting room. I was delighted to see this small girl with bright eyes showing me a notebook in which she had written the gist of my talk. Making notes of important points without missing any is very difficult, and is only possible when a lecture captivates a listener. Being appreciated by patients was a common experience, but that I could impress a child through my talk thrilled me beyond words.

In 2012, I was felicitated by a medical university for my role in advancing gastrointestinal surgery. I gave an acceptance speech attended by doctors and their family members. A surgeon approached me with a request. His daughter of twelve years felt so inspired by my talk that she wanted to be photographed with me.

My house at Deshpande Galli, Belgaum, 1931-1939

Old hostel, Grant Medical College, Mumbai

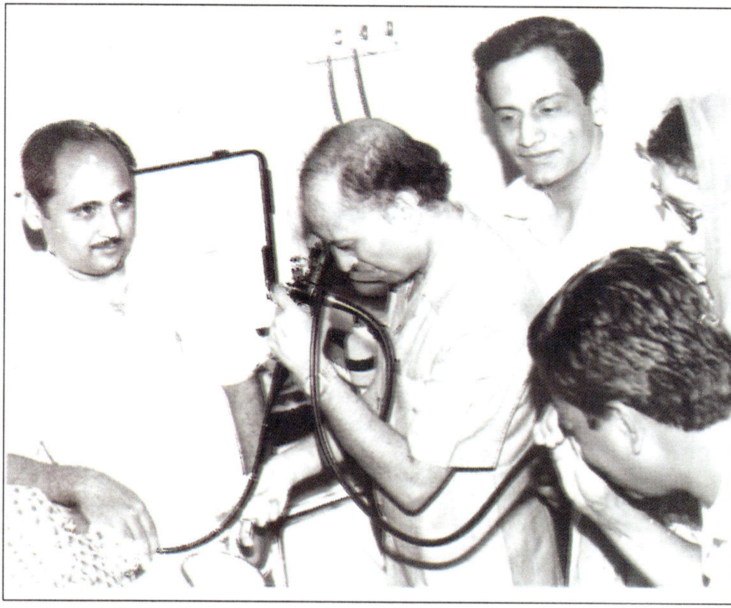

Teaching Endoscopy in Districts, 1979

Clock that never failed!

Clock that never worked!

With son-in-law Dr. Anand Nande (L)
and son Dr. Shailesh Shrikhande (R)

From L to R: With Drs. Kishor, Rasika, Jyotsna and Anand
Our team at Bombay Hospital Institute of Medical Sciences, Mumbai

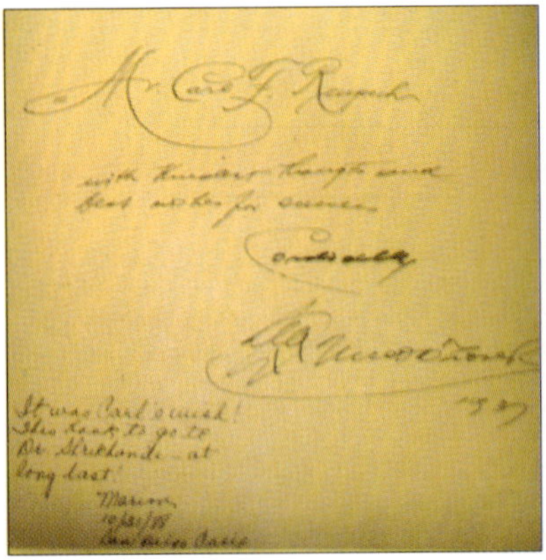

Max Thorek's book
gifted to me by
his wife Marion, 1988
(Refer page 220)

The book
'Creative Camera Art'
by Max Thorek presented
to Reupsch, 1937

Bhairu Ratan Damani Puraskar
for Literature, Solapur, 2009

I asked her, "What was it in particular that you liked about my talk?"

She read a note she had made from my talk, "Every individual has some talents. Concentrate on them rather than feeling sorry for some drawbacks in life."

I enjoy it when people, whether they are small children or senior citizens, connect with me spontaneously!

I am happy I have become an effective speaker. I am now in my 80s, and I have stopped operating, but I have no regrets at being left out from the exciting life surrounding a surgeon. Invitations for lectures on various topics keep me busy.

I have a mission to educate society in matters of health, especially in the present era, when medicine has become an industry. Doctors in the past gave hope, but now they seem to be messengers of anxiety. The message today is that everyone is ill unless proved otherwise by thorough check-ups. It is exactly opposite in the legal field where everyone is innocent unless proved guilty by evidence.

Lastly, a true story connected with speech defects.

A young boy from a village near Aurangabad had a terrible speech defect that made him the target of anger, ridicule and even beatings from his father. The mother sympathised with him, but could not utter a word against her husband. The boy failed in the school exams and got a severe beating from his father. He ran away from home to end his life. He was found by strangers lying under a tree in the next village. He was hungry and ill.

The villagers looked after him and ultimately the anxious parents traced him the next day. He had marks of injury on his body. His face was swollen because of crying. His mother gave him a bath. His father was still angry and not repentant for the cruelty he had inflicted on his disabled son. He went to bed with a severe body ache. There was a radio in the room. He turned it on and heard one of my interviews on All India Radio. He had heard my name as a famous surgeon, but did not know that I stammered.

This was a turning point in his life.

He decided that he would prove that his speech defect was not a barrier to his growth. He passed all his examinations with a first class, got admission to a medical college on merit, did post-graduation in general surgery and married a doctor. When they went to the small town where the husband lived, they saw a severely ill patient being taken to a dispensary on a rickety cart pushed by his very poor relatives walking barefoot. The sight disturbed the young couple and they took an instant decision to start a small hospital in that town. They went to a temple in that small town and took an oath to serve the poor patients there.

It so happened that his father-in-law had built a hospital in a big town near Pune. The couple felt convinced that what they had learnt must be used for poor, needy patients. This was their inner calling. His wife resigned from the government post and the couple embarked on this difficult journey. A few years later, a modern hospital with ICU, ventilators, and facilities for laparoscopic surgery was built. Grateful patients spread the word and soon, they even had patients from big towns coming to them for treatment.

It was overwhelming to realise that by chance I had influnced a life for the better. I was touched to know that he had kept a blank plaque at the hospital entrance to inscribe my name, when I would visit the hospital.

There was an international conference on tropical diseases, held in Bombay Hospital in 1976. I was not attached to Bombay Hospital then. Dr. R.J. Manekshaw, the renowned pioneer in the field of plastic surgery, asked me just 2 hours before if I could give a short speech since he liked the way I spoke. I was his registrar for 2 years till 1957 and had no clue for 19 years that he had been appreciative of my manner of presenting my thoughts! I was not even dressed appropriately for the occasion. But I accepted the offer. I said, "The past four days would remain memorable in the history of Bombay, which is known as 'Gateway to India'. It will also be now known as 'Get together in India'. Doctors from the East and the West have gathered to see how they can heal the sick.

The world is shrinking. Science of the West and philosophy of the East will meet to wipe out the tears of the suffering humanity. Dr. Christian Bernard reportedly told the press, "Indian dishes are delicious." We all know it. "Indian women were attractive." It is obvious to all. "Indian telephone services are efficient."

I took a pause and then said, "I hope one day he will be right!"

There was an applause because our telephone services were very poor then. My talk was covered in the press. What is interesting is that, I gave the talk in the same hall where Dr. A.V. Baliga had spoken twelve years before and which had motivated me to be a public speaker! (I must mention that our telephone services are now really excellent. We are progressing, I continue to be an optimist.)

Chance plays an unexpected role in one's destiny.

❑ ❑ ❑

Chapter 11

Turning Point

It is stressful to keep improving our professional career in times of rapid changes. I will illustrate one turning point in my career.

It was in 1972. I had operated on a complicated case of gall stones impacted in the bile duct of a middle-aged lady. The senior medical practitioner who was related to the patient was impressed with the way I tackled the case. The patient came for a follow-up every month. One day, I saw the patient's parents in the hospital and for a moment I was worried that something had gone wrong with my patient. I came to know that their son had abdominal pain due to kidney stones and had to be admitted under the care of the urologist. I realised that the era of specialisation had arrived. Formerly when patients had a good experience with a surgeon, he was consulted for all surgical problem. I had just crossed forty years and had to think about specialisation. We had specialists in urology, ear-nose-throat, pediatrics, orthopaedics, plastic surgery, but none in gastrointestinal surgery in which I decided to take interest.

I bought an endoscope, and within ten days detected a case of stomach cancer in a young man of forty-two who was being treated as a case of peptic ulcer. He had survived for twenty-four years, because the disease had not spread beyond the stomach. I started getting references from the three government hospitals attached to Grant Medical College. None had a flexible gastroscope because of the cost factor. Instruments for heart surgery were free from import duty, but a gastroscope was charged at 110% because it was not perceived as life-saving equipment!

(Doctors were very keen to see the stomach from within. Initially the scopes were rigid and limited the vision in a curved organ like

the stomach. A flexible endoscope with good lighting was a boon for the medical profession. Endoscopy was normally done by the physicians.)

I took one more decision. I stopped accepting urology work against the advice of some seniors. I had learnt the operation of Millin's prostectomy while in the UK, and very few were trained for this method in Bombay. A specialty means remaining faithful to the chosen field. A boy cannot remain faithful to two girls! My decision proved correct because other specialist surgeons started referring digestive problems to me. I became one of the surgeons known to have established gastrointestinal surgery in Bombay. Later I was chosen to be the first President of the Indian Chapter of the International Hepato Pancreato Biliary Association.

I met a gastroenterologist from Germany and came to know about excellent therapeutic endoscopy being done in Hamburg by Professor Nib Soehendra. I met him and realised the great potential in therapeutic endoscopy work. I spent one month with him. I attended the conference in Paris as his guest for the International Conference of Endoscopy. That evening, the professor was reminiscing about his childhood in Indonesia; how financial constraints made him leave the country and how, though he had earned international recognition, he had a desire to do something for his people at home. He said, "Professor Shrikhande, you are lucky to be in your country helping your people there." I made him an immediate offer. I said, "Professor Soehendra, I will send you the best of my residents, please train them and I can assure you that it will be the best gift you could give us."

The agreement was sealed by the clink of our wine glasses. I was so burdened with operative surgery that I had no time for endoscopy work, and so I sent my best student and son-in-law, Dr. Anand Nande, to him for training. He was perhaps the first surgeon who contributed a lot to the therapeutic endoscopy work in Bombay. He trained other residents, Dr. Amit Maydeo and Dr. Vipul Rathod, who were later sent to Professor Soehendra.

Another surgeon whom I met by chance was Professor Marcus Büchler who had organised the conference on acute pancreatitis in Europe. I went to see his work in Berne, and one evening I invited him for dinner. During the course of our conversation, I told him that I had trained over two hundred and fifty residents, but I would not be able to train my son.

"Why?" he asked

"I am now sixty-six."

He could not believe my age. He however said, "Professor Shrikhande, do not worry. I will train him." Thereafter he took personal interest in the same.

He trained my son, Dr. Shailesh, in research and academia. It is very interesting. I learnt surgery by reading books and through observation. My son-in-law, Dr. Anand, learnt surgery from me and Professor Nib Soehendra. My son learnt surgery from me, laparoscopic surgery from Dr. Anand and then pancreatic surgery from Professor Marcus Büchler. He is now the Chief of G.I. Unit at the Tata Memorial Hospital, the premier institute for cancer in India. Every generation thus stands on the shoulders of the previous generation.

I feel happy that I introduced Professor Nib Soehendra and Professor Marcus Büchler to India. Many a great association begins over a glass of wine! Incidentally, when I was in the USA, I was told that many important decisions in the UN General Assembly were taken in the many cafeterias and restaurants in New York!

Many of my residents have become good professionals in India and abroad and they in turn continue to train newer generation of surgeons. During my travels and at the various conferences I attend, it is gratifying to meet surgeons trained by my residents.

❑ ❑ ❑

Chapter 12

Memorable Cases

I remember one incident during the first week of starting work in a hospital in the UK. A patient was operated for intestinal obstruction. He had recovered well, the wound had healed, the sutures were out. He was waiting to be discharged. Instructions were given for the follow-up. He went to the changing room for putting on his personal clothes, and collapsed. The attendant called for immediate help, but by the time we reached, a couple of minutes later, he was dead. Post-mortem showed a long clot had blocked the main artery supplying blood to the lungs. This is common in the West as compared to India.

(*Movements of the legs are important for blood circulation. Passengers on long journeys by air are therefore encouraged to stand and walk in the plane at frequent intervals. Elderly, obese patients lying in bed develop a clot in the veins of their calves because of pressure against the mattress and slowing of blood circulation.*

A long clot which is not firmly attached to the vein wall often gets detached, goes into the circulation, travels through the right side of the heart and may block the blood vessel supplying the lungs, leading to sudden death. This is called pulmonary embolism. This tragedy can only be prevented by starting calf exercises soon after operation.

The incidence is more frequent after prolonged operations and in patients lying in bed with serious illness.)

I was treating an elderly patient for acute pancreatitis in Mumbai. After the operation when things seemed to be under control, he suddenly suffered from a pulmonary embolism and we lost him. The family was very understanding. His son's comment was, "Doctor, death is an event in life. You did your best."

Two years later I received a letter from him.

Respected Uncle,

I am happy to inform you I will be getting married by the end of this year. I think I can tell you more about her. She is a young widow. Her husband expired in a car accident after a few months of their marriage. Uncle, when I was in hospital with my father, I met a woman outside the ICU. She got married to a blind man out of her own desire; it was not through pity. They had been married for quite some time and I learnt with what devotion and joy she was looking after her husband. She influenced me. If a woman can marry a blind man, why can't I marry a young widow? I am sure that I can keep my wife very happy.

Love and regards.

It is now more than twenty-five years and the couple have two children and are leading a happy life. I am now a member of their family. In India, the association between doctor and patients is the envy of other professions. From a doctor, I became an uncle. I don't think I would have had similar experiences had I settled abroad. His turning point came when he was in the hospital where his father was fighting for life in the ICU.

Does our literature, film industry, theatre reflect these inspiring examples around us?

Dominique Lapierre, the author of *A Thousand Suns*, writes of a remarkable experience. He saw a small emaciated girl accompanied by a hungry dog near a village in Bengal. He gave her a loaf of bread and what he saw he could not believe.

The girl divided that loaf into two and gave one half to the dog. His turning point in life came when he saw that hunger was less important for a girl than concern for a dog.

My profession has provided me with many instances of inspiring human behaviour.

A Story of Two Clocks

Patients in India frequently give gifts after an operation. A man in his late forties underwent a planned gall bladder operation without any problem. The day after the operation, he gave me a clock. When he was recovering, he developed a fulminating chest infection and died. He had expected to go home within a week. I had assured him that he would be in excellent health to celebrate his son's marriage a month later.

In another case, a patient was referred to me from North India. He had severe jaundice with a diagnosis of malignancy. This was much before the era of modern investigations. As a last hope, he came to Bombay. It was an unusual presentation where a large stone in the gall bladder had completely compressed and blocked the bile duct which brings the bile from the liver to the intestine. The obstructed bile was absorbed back in the blood stream giving rise to jaundice. He had no pain which is almost always the main feature in gall bladder stones. Absence of pain is a feature of obstruction due to cancer. The operation was technically challenging, but he had a smooth recovery. He was discharged after 10 days.

In the first case, the patient came with the idea of going back to his hometown within a week, but did not survive, while the other patient who had lost hope, went back cured. Twenty years later, the same man, who owned a big transport agency, was killed in an auto accident. This patient had also given me a clock.

I kept both these clocks in my office side by side. Interestingly the clock given by the man who died required frequent repairs, but the other man's clock has been working faultlessly for 30 years. These clocks remind me of a great truth - that patients with simple problems may die, while some very serious patients may survive!

Muhurta (Auspicious Time) for Operation

I had finished consultations by 9 pm and as I was preparing to go home, I was called to visit a young boy with severe abdominal pain. The residence was in a congested lower middle-class locality in the city. The family was staying in a one-room tenement with an area of about 350 sq. feet. There was a low partition with a door. The bed was so small that the patient could not even lie straight. He had acute appendicitis with early signs of rupture and needed an urgent operation to save his life.

Like many Indians, the parents had a belief in astrology and told me that that day was inauspicious for surgery but the operation could be done the next morning. I agreed with their suggestion not to operate on that day. After admission I convinced them that the new day started at midnight. I removed the burst appendix within three hours of the visit and the child was discharged after three days. Arguments to convince them that their belief was wrong had no place at the time. Tact and wisdom solved the problem.

I have worked both in public and private hospitals. It was an interesting observation that many poor patients who came to public hospitals never chose an auspicious time for their treatment, while rich patients would request us to follow an auspicious time as per their horoscopes. Man has walked on the moon, but even educated people have requested us to start anaesthesia before 10 am. Luckily there is no time limit for the last stitch!

I had operated on a young man for acute pancreatitis.

(Acute pancreatitis is a disease in which the pancreas which secretes the digestive juices, swells and at times bursts and starts digesting the patient's body from inside. It is described as internal burns. It commonly happens in people who consume alcohol in large amounts or those who have gall stones. When a large amount of pancreas gets destroyed, the bacteria from the intestine invade the body and lead to a life-threatening calamity.)

He had to be operated three times and still things were not going well.

His sister, who was an intensive care specialist in New York, came to Bombay. This was in the early eighties. She asked whether she could visit the hospital and see the patient. I felt happy that I could have a joint consultation with someone who had experience in handling the problem we were facing. She was impressed by the management of the case in India, a country she had left two decades earlier. She felt that nothing more could be done and that the outlook was poor. She went back to the USA. His condition continued to deteriorate.

What happened next was interesting. I went to the ICU where I saw that his wife was reciting some prayers while the patient's brother appeared cool and composed.

As was my usual practice, I took them aside to tell that we were fighting a losing if not a lost battle. Very calmly he said, "Doctor, you do not worry. His stars are about to change; he will improve and go home cured."

I said, "I too pray to God that you are right and I am wrong."

The resident-in-charge of intensive care asked me while I was leaving the ward, "What should we give as the cause of death, so that we need not disturb you at night?"

It was my practice never to give the cause of death when the patient was still alive, but on that day I made an exception. I was proved wrong. The patient got well and was discharged two weeks later. We had no explanation to offer. His sister from America was pleasantly surprised.

The faith of the relatives helps to maintain the equanimity of their minds without interfering with the treatment. I have no right to destroy that hope. Logic does not replace long-standing beliefs overnight.

There are some eminent surgeons who do not operate on inauspicious days such as no-moon day (*amavasya*). Their attitude does not help society to become rational. I do not believe in astrology. I operated upon my brother-in-law on a no-moon Friday, something which is considered a bad combination. But in some parts of India, Friday is an auspicious day.

One must convince the society by personal example.

Never Lose Hope

A patient who had an attack of acute pancreatitis was flown from West Africa to India. He had a choice of either being treated in the UK or in his home country. His condition was critical, requiring intensive care for several weeks, five operations and over 60 units of blood. When he was discharged from the hospital, the doctors and the nurses told me, "When we had all lost hope, your optimism and perseverance against all odds was an important lesson we will remember all our lives."

Acute pancreatitis is one of the costliest diseases in surgical practice. When patients recover they are completely cured, but are often bankrupt. I have even known of patients selling their properties. Surgeon's fees are less than 10 per cent of the total bill and we are still blamed for increasing the cost of treatment. Many patients in India have no health insurance, and treating expensive diseases is a stress for doctors. Even in rich countries maintaining good health services is becoming increasingly difficult.

"In USA, the wealthiest nation on earth, no one should land in ruin because of an illness."

— President Obama
June 27, 2012

Diseases continue to ruin innumerable families in India.

The West African patient has remained well for over 20 years. Every year he sends a letter of gratitude.

How Much to Tell

I remember a case of jaundice due to cancer in the pancreas in the beginning of my career 40 years back. Sophisticated investigations were not available and it was only after opening the abdomen, that surgeons could decide on the nature of the operation. Luckily, I could operate and remove part of the pancreas, a major procedure even now. It is known as a Whipple operation, a supramajor operation rarely done in the past.

The patient recovered without any complications. Doing such an operation was like reaching Mount Everest for a climber. I had a talk with the patient's son and told him that the report had confirmed cancer, but that he should do well for several months. Patients living for more than 2 years were not commonly seen.

I suggested that he should not divulge the information to other members of the family. (This may sound odd to many, but that was an approach which I preferred in my practice in those times.)

His only sister had settled abroad, so he felt that she should know about it. He warned her not to tell the mother because she would not be able to stand the stress. However, the daughter felt guilty not to inform her mother. She also told the mother not to inform the patient.

The daughter left India after two weeks. The mother got very restless because she had never hidden anything from her husband in her life before. She ultimately felt that she could not keep the truth from him. The patient went into depression and ended his life by probably taking some sleeping pills. He had written in a note that pancreatic cancer was a fatal disease and he had no desire to suffer.

A secret remains a secret as long as only one person knows it.

There is a lot of discussion about how much we should disclose to the patient. My policy was to tell the facts to one responsible person from the family. If I had to tell the patient, the manner in which I gave the news was very important. No one likes to know the truth if it is unpleasant. Faith and trust are positive forces that support the quality of life.

How much truth do we know? Statistics do not help in an individual case. We were told an anecdote when I was in Edinburgh that a surgeon operated on a woman and found that she had advanced stomach cancer. He told the relatives that she would not live long. Her sister had a similar stomach problem, was operated on by the same surgeon and he found that she also had only a few months to live. Finally, both the sisters attended the surgeon's funeral. I do not know if the story is true, but doctors should be cautious when making the prognosis.

I had operated on my friend for cancer of the colon which unfortunately recurred after 20 months. The operation had to be done for recurring intestinal obstruction. He was told that the obstruction was due to adhesions and not because of cancer, but his wife knew that he had a recurrence. The family was keen that he should be flown to USA to some well-known medical center. I accompanied him to the USA.

I knew the professor and requested him not to disclose everything that we feared. He saw the patient, assured him that there was no cause for worry, and that the exploration was planned the next day. A resident came to see him in the afternoon and my friend asked him some questions.

"What do you think is the cause of the obstruction?"

"Most likely, recurrence of cancer."

"What will be done?"

"Depends upon what we find."

"What is the outlook? "

"Not good, but we will do whatever is possible."

"What is my life expectancy?"

"Difficult to state, but perhaps a few months."

The patient was devastated, and decided to return to India. The same evening he got a massive heart attack and inspite of the determined efforts by the cardiologist of the ICU, he died. The previous day the investigations had shown that he had a healthy heart. Do patients really want to know the truth?

How much to tell, what to tell, when to convey the unpleasant information? We must keep a balance between false hopes and unpleasant truths. How we convey something is far more important than what we convey.

A short, fat lady in her mid-forties got severe pain in her upper right abdomen. The diagnosis of an inflamed gall bladder due to a stone was straightforward. She had uncontrolled diabetes, high blood pressure and was obviously a high risk case for operation. But as her condition was worsening, the relatives agreed for surgery. Her gall bladder was full of stones and had burst, with collection of pus around the liver. The necrotic gall bladder, all the stones and pus were removed, and a tube was placed to drain the area before closing the abdomen. She had a stormy convalescence which required ventilatory support and 10 days' stay in the ICU.

Pus dissolves the sutures used to bring the muscles together and as expected, she developed a hernia at the operation site. I was called for a visit to her residence. I advised her to remain physically active and reduce some weight. Surgery on bedridden patients carries high risk.

Six months later, she consulted me again. She had not reduced weight and complained that her hernia was a big bother to her. I explained that the main risk was that when the intestines were placed inside the abdomen and we put a mesh to cover the defect, the pressure inside the abdomen would push her diaphragm *(partition between the abdomen and chest)* up, leading to breathing difficulties. She pleaded that she would get her weight down once she got rid of the troublesome hernia. She came from an affluent family and I was told that I would be paid handsomely for the surgery.

The daughter was hurt when I declined to operate. A few days later, I saw the relatives outside the ICU and learnt from them that she was operated on by another surgeon. They could not look into my eyes. The patient could not be saved! It was too late for regrets.

Money makes some people believe that they can buy any service.

Death of an Engineer

Soon after I started my practice in Mumbai, I saw a young engineer for treatment of phimosis.

(Phimosis is a condition in which the foreskin remains adherent to the glans penis. At birth the foreskin is always adherent, but by the age of 7–8 yrs it automatically gets separated from the glans. This is nature's mechanism. If in due course it does not get separated, the secretions of the glans get collected in the form of smegma which

may lead to infection and cancer. Cancer of the penis is common in India among Hindus who do not have the ritual of circumcision.)

He was told by the skin specialist a few years earlier that he would require an operation at some time convenient to him. When I saw him he had already developed cancer and unfortunately the disease was advanced.

He was just settling down in Mumbai and had invested in an apartment. He wanted me to attend the housewarming party he had organised on his wife's return from Kolkata with their new-born baby.

I knew that he was not going to live long. I convinced him that he would recover faster because of excellent help and family support in Kolkata. He died leaving behind a young wife, a two-year-old son and a devastated family.

Why was the treatment delayed? The skin specialist had advised him to get the operation done at some convenient time. The young man was an extremely talented, creative engineer who was trying to settle down and therefore no time was convenient to him for medical treatment.

Only when he found the tip of the penis swollen and there some foul discharge, did he approach me. In India, many patients delay treatment as long as there is no pain.

The patient died young. Both his parents died of shock. The family kept in touch with me. His son wrote me a letter on his 7th birthday: 'I will get a gun to kill cancer.'

His brother wrote to me 16 years later, *"I remember the day in March 1966, when I visited your clinic in Bombay while accompanying my ailing brother. You did not accept any fees because you felt a tragedy was about to occur in the life of a young man trying to settle down. You sent me a letter of condolence after the sad demise of my brother. I do not know how much more generous a busy, eminent doctor can be!"*

If only the dermatologist had told the patient to undergo surgery without delay, this tragedy could have been avoided.

'Doctor, I Can Swallow Comfortably!'

I operated on a man in his late fifties for some difficulty in swallowing. He had a large diverticulum in the gullet due to an abnormally tight sphincter between the food pipe and the stomach. On the fifth day I asked him to drink water, and I still vividly remember his expression of surprise when he said, "Doctor, it has gone down!"

I was a bit surprised by this comment.

He said, "This is the first time I could swallow with such ease."

He had been suffering for many decades, but it was only after the surgery that he realised what a blessing it was to be able to swallow without discomfort.

We get used to discomforts and consider them as normal. Often we realise our sufferings only when they pass.

I remember the evening I passed my F.R.C.S. in Feb 1959; the torture of examinations from school days was finally over forever. I was free. I could now enjoy life.

A patient with his lungs destroyed by smoking spent the last months of his life sleeping in a sitting position. One morning he greeted me with a smile because on the previous night he could sleep lying down with only three pillows.

Only suffering makes us realise the simple joys in life.

G.K. Chesterton, well known writer, had a fall, and one leg was put in plaster. He wrote something like, "Now I realise the blessing, the beauty of two legs. If you want to understand the beauty of two eyes, wink at the world with one eye."

Every year, I get a diary from a patient whom I had operated on for cancer of the rectum in 1974. The diary is not important, but a patient remembering me for forty years makes me feel good.

An elderly lady in her eighties died after intestinal obstruction. Her relatives from the USA wanted to file a case against the hospital and me; they did not remember that I had sucessfully operated on the father when he was in his 90s.

I am happy that I did not settle down in the USA where the surgeons always have the sword of litigation for negligence hanging over their heads.

A patient who had undergone an operation for severe abdominal pain was referred to me. In those days, chronic peptic ulcers were treated by cutting the vagus nerves supplying the stomach to bring down acid production, which was considered the cause of non-healing ulcers. The ulcer area was bypassed by joining the stomach to the upper small intestine. In spite of the operation the pain continued and therefore the patient consulted me. I had taught students that if a properly done operation not give the expected relief, the diagnosis must have been wrong. Have the courage to change the diagnosis.

I had operated on him in December 1972. It was a difficult operation because the tissues were stuck together as a result of the previous operation. The patient had a gall bladder full of stones. It had ruptured into the duodenum, and this hole was seen as an ulcer on barium examination. The gall bladder was removed, the hole in the duodenum was closed. The surgeon who had done the first operation was a well-known surgeon, but at that time it was believed that gall stones occur in fat, fertile females of forty and are rare in males. The patient was a thin male.

His pain disappeared and every year on the date his operation was done, he would send me a simple post card saying, "I have not experienced any abdominal pain even once. It is because of your blessings I am enjoying a rebirth." This simple post card was a new year's greeting that I received for over thirty years.

The teaching had stood the test of time. If the treatment does not give expected results, change the diagnosis.

An old man in his eighties required an emergency operation for a strangulated bowel. It was past midnight when he was wheeled into the operation theatre. The family was quite tense and worked up. Luckily everything went well and he was discharged few days after the operation.

What he told me when he came for a check-up was very interesting: "I knew that my end had come near. I said goodbye to my family members, gave a last look at the trees through the window, hugged my grandchildren before I was wheeled out of the room. My fear as I entered the operation theatre disappeared because of the unexpected serene atmosphere I experienced there. I heard a devotional song so soothing that I felt that I could not have chosen a better place for taking leave of this world. Your smiling face and the confidence you gave me by the touch of your hands was very reassuring. My recovery was a surprise for all."

Before leaving my office he added, "And one more thing I must tell you - when I go to sleep, I hear the same music which I heard when undergoing anaesthesia."

Words of comfort, skilfully administered, are the oldest therapy known to man. All healers have this capacity, but unfortunately the word 'healer' has taken on a wrong connotation in this world of scientific medicine.

Music is a great tranquiliser. I stayed for two days with a German endoscopist in Hamburg. I gave him two tapes of instrumental classical Indian music as a gift for his wife. She thanked me but said that she did not understand Indian music. I told her that music had no language, race, or nationality. She should just listen and enjoy the experience. Some months later, when she visited India, she told me that whenever she felt low the music elevated her mood like magic.

Medical Student with Acute Appendicitis

A medical student came to my consulting room once with acute appendicitis. He needed an emergency operation but wanted only me to perform the same and I had no facilities to operate in the hospital where he was studying. His parents lived in Iran and it was impossible even to contact them. I put myself in his situation: what if I were a medical student in a foreign country with acute appendicitis. I had no choice but to operate on him in a private clinic late at night. I did not charge any fees and even paid for the hospital expenses because of his personal problems. Luckily everything went off well and I was relieved of the big burden of operating on a foreigner without his family being present.

Some months later when I had gone to the USA, his parents came and left a crockery set for me. They expressed their gratitude for looking after their son. When I returned I saw the set which was not new. The student met me and what he told me touched my heart. There was a lot of discussion in his family about what should be given to a surgeon who had saved a life, and that too without charging any fees. Ultimately they decided that I should be given the most precious possession they had—a crockery set which was over eighty years old!

After his graduation, my former patient settled abroad. Some years ago he sent me a letter, in which he wrote, "I often remember what magnanimity you showed in looking after me. Whenever I see a poor patient, I give a concession or even free treatment. I feel that my gesture is helping poor unknown patients and the service given without any expectations is a source of great contentment and happiness."

How Much do you Smoke?

A young couple brought their four-year-old son to me for a hernia operation. They had many questions to ask including whether I would also operate on the side where there was no hernia. Finally they were satisfied and the date was fixed. As they were about to leave, I noticed a pack of cigarettes in the shirt pocket of the father. I spontaneously asked him how much he smoked.

The question was so unexpected that he suddenly became serious and I noticed that his wife looked very upset.

I said, "You can tell me that I have no business to ask that question because you have not come to consult me about your health. But your son is now my patient, which means I am concerned about his health. Your smoking will harm him in the future and the influence of a smoking father on a son cannot be underestimated."

The couple looked upset when they left my room and I was sure they would go elsewhere for the surgery. But surprisingly they came back, the surgery was performed and the boy went home on the same day. A few months later, I was told by my secretary that a lady had come without an appointment and wanted to meet me for only two minutes. As she walked in, I recognised her as that boy's mother. She gave me a bouquet of flowers, and with tears in her eyes said, "My son is fine, but I wanted to give you another good news. When we left your room that day, my husband was very upset, but after reaching home he threw the cigarettes in the dustbin and has stopped smoking since. He used to get angry whenever any of us would request him to stop smoking. You have blessed our family."

The couple was rich. The thought that I may lose a rich patient did not prevent me from giving good though unwanted advice. I did what a good doctor should do.

Doctor, You Look Rundown

I operated on a patient who was suffering from ulcerative colitis since many years. I had to remove 90% of his colon. Some time later when he came to know that I was being interviewed on TV, he made special arrangements for the villagers to view the programme by arranging a big screen. He wrote to me, *"It was a great moment for the villagers to see the man who had given me a new lease of life. You looked rundown so I am sending you a jar of cow's ghee (clarified butter made from cow's milk) which will give you energy. I will send you again when this gets over!"*

An illiterate villager giving instructions on health to his surgeon! My life is blessed with such goodwill.

(Ulcerative colitis is a disease of large intestine where ulcers develop and patients suffer from intractable diarrhoea with blood. Drugs can control the disease but cure is not possible. In some cases,

colon has to be removed by surgery and small intestine brought to the abdominal wall and the faeces are collected in a bag placed on the abdominal wall.)

I Did Not Lose My Appendix

I was in a bookshop. A lady stopped me and asked, "Are you Dr. Shrikhande?"

"Yes."

"Do you recognise me?"

"No."

"I had come to you for appendix operation thirty years back. You asked me many questions and told me after taking the detailed history that my abdominal pain had nothing to do with the appendix."

She had a book in her hand, and she wrote on it, "Dear doctor, we met last in 1977 when I did not lose my appendix. No words to express my thanks."

How To Avoid Unindicated Operations

I had prepared a note for educating lay people many years back. There is a general belief that unnecessary operations are performed for monetary gains. My note instructed patients about the questions they must ask when an operation is advised:

Doctor, what is the problem with me?

What will happen if the operation is not performed?

What do I do if the operation does not relieve my symptoms?

Will you send the specimen for examination to the pathologist?

Will you give a written report with relevant details?

Many doctors don't give detailed reports to the patients and patients too do not preserve their medical records. Many reports mention only the name of the operation in handwriting which is difficult to read.

Both, the medical professionals and lay people, must realise that medicine is not an exact science. Patients and law makers are also responsible for the high expectations from an imperfect science.

A Case of Missing Bangles

I had a very unusual experience at the beginning of my practice.

I had done an operation for colon cancer the previous evening and the night call informed me that the patient was doing well.

When I went for a round the next morning, the first thing I heard from the relatives was that the gold bangles the patient was wearing when she was taken to the operation theatre were missing. I said, "Let me see the patient first and then talk about the bangles." The patient was doing fine.

I made enquiries and I was told by everybody that the patient was not wearing any bangles. This was confirmed by the anaesthetist who always checks the patient before starting anaesthesia. I knew that the hospital had a reputation for integrity and good services.

I tried to explain to the relatives that this was the first time I had such a complaint in my experience of over ten years, but the relatives were not satisfied. I had two options before me. Either to report the matter to the police in which case it would cause great embarrassment to the hospital, or accept the responsibility. I chose another option. I deducted the value of the bangles from my professional fees and the matter was closed. The hospital staff were relieved and I was happy with my spontaneous gesture.

One more check was added; while shifting patients to the OT, it was made mandatory to check that they were not wearing bangles, rings and necklaces!

Our friends from USA would tell us how efficiently and quickly the airport checks were carried out for departing passengers, unlike the time-consuming procedures in India. Everything changed after 9/11 when four planes which took off from Logan airport were hijacked leading to chaos.

It is when things go wrong that we get an opportunity to grow and learn.

There is a lot of criticism against doctors for the way they over charge and exploit the suffering patients. However, doctors have the same characteristics that society nurtures. A greedy society should not expect dedicated doctors and an honest society will never produce dishonest professionals.

Case of a Bounced Cheque

A patient coming from far was found to have an inoperable cancer during surgery. I told her husband that the outlook was poor and that she was unlikely to live long. The relatives who were educated and appeared well-placed, thanked us for our services at the time of discharge. The cheque they gave bounced. The letters sent to the address were returned stating that the place did not exist.

Why are hospitals criticised for demanding deposits in cash before admitting patients?

A patient had not paid the full amount and therefore Bombay Hospital was not ready to discharge as per the hospital rules. The patient requested me to sign his discharge on assurance that he would deposit the money with the finance department of the hospital after a few days. He never paid and the hospital deducted that amount from my fees. Are such instances ever shown on TV programmes where actions of greedy doctors are discussed with relish? Ours is one of those rare professions where even eminent members give free service to society. We have a legacy of eminent doctors who served the society well, and trained us to carry on the noble traditions of our profession.

A Case of Liver Transplant

I was making rounds with Prof. Marcus Büchler, in the famous Inselspital, University Hospital Berne, where a patient was obviously upset. His gestures were rude and professor was trying to keep cool. I did not know the language but the patient was certainly not thanking the surgeon!

The reason for the patient's outburst was that he expected to go home in fifteen days after the operation but it was now twenty days. He had undergone a liver transplant for liver cirrhosis resulting from alcohol abuse.

Patients' expectations are fuelled with assurances that the modern medical approach has the potential to defeat all diseases and disabilities. That surgery can be avoided with 'laser treatment' (term used by lay people for endoscopic, laparoscopic and interventional radiology techniques) is a common expectation.

While medicine can really do a lot more than what it could do three decades ago, the patient-doctor relationship has taken a severe beating. Today patients are unhappy; doctors are unhappy; insurance companies doubt the patients and question the doctors. The sad aspect is that we are losing even clinical autonomy. The best among the students are rejecting medical careers. The rising cost of health services is creating serious problems in India with a large section of the population still below the poverty line.

Like divorce rates, medico-legal cases are mushrooming. Defensive medicine will not prevent them.

I had another case of a man past seventy who was getting frequent attacks of pain in upper abdomen, and fever with rigors. The patient had diabetes, was a chain smoker and consumed whisky regularly. The relatives were told that the operation carried a lot of risk but the risk of not operating was also high.

His son said, "But now he has stopped smoking, not taken a drink for three weeks and blood sugar is normal!"

We had to spend a lot of time to explain that an operation was a big injury and recovery was not easy. Stopping alcohol and smoking for three weeks did not mean that there would be no complications. Years of practice help us spot troublesome patients and relatives, and so a detailed consent was taken with a list of all complications that could follow.

The operation was done. The gall bladder was very thick-walled, and contained pus because a large stone had blocked the outlet. He was well for two days but started showing signs of chest infection which could not be controlled, and after eight days we lost the battle.

Now started another battle. The relatives became violent, and started shouting and damaging the nurses' station. The security guards were summoned, and with difficulty a worsening situation was brought under control.

Questions were repeatedly thrown at me, "When you knew that the patient was going to die, why did you operate? We would have taken him home."

"You did so many investigations, we have spent so much of money in the ICU and still he died. We will sue you for negligence."

I remember another high-risk case we lost, again because of severe chest infection. His daughter, who was a medical practitioner, was so annoyed that she said, "Doctor you will realise my tragedy when you lose your father."

I refused to give a cause of death and asked for a post-mortem. Only after getting a written apology from her, was the cause of death given. If doctors can be so unreasonable, what can we expect from illiterate patients?

The stress among doctors is increasing. In the past I have done major operations in small set-ups because patients had faith in doctors and death was considered a possible event in the course of treatment and not related to medical negligence. Surgeons work in isolation and function with incomplete data and faulty infrastructure.

It is important to remember that one can face an emergency even on the last day of a brilliant career with a record of safe surgery.

❑ ❑ ❑

Chapter 13

'Doctor, You Must Cure Me!'

Large numbers of patients crowd hospital consulting rooms, laboratories, ultrasound, C.T. Scan, MRI, and endoscopy clinics either on medical advice or even on their own, in search of a cure for their ill-health. They present a typical pattern. They have not been well for several years, complain of lack of energy, weak digestion, acidity, backache, chest pains, gases in the stomach, excessive belching, constipation or loose motions, and poor sleep. They do not feel refreshed even after sleep, and have no taste in their mouth. They experience extreme weakness, joint pains, and loss of interest in life. They carry thick files of investigations and treatment. They are accompanied by anxious relatives who share their worries, but at times there are also verbal disagreements between the couple such as, "You have no time to look at me, how do you know my suffering?" Some have complaints of ill-health from childhood; they had never enjoyed good health.

If patients have symptoms for many years but there is still no loss of weight, no fever, and no anaemia, the patient probably has a functional disorder. The clinical model is reliable. These patients keep the medical industry, pathology laboratories, ultrasound, CT scan, MRI and endoscopy departments busy. Like octroi collectors, the medical industry is very happy. Patients remain unhappy if the symptoms do not disappear. Then they change the doctor, who makes some changes in treatment, and repeat the same investigations.

Even highly competent doctors cannot analyse symptoms such as gases, bloating, and acidity, but it is a safe assumption, that severe pain does not last for a long time, and pain that lasts for a long time cannot be severe. The conclusion that there is no serious problem is easy, but management requires a personal touch with empathy.

The other side of the story is that patients remain unhappy if they are not investigated. "When I am suffering so much, how do you say that nothing is wrong with my health? Do anything, but relieve me from this intolerable suffering. It was with such hope that I consulted you, and if you do not cure me, what is the use of living such a life of suffering? I am willing to bear the costs but I want to get well."

But doctors take no chances and go on investigating, to avoid being dragged to the consumer courts in case they miss a diagnosis.

If allopathic medicines do not work, they go for alternative medical therapy. The hospitals, doctors, and medical industry thrive on these patients. I advise my patients:

"As long as there is no anaemia, weight remains constant and physical activity leads to no serious discomfort, do not go for exhaustive investigations.

Take daily exercise, eat plenty of vegetables, remain cheerful, avoid the company of negative people and count your blessings."

People are worried about everything. They see danger lurking in every corner. Many take common ailments as heralding disaster. If there is a common tummy upset because of late dinner or drinks, they think of cancer or ulcer. Internet sites are accessed, and they are convinced that they have a serious disease.

In law courts a man is held innocent unless proved to be guilty. Nowadays everybody is ill unless proved to be healthy by investigations.

Medical literature for lay people conveys the impression that living is a dangerous activity. Doctors must reassure the society that life is sturdy and all of us need to lead a sensible life. People need to be told that we have armaments given by nature for our body's defence. But society is becoming neurotic. People give a sigh of relief when they see that the toilet seats are marked 'sterilised for your use'!

Many people do not realise that man with his intelligent methods has made living less dangerous. There are no longer epidemics of plague or small pox, influenza or polio which claimed millions of lives in the last century. I know of some close relatives whose entire families died during epidemics of plague and cholera.

We take so many things for granted that we have no gratitude for what nature has given us and what science has achieved to save labour and time. Very few realise that we also have internal enemies of greed, hatred and lust. Man can escape man-made laws but he cannot ignore nature's laws. Our wise saints from the ancient times have stated that those who have exploited others for personal gains can never find happiness in life. These laws are as true as the laws of gravity. On the other hand, I have seen patients with serious diseases, bearing physical discomfort, disability and pain, in the face of death, with courage and equanimity.

Money, status, and power do not guarantee happiness. Generosity, ethical conduct and helping the needy without any expectations is an enriching experience and an eternal source of happiness.

Unhappiness is increasing in all strata of society. When life is not lived with gratitude towards several benefits science has showered on us, but is wasted on amassing wealth and seeking honours; it proves an invitation to a feeling of worthlessness in the later years of life's journey. Contentment can be achieved only if we can lend meaning to our existence by contributing to society's general happiness. Selfish individuals will always be cursed with unhappiness and innumerable body complaints which no medicines can cure.

When we explain to them that the symptoms are a result of stress, they accept it because stress is a fact of everyday living. There is a big difference between stress and distress. Driving to the airport through traffic jams is certainly a stressful experience. The stress of traffic jams is a good stimulus for finishing work in time and reaching the airport early. However, to worry about a bomb or a hijacker in a plane, or catching a bad infection or loss of baggage will cause distress. Stress is essential for staying focussed and alert, while distress is destructive. How to change the attitude is the responsibility of the patient. The brain, which is a stationary organ as compared to the limbs, heart, lungs and intestine, requires the maximum amount of oxygen in spite of its small size. Controlling thoughts is the essence of Yoga and is a conservator of energy. Imagine a busy airport without Air Traffic Control.

Giving enough time to listen to the patient, making notes, and going through their papers will have a great therapeutic effect on the patient. Many a times we can diagnose the condition within the first few minutes of a patient's narration, but a good doctor will listen to his innumerable complaints with attention and empathy. Some patients show dramatic improvement, but many will continue to suffer. Society is getting addicted to taking medicines, but doctors should prescribe hope and not drugs!

Some years ago, when I had gone to Europe, I was invited for dinner by a patient's friend. The host requested me to examine his wife who had been unwell for quite a long time! I took a detailed history and came to the conclusion that she had no serious problem. I assured her that there was no cause for worry and advised her to make some changes in her diet and lifestyle. She told the guests who had come for dinner, "Dr. Shrikhande is the first doctor who has examined me by touching my abdomen. Earlier when I went to a hospital, I was made to sit on a chair. One look at me and the doctor started to work on a computer as if I didn't exist. Then I was handed a list of investigations. I went to the lab and radiology department, and submitted myself to whatever tests they did. When I took the results of the tests to the doctor, some other doctor would see me, go through the reports and give me a prescription. In all my visits to the hospital I have not really met anybody who had time to listen to me."

Some months later when her husband visited Mumbai, he told me that his wife was keeping well and she was very happy with the way I had examined her. The problem today is that doctors have no time, patients have no patience and stress and fear are the engines that run the medical industry.

Parent Child Discord

A well-built youth of seventeen consulted me for intractable abdominal pain that had been going on for two years. His investigations showed no abnormality. Treatment proved ineffective. I assured him and his father that there was nothing to fear and that he could contact me after four months if he needed help. But he again contacted me 10 days later and insisted that he would come alone. I understood that he had something to disclose.

His father was a creative artist, interested in literature, music, art, poetry, and photography. He enjoyed an occasional drink and invited the son to join him. The son enjoyed his father's company. In contrast, his mother was glued to the television, very dogmatic in her views and continuously complaining about everything. She wanted everything neat and precise as per her perception and was very particular about her own appearance. She suspected that her husband was having an affair, making things very tense at home and affecting his studies.

I asked him, "Is he having an affair?"

"I am not sure, but if he is, I can understand because he is suffering a lot by putting up with my mother's temper."

"What does your mother do?"

"Graduate from Delhi, active member of social organisations and gives lectures on lifestyle management!"

"If your mother and father do not change then can you change? You must learn to accept what you cannot change."

I prescribed him no medicines. Three months later when he met me, he was a changed young man. He never met me again, but his greeting cards are an indication of my effective advice.

Retirement Blues

One day a lady walked into my consulting room with a thick file of investigations. She looked ten years younger than her actual age of 48. She had consulted many specialists for abdominal pain for over two years but without relief. She looked quite graceful even without any make-up. I listened to her carefully while observing her body language as she spoke.

In spite of her ill health for over two years, she had not lost any weight, had no fever. She was not a diabetic, had no urinary symptoms, was physically quite active and could climb four flights of stairs without any discomfort. Physical examination was normal. I was sure that she had no disease; she was in distress.

I was taught in my college 60 years ago that it is more important to know the patient who has a disease rather than about the disease which the patient has.

She came from a well-to-do family, and had a married daughter settled in Canada. Her bachelor son was in a multinational firm in New York travelling between Singapore, Paris, and London. Financially the family was so sound that the husband took VRS to get away from the drudgery of travel through the traffic jam in Mumbai and bringing work home.

The couple went to Canada and USA for a four-month holiday when the trouble started. The couple had nothing to do there. The streets were deserted except for speeding cars. In Mumbai there were crowded footpaths and crawling cars: in either situation going for a walk was not possible. The daughter and son-in-law were out of home for the whole day with a tight schedule of work in different offices. By the time they returned, they looked exhausted. The son, who was staying in a highrise building in Manhattan, had no fixed schedule. He had to travel a lot and hardly had any time to look after the parents. The couple who had gone with a grand plan of enjoying their holidays started looking forward to returning to the familiar surroundings of home.

On their return to India, things started getting worse. The husband did not know how to handle his spare time. He would sit in the drawing room all the time watching television. He lost interest in life, became moody and would not shave for 2–3 days. He had no interest in outdoor activities, books did not interest him. He had some friends but they were busy in their world. His wife was exactly the opposite. She was interested in social activities, attended music programs, and was a member of a book club. Previously she had the freedom to engage in her activities when the husband was busy with his office work. Now he would remain at home leading to a clash of interests. They had a very spacious apartment and servants at home. She stopped inviting friends home because her husband did not like it. It was obvious that this woman was suffocated in the company of her husband who had no knowledge of how to handle spare time.

We take so many things for granted in life such as going to work, answering telephone calls, writing letters, and attending social and official events. There is always some work that remains undone and keeps the mind engaged. It is a blessing to be busy. Unless a person has variety of interests, spare time becomes a nightmare and an invitation to depression. Life without a structure leads to boredom. This structure has to be developed before retirement. Whatever the demands of one's professional work, to develop a balanced life, one must spare some time for reading books, making friends, and doing some physical activity. Individuals who have limited interests in life can be compared to a television with only one channel. The convenience of having several channels is a blessing of modern technology. Depending on the mood, one can see a hilarious comedy, a detective story, sports, music, history, wildlife or the stars in space. Utilising one's time effectively is a great art, work is a blessing, and leisure without work is a punishment.

Marital Disturbance

A lady in her 50s suffering from vague symptoms of joint pains and poor digestion came with a big file of treatment and inconclusive reports. The picture was so typical that I had to conclude that there was no serious illness bothering her. She was accompanied by her husband. I reassured her that there was no cause for worry.

Two weeks later she came alone and her story was an eye-opener. She said, "I could not tell you everything in the presence of my husband. We were a happy family. We have two sons, who are settled abroad. I stay with my husband and his parents in a spacious bungalow. Five years ago, my husband's cousin, who was working abroad, had an accident, and was taken to England for treatment of a back injury resulting in permanent paralysis of both the legs. He was sent back to India with full monetary compensation that would take care of him for the rest of his life. His wife had an excellent job in the bank. The couple had no issue. My husband would go to their residence and help the couple. That is the time the trouble started. My co-sister and my husband developed a relationship disturbing our marital bliss."

I knew that she had no health problem. Her reaction was natural. Now my role was of a friend, philosopher and guide. I asked, her few questions.

"Is he neglecting the family?"

"No."

"Do his parents know that he is having an affair."

"Yes."

"Have they tried to disuade him?"

"Yes."

"Does he neglect you?"

"No. Doctor, he is essentially a good man. Never rude to anyone and very good to the staff and servants in his office. I only wish that he has no affair with any other woman."

"If he does not change, you can change your outlook, take a decision one way or the other instead of remaining unhappy all the time."

She left my room not in very happy mood. Sometime later I happened to see her at a social function when she said, "Thank you for your advice." I didn't expect this. Wisdom lies in accepting some problems which have no solution.

Professional Dissatisfaction

An eminent criminal advocate consulted me for intractable abdominal complaints that he had been having for over ten years. He had a big file of investigations and ineffective treatments. He had not lost weight, he had no cough or fever, did not smoke, but enjoyed a few drinks on Saturdays. He was taking tranquilisers for sleep. There was nothing obviously wrong with him.

It is my pratice to not look at the reports of investigations before examining patients. A physical examination is something I insist on even when I am convinced about there being no cause of worry. Apart from eye contact, a doctor's personal touch works wonders to build a patient's confidence.

"Your personality must have been a subject for a photographer's camera and an object of envy among boys and girls during your college days."

He was now a changed man.

He said, "I was a hero during my college days. I was surrounded by pretty girls, but I zeroed in on two of them. One girl wanted me to grow a beard and the other was happy only with a smooth shave. I had to make one unhappy."

I was curious and asked him how he finally chose. "I decided with a coin toss. I am very happy in my marriage."

"You have been successful in your profession. What is bothering you?"

"At times I wonder whether I am defending criminals who ought to suffer long-term imprisonment. My success is bringing me more and more complicated cases."

"Can you give me one instance?"

"I was defending a man who had committed a rape. I saw the expression on the face of the victim's husband and her frightened children and suddenly remembered my own family. It was a turning point in my life."

"What did you do?"

"I took interest in non-criminal legal matters. But even in those cases I was troubled by knowing how illiterate, uneducated clients were duped by individuals in power."

He said that he was losing faith in the judiciary. It seemed to him that every man had a price, and he was worried that he had become an instrument for injustice.

I asked him whether it was possible for a lawyer to handle only just cases. He was not sure.

I told him that societies were never just. Justice is a concept absent in the animal world. Humans have introduced the judiciary system. But law makers are not perfect, all those who collect evidence are not men of integrity, and judges are not gods.

Human beings have exploited one another and their environment since since time immemorial. However, there are always some individuals in every walk of life who stand apart and spread messages of truth, beauty, and justice. They are the true pillars of mankind, the lighthouses to guide ships that have lost their direction. We have to play that role in life. I suggested that he take on *pro bono* cases where he could defend poor individuals who were suffering any form of injustice, but who could not pay lawyers to fight their case. Serving the needy without any expectations is one of the surest paths to happiness. This law of happy living is as immutable as the laws of gravity.

It is not necessary to do great acts of charity to give meaning to our lives. Everyone has many opportunities for small acts of kindness through which they will experience contentment. It is by giving we enrich our lives; a simple remedy but difficult to practice in this acquisitive world.

One day, I had gone for a walk while on holiday at a hill station. There had been rainfall the previous night. I saw an earthworm struggling to move on the dry tar road, like an exhausted traveller dragging his feet in a vast desert. I picked up a small leaf, lifted the earthworm and placed it by the side of the road where there was mud. It was a wonderful feeling when I saw it gliding gracefully on its home ground. Had I not done it, it would have left a sense of guilt in my mind. I felt happy. Small acts of kindness, done without any expectations have a cumulative effect on our mind.

"I did not expect to have such an experience in a doctor's consulting room. I am happy that I met you," said the advocate when he took my leave. I never saw him again.

While going for a morning walk, I saw a poor couple sleeping on footpath with their little son lying naked. These sights disturb me and I feel guilty with my comfortable life. The next day, I took a shawl with me and covered the naked child. I felt very happy.

Three days prior to completing this book, I saw a blind college girl unsure of taking steps to cross the road. People passed by, looked at her, but didn't stop. I helped her to cross the road and was rewarded with the grateful smile on her face. I was engrossed in giving final touches to my book, had not slept well and decided to go for a walk for twenty minutes. Somehow the small act of helping the blind girl renewed my energy, and I walked on for fifty minutes with a spring in my step. I have experienced that any act to help others without any expectations gives us blessings beyond description. The sleeping child never saw me, the blind girl could not see me and they would never know who I was.

❑ ❑ ❑

Chapter 14

Stress in a Surgery

Every human activity has a potential to turn into a life-threatening situation. We create a life-threatening situation in every operation to make an ill patient better. Millions of surgeries are done every day and accidents do occur like they do in any other field.

Constant vigilance is essential to prevent tragedies. People who live in constant stress are likely to become indifferent, careless to seemingly unnecessary rituals and intolerant of small lapses. It is argued that in our present national climate of disregard and indifference to law, it will adversely affect every human activity not excluding the OR (operating room). If there is indiscipline in the society, it will also be seen on roads, in construction activities, supplying midday meals to school children and in operation theatres.

I will mention a few examples of stress in surgery from my career.

Operation on the Wrong Side

I got a telephone call from a high court judge informing me that I had done his father's operation on the wrong side. This is an event which every surgeon fears. I had a sinking feeling.

I accepted my mistake and explained to the family that this was the first time such an accident had occurred in my long career of 42 years. He asked me what could be done and my answer was that I would operate on the correct side. My offer was accepted.

The operation was done the next day and patient was discharged two days later.

This is the protocol followed when the patient is wheeled into the operation theatre:

The patient's file is checked for:

- Name, age, disease, which side?
- Blood group, any allergies, medication given
- Is blood kept ready?
- Diabetes, High blood pressure
- Any eye lenses, dentures, ornaments
- Is the stomach empty?
- Consent of the patient

Failure to follow this routine that looks so simple results in mishaps all over the world. It is the duty of the ward sister, residents, surgeons, and the anaesthetist to do this check.

How often in every day life, do we forget to take the house-keys before locking the house, forget to charge the mobile phone, even forget to take medicines ?

When I conducted lessons for the students, I always quoted the story of four people who were found in all institutions; namely anybody, everybody, somebody and nobody. In this case nobody had done the check. Flouting the basic rules is invitation to chaos.

How did this happen in spite of the many checks in my practice? I note in bold letters on which side the patient has the hernia, the patient shows my papers on admission, my resident makes a note again, the exact side is mentioned on the operation list, and this is confirmed in the operation theatre by the sister and the anaesthetist. I am always in the theatre before inducing the anaesthesia to comfort the patient and also to make sure about some relevant details. This is particularly important when there is a heavy workload with long operation lists.

It was a series of mistakes that had led to this tragedy. The patient also had a urinary problem for which the urology colleague had planned an endoscopic examination before the hernia operation.

The urology resident had made the notes. His handwriting was so bad that the Rt side (correct side) was interpreted as the Lt side. My resident, without examining the patient, copied the notes made by the urology resident. The patient had not brought my notes.

Normally my anaesthetist always asks the patient to mention the side on which he has a problem before starting anaesthesia. On that day the anaesthetist was new and she did not ask this question. The cystoscopy was done. When I entered the OT, I asked for my papers and they were not in the patient's file. I always talk with the patient prior to the induction of anaesthesia, but because of the prior endoscopic examination the patient was already anaesthetised. Unrelated events came together in one single case that led to the disaster.

The aggrieved party is not interested in how things happened, but what is to be done. I took the entire blame and prepared to face all the consequences.

When there is no defence, do not find scapegoats and argue. 'Accept the blame' was my advice to my residents.

I was lucky that I was spared the medico-legal consequences expected in such a situation.

Wrong Eye Removed

I have heard a story that in Germany, a child's eye was to be removed due to cancer. The surgeon realised at the end of the operation that he had removed the normal eye. He went to the toilet and committed suicide by putting a bullet through his head.

A well-known neurosurgeon in New York's Memorial Sloan Kettering Cancer Center operated on a noted actress's mother on the wrong side of the brain for a tumour. The reason was he saw the CT scan of another patient!

When the work load is very heavy, things go wrong. A child underwent a tonsil operation, and the blood with a wrong blood group was transfused because two patients with the same name were on the list. The name without the date of birth is not adequate to confirm the identity. It is very rare that two patients with the same name are admitted for operation on the same day but that shows that there is always a first time. I know of a case where the X-ray plates were named wrongly and the wrong kidney was explored for stone removal by an eminent surgeon in Bombay.

Bleeding on the Operation Table

I was urgently called to the operating room for a serious complication. The atmosphere was one of confusion and chaos. The surgeon was shouting because the light was inadequate, the instruments were not proper and sponges were in short supply. The floor was full of blood-stained sponges, the suction was not working, the sister appeared helpless and the young anaesthetist's hands holding the mask were trembling. The bleeding area was not seen and the blood loss was appreciable. The patient had a rapid pulse. In a rare gesture, I raised my voice and ordered silence and remembered what I had learnt during the early years of training —If you cannot stop the bleeding, hide it.

Excellent one-line advice.

I took the sterile sheet of cloth used to cover the patient on the operation table and pushed it inside the abdomen and kept it pressed with the force of both hands to stop the bleeding.

We had now time to breathe. I told the anaesthetist that I would not do anything till blood arrived. Telephones were not working, so someone was sent to the blood bank to get four units of blood. The stock of gauze sponges was over and the fresh stock would take more than an hour to be ready. I instructed the sister to get the proper instruments sterilised, and arranged for the floor to be cleared of blood and blood-soaked sponges. The chaotic scene in the theatre was now replaced by normalcy.

An additional suction machine was made available because they tended to get blocked with clots and did not function when we needed them the most. It took two hours to stabilise the situation. The sheet was removed and when a small hole in the blood vessel was clearly seen it was closed with a few stitches. We waited for some time to make sure that there was no other source of bleeding before closing the abdomen. The patient walked home after 10 days.

Surgeons of today cannot imagine the stressful working conditions during emergencies forty years back. The lights were not proper, the suction machines did not work and the cautery was moody. There were no cell phones and communications were poor. The quality of equipment and gadgets was no match for what is available today and life in the operation theatre was extremely stressful.

Presence of mind, quick reflexes, avoiding blame game, keeping the atmosphere tension-free in the theatre are the keys to handle an emergency; skillful hands alone are not adequate. Many stories are told about great surgeons who remain cool when faced with bleeding. No surgeon likes to see a patient bleeding but he has to train himself to remain cool and keep the atmosphere stress-free.

An Operating Room is a place which has potential for innumerable emergencies either because of us or in spite of us. We must expect the unexpected and this is the only attitude which keeps us vigilant in everything that is done in there. As soon as we put a gown and a mask on and enter the sacred place where the patient has placed his life in a surgeon's hands, we should reciprocate their trust by our deep involvement and commitment to their precious lives.

Power Failure During an Operation

I had started an operation for a gastric ulcer (*ulcer in the stomach*) in my own hospital. The patient was well-built, his ulcer had not responded to treatment and there was one episode of bleeding. I separated part of the stomach which I had planned to remove. The clamp was placed over the duodenum which is beyond the stomach and the duodenum was divided. *(The duodenum is part of a small intestine that connects the stomach to the rest of the intestines.)* At this stage, the lights in the OT suddenly went off. I called my hospital's manager to make enquiries and within a short time, he came with the frightening piece of news that the power failure had affected a large part of the city and that the power would be restored after several hours. This was my first experience with power failure after I started my practice in Mumbai.

The operation had reached a stage of no return. We had two hand-held torches but they would not last long. My friend Ravi Desai had already deputed his assistant to fetch two big torches and twenty-four large dry cells. The situation was difficult because with power failure it was impossible to do any suction during the operation. In a major operation the operative area fills up with blood-stained fluid that obstructs the vision for surgery. Taking stitches through the stomach wall too becomes difficult without good light and suction. I kept my mind cool and completed the operation after a gruelling three hours of struggle. I must have aged a few years during those few hours.

The patient was a police inspector. It is a common experience that when we operate on doctors, lawyers, judges, or police, something goes wrong! In places outside Mumbai where power failure is very common, doctors have to maintain generators. I did not have one because in Mumbai such power failures were a rare occurrence and if one did occur, it lasted only for a short time. At the end of the operation, I had a tremendous sense of relief. I was drenched with sweat and was exhausted. There was no complication following the operation. If my friend had not arranged for the torches in time what would have happened to me was a scary thought. The next day I bought a generator which has not been used for many years, but the mere fact that it is there gives me relief from anxiety.

These experiences are very important when working in Indian conditions. It is easy to do major operations when everything is available efficiently. Many a times surgeons who have done very well abroad may fail when they are faced with the unexpected situations in the Indian setup. I have taught my students that they must train themselves without the luxury of comfort.

Serious Case

Once I had to do an emergency operation on a serious case of perforated intestine. The only person attending on him was his twelve year old daughter. Her mother had died of tuberculosis. The operation was very risky. The patient requested me with folded hands and tears in his eyes that there was nobody to look after his daughter in case he died. Luckily his friends had come to the hospital and they assured him that they would look after the daughter. The patient was a slum dweller and friendship among the poor is often stronger than those who live in the apartments of high rise buildings. We are never aware of this reality while studying in medical colleges!

I had to remove thoughts about that girl from my mind when I started the operation. Emotions which have a potential for destroying concentration have no place in a surgeon's life. To keep emotion away yet not to lose sensitivity of mind requires regular practice. This attitude is not connected with skill but with mental discipline. Luckily his life was saved. Reverence for life doesn't mean emotional involvement which will affect a surgeon's performance.

Emergency on a Sunday Afternoon

I was called one Sunday for management of a rectal injury that occured during the surgery for removal of the uterus in a small hospital. The patient was very fat, the operation table could not be tilted and adequate positioning of the patient was not possible. The operation table lamp was ineffective, the staff was not trained and the anaesthetist expressed her lack of ability for any prolonged procedure. Long instruments and suture materials were not available, and no blood bank could supply blood.

A quick decision was necessary. The tear in the rectum was irregular, the edges were frayed and proper closure was impossible. A few stitches brought the torn edges together.

A thorough wash of the pelvic cavity was done to remove all the faecal matter in the abdomen. Tubes were positioned inside to drain the pus that would collect. A loop of the intestine was brought out of the abdomen and opened to evacuate the faecal matter to prevent it entering the damaged rectum. The operation was over, the patient was shifted to a major hospital where she had a difficult recovery. She was re-explored after three months, the rectum was neatly sutured and after some weeks the intestinal loop was closed and dropped inside the abdomen.

Any attempt to do more at the time of injury would have proved fatal. Judgment of the whole situation is more important than mere skill.

Accident on a Modern Operation Table!

I had started my hospital with an operating table made by a reputed company abroad. The company had brought one to India as a prototype, but the cost was so exorbitant that there would have been no market in the country at that time. The table was simply lying in a warehouse. I was able to approach the company, who offered me the table at a much reduced price. However the table required some overhauling which was accomplished soon enough. It was very sturdy and its various manoeuvres could be controlled by pulleys at the head of the table—a job that was to be done by the anaesthetist. Back then, all tables had revolving wheels, so that it was possible to rotate the table into various positions—head low, leg low, rotate on either side. Needless to say, at that time, this table was a source of great curiosity. I trained all my staff in its proper use, and also informed every anaesthetist about the ease with which the pulleys at the head end could change the positioning of the table.

A few months later I was operating on a well-known artist who had an enlarged thyroid. The anaesthetist passed a tube through the mouth across the larynx into the trachea. The thyroid is a gland in the neck that surrounds the trachea in the front as well as both sides. It is important that the anaesthetist carefully maintains the patency of the intra-tracheal tube, through which the anaesthetic gases are given during the course of the operation. The patient was draped and just as we were about to start the operation, the table suddenly tilted with its legs down and head up and the patient with the intra-tracheal tube landed on the floor. The anaesthetist was trying to adjust the position of the table but the mechanism of the pulleys was so delicate that with a slight increase in the pressure, the table tilted to a dangerous level. The patient was put back on the table, and we first made sure that the tube passed by the anaesthetist was in the correct place. I had never experienced such an unusual crisis before. I doubt if any surgeon in the world has faced such a crisis.

My mind was flooded with worries. Was there any internal damage due to the fall? Was there any injury to the spine, any damage to abdominal viscera? If there was indeed even the slightest bit of damage, I had no business to continue the operation. If there was no damage, I had no reasonable explanation as to why I didn't perform the operation. There are many individuals who like to play safe and postpone the operation and give some false excuse.

After waiting for half an hour, I finally made the decision to go ahead with the operation. I cannot explain in words why. We cannot be right every time, but experience teaches us that we can be correct most of the times. However, I had to make one thing very clear to myself—in the worst case scenario, if something serious did happen, I would have to face the consequences of the accident, as well as my decision to go ahead with the operation after the mishap. In such a situation, nobody could save me. Luckily, the patient did not have any complications, not even any pain in his back. He was safe and I was lucky. These are moments of great stress which surgeons have to face and handle. And in most cases, the decisions that we take at such times are not based on intelligence, skills, or statistics but on intuition. If a patient had sustained serious injury, my career would have been ruined at a young age.

Cardiac Arrest During an Operation

In May 1972, I met with a car accident and was out of pratice for two-and-a-half months. When I restarted work, the very first case I treated was a young man with phimosis.

Circumcision is a small operation. The anaesthetist induced anaesthesia. Just when I was getting ready to begin the operation, the anaesthetist informed me that the patient had cardiac arrest. I quickly gave an external cardiac massage by forcefully thumping the front of the chest wall. By doing this, the heart muscles get mechanical vibrations which cause the heart to start beating again. The heart may start, but if the brain does not get oxygen supply for 180 seconds, there is permanent damage to the brain. This is a vegetative state wherein the heart continues to beat, the patient continues to breathe, the intestines, liver and kidneys function automatically but patient remains unconscious. I was forced to ask myself whether I should proceed with the operation. I shone a light into the patient's eye, and the pupils suddenly contracted. This indicated that the brain had not suffered any permanent damage. We continued with the operation and I felt relief when the patient regained consciousness. The patient was the only son and his parents were old and completely dependent on him.

These are the stresses that a surgeon has to face throughout his professional life. I know of instances where one terrible tragedy has ended a surgical career.

Full Stomach can Lead to Disaster

When I was in England I was told by an anaesthetist that there was a confidential report on deaths in operation theatres and the commonest cause of death was anaesthesia in pregnant women during application of forceps. During anaesthesia the contents from the stomach can regurgitate into the throat and then enter the wind pipe to drown the patients with her own secretions. Normally the stomach empties completely in five hours after taking food but when patients are in pain, the stomach may remain full for many hours. Unless the stomach contents are emptied by a tube, anaesthesia can lead to death.

The risk of aspiration is very high in children. They should be operated first thing in the morning. In case of delay, if they start crying because of thirst or hunger, the frightened mothers give them water or some milk to keep them quiet.

A good suction machine must be kept ready all the times during anaesthesia. Delay in suction may cause death. So many checks are necessary every day in operating rooms.

'For want of a nail the kingdom was lost...'

I understood the profound meaning of this rhyme with increasing experience!

❑ ❑ ❑

Chapter 15

Skill and the Surgeon

A surgeon's hands are believed to have a magical quality about them. However, them being long with tapering fingers, is more fiction than fact. I have worked with a surgeon who had thick shapeless hands because of acromegaly but the strokes of his knife were a delight to watch. It is impossible to judge the voice of a singer by inspecting his vocal cords or a runner by his long legs or intelligence by the size of the head.

(Acromegaly is a disfiguring affliction of the body due to tumour of the pituitary gland in the brain. Pituitary is considered as the conductor of the endocrine gland orchestra in the body. These patients have thick hands, big fingers, big feet, massive height, jaws and tongue, and a prominent forehead. Removal of the tumour by surgery in time prevents the progression of the disease and the patient is cured because luckily most tumours are simple and not malignant.)

Skill is an essential requisite for a surgeon. It is a delight to watch some surgeons operate with graceful hand movements while it is a torture to see clumsy hands meddling inside the human body. A surgeon is an artist but his performance does not depend on his moods unlike that of some temperamental musicians, actors, painters, sculptors etc. On the contrary, a surgeon has to create a positive atmosphere when a situation is difficult, and play the role of a captain of a ship.

He often feels lonely but his only comfort is in knowing that he is doing his best for the patient, and has a team which trusts his competence and respects his decisions. Surgery is not a one-man show. Reinhold Meissner from Italy has the unique distinction of climbing all the fourteen peaks over 8000 metres. There will never be a Meissner in surgery. Apart from skill, speed is yet another hallmark of talented surgeons. It is insightful to read of the patients' suffering vividly described in the following words, "*Before the days of anaesthesia, a patient preparing for an operation was like a condemned criminal preparing for execution. He counted the days till the appointed day came. He counted the hours of that day till the appointed hour came. He listened for the echo of the surgeon's carriage in the street. He watched for the pull at the door bell, for his foot on the stair, for his step in the room, for the production of his dreaded instruments, for his few grave words and his last preparations before beginning and then he surrendered his liberty and revolting at the necessity, submitted to be held or bound and helplessly gave himself up to the cruel knife.*"

This was the reality as late as 1846 when speed was so important that amputation, a common operation, was over within two minutes! It took some years for me to appreciate that speed in surgery was dependent upon teamwork and not as much on a surgeon's skill. The operation theatre sister assisting the surgeon knows the next step of the operation and hands over the correct instrument without any cue from the surgeon.

A gentle handling of tissues is far more important than speed. Operations in skilled hands take less time, patients bleed less, the postoperative pain is less and recovery is fast. The sense of touch in a surgeon's hands is as important as the sense of tune for a singer. Intuition and awareness of dangers are unique characteristics seen in outstanding surgeons.

Is there any connection between skill and speed? An uninformed observer confuses movement for speed.

As young residents we were impressed by fast hand movements which we mistook for speed. Competent surgeons often appear slow but with every step, the operation progresses steadily and surely.

The most difficult part of training for a surgeon is to nurture attitudes like caution, concern, concentration, compassion, humility, presence of mind, quick reflexes and taking split second decisions in a confusing, highly stressful situation, all the while maintaining a tension-free atmosphere in the theatre.

Surgeons require skill, ability to take decisions, intelligence, enthusiasm and stamina to work long hours but if he has NO integrity, forget all other assets.

❑ ❑ ❑

Chapter 16

My Travels

I went to the USA in 1976. On the very first day, as ill luck would have it, my hostess put my trousers in the washing machine with the passport still in the pocket. I always worry about losing my passport when I go abroad. I went to the Indian consulate in New York to get a new one. I thought it would be a straightforward job because all the details were clearly visible though the passport was damaged. I was the first one to enter the office as most of the staff had not come to work, a common occurrence in any Indian establishment in those days. I had to wait for almost forty minutes before I could meet the concerned officer.

I told him what had happened. I did not expect a helpful attitude because I had heard frightening experiences from others in similar situations.

"Why did you not take care of such an important document?"

"My trousers needed a wash after my Europe tour and my hostess placed it in the machine without checking the pockets."

His annoyed expression was an indication of the rough time ahead.

"First get a black-and-white photograph taken and then come back to me." The word 'Please' was conspicuously missing!

"Where can this be done?"

"I do not know!"

I spotted a studio hardly five minutes away from the consulate building. I told the girl at the counter that I urgently needed a photograph for my passport. She told me that it couldn't be done immediately and that I would have to wait.

I asked her, "How long?"

"Fifteen minutes."

This was my first lesson in the USA. America respects time, an attitude foreign to our representatives working there. The man at the desk was surprised at my quick return. I felt sad that a person who had worked there for a long time had no desire to help fellow-citizens in distress.

I completed all the formalities, paid the amount and asked him when I would get the new passport. I was shocked when he asked me to come on Monday because the office was closed during weekends. That was Friday at 12 noon. I requested him to issue the passport the same day because the next day I had to go to Canada. He expressed his inability to help me but suggested that I should see his boss, the ultimate authority.

I was asked the same questions and I gave the same answers.

He said, "Come on Monday."

"Can I get it today?"

"No."

"Why do I have to wait for two days?"

"Doctor, we have many jobs to do and if we start spending time on issuing new passports for individuals who do not know how to keep them safely, our work will become unmanageable."

"This is the first time my passport has been damaged. I have been travelling abroad for twenty years."

"I cannot help you. Today is Friday; come on Monday."

This was a bureaucratic response typical in India.

I thought that if he was talking to a responsible citizen in such a shabby way, how must he behave with others? I could no longer remain silent.

I raised my voice, "How many times have Indians come with similar complaints to your office? You are our servants and not our masters; we maintain you by paying taxes. You are short of time because you come late to the office, do not work with efficiency and leave the office much before time."

He was taken aback and I continued my attack. "Today, no one was present in the office when I came here. If I do not receive my passport today, I will not keep quiet. I assure you that I will lodge a complaint against you and your office after I go back to India. You are here to help us when we have a problem. You can harass me, but I will not spare you either."

He did not expect such a sharp reaction. He had enjoyed a comfortable life in his cosy chair of authority. He was visibly upset.

"Come back at 4 p.m. and if it is ready, take it."

"If I do not get it at four, I will create a ruckus", I again threatened him.

I came out of his office and everyone was looking at me. Obviously, they had heard my outburst. I speak loudly when I am upset. I was going to the cafeteria when a young girl who was working in the office stopped me. She asked me whether I was from Mumbai because her sister was doing medicine and had worked with one Dr. Shrikhande for a surgical term. She felt happy that her sister was my student. While we were drinking coffee, she complimented me for my outburst and agreed that there was no proper work culture.

I got a new passport within an hour.

I should mention another example of cold bureaucracy. Getting foreign exchange for attending a conference abroad was a nightmare till 1991. One had to waste three days visiting different departments in different buildings and present necessary documents. I once requested foreign exchange for an extra day. At the age of 60, I needed it to recover from jetlag. I was denied it because there was no provision in the rules to consider jetlag as a valid reason! Ironically, those who had no respect for the law, could have wads of dollars in their pockets. Luckily the situation has changed completely; now I can have plenty of foreign exchange, but I don't need it!

The main purpose of my USA trip was to visit Lahey Clinic in Boston. This was connected to an interesting episode that happened in London in 1971.

I had passed F.R.C.S. England and Edinburgh in 1959, and got a job in a busy district hospital where I learnt surgical work on my own. I kept illustrated surgery books in the operation theatre, referred to them before starting operations and at times during surgery, the anaesthetist would show me the illustrations for guidance. This is unthinkable in today's era but I learnt surgery in the 1950's. I was cautious but not timid; bold but never rash; and earned a reputation as not only a skilled, but a safe surgeon.

On my return I worked in Mumbai for ten years and knew that I was on the right track. I knew what my strengths and my limitations were. My one urge was to see how master surgeons worked and that urge took me back to England for a few weeks. In 1971, I visited St. George Hospital in London to see Dr. Rodney Smith, a known authority for gall bladder and pancreatic surgery.

I had to observe the operation from the observer's gallery which gave me the occasional opportunity to see what was going on when the heads and shoulders of the members did not obstruct my view! What can anyone see from such a long distance and that too, what was happening inside the abdomen?! But that was the only possibility available to me.

The surgeon's comments were more helpful than what I actually saw. How fortunate surgeons of today are! They can sit in a hall and observe the steps of the operation on a big screen, even better than the assistants helping the surgeon.

One day, an elderly doctor joined me in the gallery. He gave me a warm smile and said, "How funny the English are! There are no pockets in their shirts or trousers. I have to keep my travel documents, passport, and cash in my gumboots."

His accent was typically American. His interactions with Rodney Smith showed that they were close friends.

Rodney said, "Ken, pardon me. Our operation theatre is ancient. We do not have your sophisticated American set-up."

"Ron, I have come to see good surgery, not modern operation theatres."

I was curious to know who the visitor was. I said, "It seems that you are from America."

"Yes."

"Where do you come from?"

"Boston."

"Your field of interest?"

"Bile duct strictures and pancreas."

"Your name?"

"Kenneth Warren."

"Lahey Clinic?"

"Yes."

I had met a giant among surgeons.

"How fortunate I am to meet you in such an unexpected way. I have heard so much about you and Lahey Clinic. I have not visited your country but when I come, I would like to see your work."

"Most welcome. Let me know when you are coming and we will show you a lot of work."

I could not believe that I was meeting a world-renowned surgeon in the field in which I had decided to develop expertise. This has always been my experience. When I decide on a particular goal, everything falls into place. Five years later, I visited America and Kenneth Warren kept his word.

Kenneth Warren was a remarkable surgeon and an outstanding human being. He took me to the hospital cafeteria, insisted that he would pay and continued to do so for the whole month. He said, "Do not feel embarrassed. I know how difficult it is for you to get dollars in your country."

Such a gesture from an eminent surgeon was a rare experience for me. It struck me as unusual that Dr. Warren was standing in a queue behind a dark-skinned maid. This was then unthinkable in India. I had heard from a friend that an Indian doctor in the 1940s could not sit at the same table as the whites. I do not know if it was true. America has changed. Now they have an African-American president! I am also happy to see that a boy who once sold tea on railway platforms has become the Prime Minister of our country. Such unusual events occur only in a democracy. More than fifty crores of people voting in a peaceful manner is a miracle in human history. In a dictatorship, dictators are replaced only by dictators. In a democracy, no ruler can take the masses for granted.

I regularly attended his operating sessions. I saw a variety of complicated operations on the gall bladder, bile duct and pancreas. I would stand next to him, and he would from time to time, let me peer inside the abdomen to explain the details. I have followed the same system throughout my career.

Dr. Warren showed me his room which had been Dr. Frank Lahey's office. I was sitting in a place where important events in surgical history had taken place. My experience was beyond any words can describe.

I learnt many facts about Warren's personality. In spite of his great fame, he was most unassuming and friendly towards all. Whenever he was in Boston, he never missed his rounds even on a Sunday or Christmas Day. If I recall correctly, he told me that when Boston had a severe snowfall he and Dr. Richard Catell reached the hospital by skiing down the vehicle-less streets! Some years later when I met him again, he took me to a new ward which was built and named after him. On a plaque at the entrance to the ward was a list of donors. The names of the donors were in alphabetical order and not according to the amount each had donated! He said that the man who gave less money did not have less regard for him and therefore it was only proper that the names be in alphabetical order. This one instance showed the fine character of the man.

Many years ago, I referred a very complicated case of bile duct injury to Dr. Warren. The family was very rich and willing to pay for treatment anywhere in the world. They were very keen that

I should repair the injured duct in Bombay, but the injury was one month old. (Earlier in the book, I have mentioned the case of Sir Anthony Eden who was flown to Lahey Clinic after the bile duct injury in London.) I explained to them that the best expertise should be offered to the young man. The patient was flown to the USA and underwent three operations. Unfortunately, he died after forty-five days in the intensive care unit. Dr. Warren told me that it was one of the most difficult cases of his own career and everything possible was done. (I had referred only two cases to surgeons abroad, the other to London, because I knew the problems were beyond me. He could not be saved.)

Every day Warren would go and speak with the patient's relatives. When the patient died, he sent his assistant to place a wreath on the coffin, while they were waiting at Logan airport to return home. The bill was very high and Dr. Warren slashed it by 50 per cent. The relatives were very grateful to me for referring the patient to a good surgeon. I learnt that an article appreciating the doctors' services had appeared in a regional newspaper in India!

My association with such outstanding human beings has enriched my life. I met a remarkable American couple during my visit to the USA and remained friends till they passed away. I met Carl and Marion Reupsch who had come to receive us when we reached San Diego. I felt embarrassed to tell my hosts that I had lost the keys to my suitcase.

Karl said, "No problem, I will make one for you". He picked up my suitcase and carried it downstairs to the basement workshop. He made the key within ten minutes and said, "I was taught by my father to do as many things as possible with my own hands and I have made it a habit." Like most Indians, I am not a handyman. I cannot handle simple tools for minor jobs around the house because service people such as electricians and plumbers are easily available. Americans are very 'do-it-yourself' in contrast. Four days later when I left San Diego, we knew that it was the beginning of a new friendship. During my next visit to San Diego in 1981, I saw the hoarding of Ryan Corporation while Carl was driving me home from the airport. I remembered

Ryan Corporation had made the plane the Spirit of St. Louis in which Charles Lindbergh had made the first transatlantic nonstop flight from Long Island, New York to Paris. I had also read the biography of Charles Lindbergh. Karl was so surprised at my interest that as soon I had settled down, he took me to the San Diego airport and introduced me to the Director as 'a surgeon from India who knows more about Charles Lindbergh than many in the USA.'

I was shown the diagrams and photographs detailing the way the plane was built. We had coffee and snacks, and it was a very interesting experience for me.

The room where I would stay with the Reupsch family was referred to as 'Dr. Shrikhande's room'. I was happy that I owned property in America without earning or spending a single dollar! Marion would wash and iron my clothes, and it was a joy to spend time with the couple at their home. She always greeted me on arrival at the airport, but never came to see me off because she was sure she would break down. Carl dropped me off at the airport, but I didn't realise that it would be the last time I would see him.

I did not know that Carl who was a director of the port at San Diego, was an individual of national fame until I read his obituary in the newspapers during my visit to the USA in May 1983. My visit was completely unplanned. I had accompanied my colleague for treatment but unfortunately he died before surgery of a massive heart attack. The next day I left USA with his coffin. I could not meet Marion but sent a condolence letter.

My dear Marion,

My mind was in 3335 Sterne Street, San Diego and all the events of our association since we all met in August 1976, passed through my mind. We met as strangers and within a couple of days became close friends as if we had known each other's families for a very long time.

We live in distant continents, but my mind constantly visits your home. In times of distress, friends do comfort us, whatever the physical distance. We are going to miss Carl. He was a stalwart among men, a person with multi-faceted talents, unassuming, humane and kind. Such individuals are difficult to meet and I was privileged to know him personally.

You were fortunate to have spent almost fifty years with him. The pangs of separation would be mellowed by memories of happy times. Carl loved the sea. I read in the newspaper report that after cremation the ashes were scattered in the sea. He has now become part of the sea for eternity and both would be richer by this association.

Please look after your health. We would feel happy if you could come and spend some time with us. We have a home in San Diego and you have one in Bombay. I firmly believe that there is a purpose behind life and even when bodies depart the spirit continues to live. Carl would know that he has left behind many friends like me who share your grief. May his soul rest in peace.

Marion flew all the way from the USA to Mumbai for my eldest daughter's wedding. I told Marion several times that she would receive a warm welcome any time and could stay with us as long as she wanted. In case of illness she would get the best medical help at no cost in Bombay. She was a globetrotter and visited even Tibet and Antarctica at an advanced age. She would send me handwritten postcards of her travels which were not legible for me. I told her that she had a doctor's handwriting.

My next visit was in 1988. Carl had in his will expressed a desire that one of his precious possessions, a book on photography, Creative Camera Art written by Dr. Max Thorek in 1937 should be given to me. Carl was a close friend of Dr. Thorek, a surgeon from Chicago who founded the International College of Surgeons and was also a well known photographer and President of the Photographers' Society of USA.

Marion gave me that book in which she had written, "It was Carl's wish that this book should go to Dr. V. N. Shrikhande. At long last." The date was October 31, 1988. The book changed hands after fifty-one years and is now in my grateful possession. How lucky I feel.

Years later, I received a letter from Marion.

"Just a week ago something important happened in my life since Carl left Earth... and now I am ready to share it with you."

"Carl was involved with the Cabrillo National Monument, the second-most visited National Park in America and very probably the most visited in the world. Cabrillo sailed into SD Bay in 1542 and sort of discovered it all. He died and probably was buried in one of the Channel Islands above Los Angeles but the most important man to our city history is this Portuguese-Spaniard explorer."

"Two years after Carl left, I decided to sponsor the deteriorating statue which itself had an interesting history, even kidnapping. This statue has stood above our harbour since the early 40s. There was a magnificent and beautiful dedication on February 28. I am enclosing just a couple of newspaper clips but there has been much publicity since April 1985 when I announced my decision."

"Although there has been publicity in the Los Angeles Times too... I have never told anyone out of the city... until now to you."

"The Portuguese sent one of their warships over with a crew of 100 which arrived at the entrance to our harbour with a 21-gun salute. They had the crates with Cabrillo aboard. I was invited to the captain's cabin (in my Shelter Island walking clothes) and the next day Cabrillo was set up in the most beautiful place overlooking all of Southern California."

"I have done something most worthwhile for my city. One friend wrote a note hoping that Carl was on a "front row cloud" during the festivities. There were VIPs from Lisbon, Washington D.C, NYC, San Francisco and Sacramento."

One day I got a letter from her daughter MerrieAnn that her mother had passed away. I wrote to her daughter that whenever I looked at a map of the USA I would first look at San Diego. Now for me San Diego is lost and America is lonely. She wrote to me that she now had a home for me near Seattle and that

I must continue to keep in touch with her. I went twice to her house and enjoyed her company and that of her husband, Jeff Martin.

Some years later I learnt that Marion had sold her two homes, spent that money to renovate the statue and had Carl's name inscribed on it. I would have visited it had I known about it. Marion never told me about this part of her contribution to the project.

How did I come to know the Reupsch family? A director of a port in India consulted me in 1970 for his wife's surgery for varicose veins. He could not believe it when I opined that operation was not necessary. He kept in touch with me and told me that if ever I planned to go to America I should inform him because he was friends with a remarkable couple, Carl and Marion Reupsch.

xxx

Bombay Hospital held an international conference on surgery where I gave a live demonstration of a gall bladder operation. I met Dr. Rupert Indar who mentioned his training at the Lahey Clinic and his association with Dr. Richard Catell. He contacted his daughter who was kind enough to send me his biography. I replied:

August 1, 2001

My dear Mrs. Virginia Dunmore,

I was happy to receive your book 'On the Cutting Edge'.

I am practising in Bombay for the last thirty years and even when I was a medical student I had heard of your late father Dr. Richard B. Cattell who had operated on Sir Anthony Eden. I had the privilege to meet Dr. Kenneth Warren on several occasions. I wanted to know about your father whom I never met. Luckily I met Dr. Rupert Indar who had worked with your father.

I am a lover of history because understanding the contributions made by outstanding individuals inspires us to travel the road of excellence. I go long distances to meet exceptional individuals, and read their biographies to enrich my life.

It was stated in the book that had Catell not become a surgeon, he would have become a priest!

I had also read the book about the Mayo Brothers and my other dream was to visit Mayo Clinic. During my first visit in 1981, I spent about 10 days there visiting the various facilities. I wrote to the professor of surgery after my return to India, "I had heard and read about Mayo Clinic from the time I was an undergraduate student. I came there as a pilgrim... what I saw was a dream come true..."

I referred to my experiences at the Mayo Clinic in my conversations with my family, friends, and students. I even gave a talk at a surgeon's conference about my visit—One man, Dr. Mayo had a vision to build an institute in a small village in the north. He was fortunate that both his sons shared his dreams to serve the sick with excellence, without thinking about the monetary considerations. Patients and doctors flooded to the clinic. An airport was built to facilitate their travel. Institutions become famous because of the men who work there... now the Clinic is known for the enormous amount of research work done in the hospital.

The story of Mayo Clinic will continue to inspire many like me.

I developed a good rapport with Professor Mcllrath of Mayo Clinic in 1981. In one of my letters I wrote, "As a medical student I had heard about the work at Mayo Clinic. I was influenced by Osler's writings and Halstead's dedication to training residents. Their teachings were reinforced by the conviction that we must do our very best to both train and work with devotion and excellence. I wonder whether I have sent you a description of the work we are doing in Bombay. The surgical practice in our country is totally different from what I saw in America. You might find the work done in a miniature set-up such as ours informative.

I have been sending my postgraduates to visit Mayo Clinic because I feel they must be exposed to centres of excellence so that they have a good model to follow in life. I am thankful to you for the courtesy you extend to them when they visit Mayo Clinic."

He wrote in July 1987, "*I am sorry to report that my wife, Connie, passed away last November. She was very fond of you and enjoyed the time the three of us spent together.*"

I replied, "I was sorry to hear about the sad demise of your wife Connie. The first time I met you both was on the 19th of October, 1981. I still remember the day because it was my daughter's birthday and the 20th anniversary of my starting a career in Bombay. During our conversation, I saw Connie fighting back tears. It is in my nature to develop personal contacts. May her soul rest in peace!"

Thompson Retractor

It was in 1993 that I went to San Francisco to attend the American College of Surgeons meeting. It is the biggest event in the world of surgery. I bought a retractor at this exhibition, a very expensive one, but one that I felt would be very useful for my work back home in India. While having a talk with the manufacturer I heard a very interesting story of how the retractor was invented. The surgeon was operating on a gall bladder, and during the removal of the gall bladder, there was sudden bleeding from the liver bed. This area was inaccessible. They had to repeatedly adjust the overhead lamp and the inclination of the operation table. Only after a struggle of two hours, was the exact site of the bleeding identified and the bleeding controlled.

The anaesthetist standing at the head of the table had the idea that a retractor would make the surgical team's job simpler and avoid such embarrassing situations. The name of the man was Thompson. I wrote a letter to Thompson who sent me a reply, "*I invented the retractor in 1960. The development was interesting. I sold the patent rights to a company but their President was killed in an auto accident six months later. The retractor remained on the*

URL Foundation Puraskar for Literature, June 2009

With Dr. Krishna and Kalpana Patil, at their son's wedding

With Dr. Ajay Vaidya

Full Moon at Leh

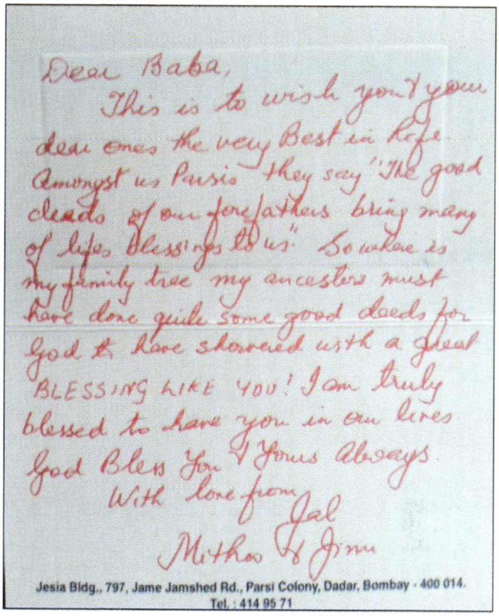

Dear Baba,

This is to wish you & your dear ones the very Best in Life. Amongst us Parsis they say "The good deeds of our forefathers bring many of life's blessings to us". So where is my family tree my ancestors must have done quite some good deeds for God to have showered us with a great BLESSING LIKE YOU! I am truly blessed to have you in our lives God Bless You & Yours Always.

With love from

Jal

Mithoo & Jimu

Jesia Bldg., 797, Jame Jamshed Rd., Parsi Colony, Dadar, Bombay - 400 014.
Tel. : 414 95 71

Mithu Jesia's letter

Son Shailesh, awarded Hon. FRCS, England, March 2015, with my wife Dr. Suhas and daughter Dr. Neena Nande

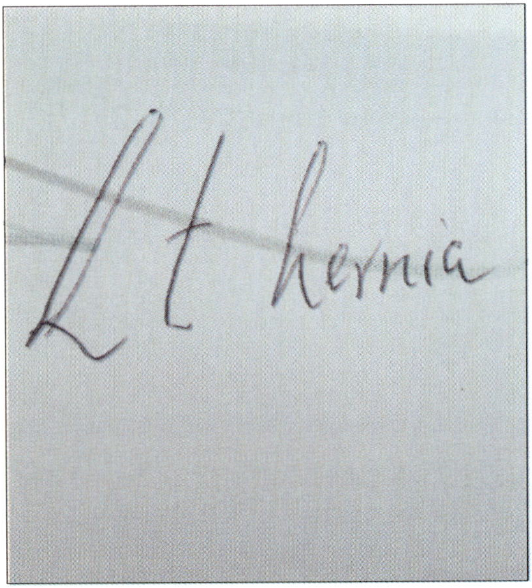

Is it Left hernia or Right hernia

'Aani Don Hath', my first book in Marathi

shelf until I took it back in 1977. I worked on it for a few years to improve the design and market it worldwide. I did this work in a garage and sold it to twenty-six foreign countries and in USA, but the apparatus had some faults. I sold it to Dan Farley. He perfected it and now guarantees its reliability. I am proud of him."

Dr. Richard C. Thompson
San Mateo
October 19, 1993

I was in Chicago for another annual conference of the American College of Surgeons. Chicago was once the hotbed of crime and is also known for its architecture. Indians associate Chicago with the rousing address of Swami Vivekananda at the Parliament of Religions in September 1893.

"I am proud to belong to a religion which has taught the world both tolerance and universal acceptance. We believe not only in universal toleration, but we accept all religions as true. I am proud to belong to a nation which has sheltered the persecuted and the refugees of all religions and all nations of the earth. I am proud to tell you that we have gathered in our bosom the purest remnant of the Israelites, who came to Southern India and took refuge with us in the very year in which their holy temple was shattered to pieces by Roman tyranny. I am proud to belong to a religion which has sheltered and is still fostering the remnant of the grand Zoroastrian nation. I will quote to you, brethren a few lines from the hymn which I remember to have repeated from my earliest boyhood, which is every day repeated by millions of human beings.:

"As the different streams having their sources in different places all mingle their water in the sea, so, O Lord, the different paths which men take through different tendencies , various though they appear, crooked or straight, all lead to Thee."

I was staying close to Michigan Avenue where he gave this speech. He was convinced that East and West could come together for the good of mankind. Vivekananda's message to the West was that India was in possession of an enduring and altruistic philosophical legacy that was crucial to keep humans connected, not only with one another, but also with their environment.

Chicago University established a Chair in memory of Swami Vivekananda. When I was young, the sprit of patriotism was in the air, and we were influenced by India's past; Vivekanand was a hero.

xxx

I went to Japan three times to see surgical work. I had operated on Professor Naresh Mantri of Tokyo University and through him, I had an opportunity to meet some eminent intellectuals from both the social and academic circles in Tokyo. I learnt a very important fact about Japan. The country was isolated for many years. A time came when they realised that isolation was no longer possible. They wanted to absorb the best in the world. They sent their lawyers to America and England, their students of literature, art and music to France, engineering students to Germany. They planned 100 per cent literacy in Japan and their main discussion was whether to teach them English or Japanese. In the end they decided that the mother tongue was the best way to educate a child so that they became creative and mature in understanding. I felt happy because I held the same views about the importance of mother tongue in bringing up children.

I had a discussion with a lady in London some time in the 1980s. She was an expert in the field of language education for immigrant students. She told me, "Please tell your countrymen not to neglect their mother tongues. The initial development of the child must take place through the mother tongue because that is a rich source of creative thinking. They are quick to pick up many languages, but understanding the environment must come through the mother tongue."

I once operated on a patient from Delhi. A child of five could speak in four languages! She learnt Marathi from her mother, English from her father, Sanskrit from her grandfather and Hindi from the maid! Words should not be translated. My son when he was hardly seven, asked me, "What is the English word for telephone?"

xxx

In Tokyo, I met Dr. Takashi Takahashi, a cancer surgeon, and later during his visit to Mumbai, he stayed with me.

He was impressed with what he saw in my small hospital and said, "We call this faultless technique. I want to give you a gift the next time I come, which will make your work very convenient."

He presented me with a self-retaining retractor which is attached to the right costal arch and is connected with a wire that goes to a stand fixed to the operation table. This was a great help because now there was no need to have an assistant standing on my left side holding the retractor. It was a novelty three decades back and looked so simple in hindsight!

xxx

I went to Egypt known for its pyramids and the Nile cruise. When kings and queens died in Egypt, they were mummified and buried with their treasures, food, fruits and everything that they needed to live in the afterlife. This was so that they could make use of all those things once they were born again. All these tombs were on the western coast of the Nile since the sun set in the west. And just across the Indian Ocean, Indians believed that though our bodies perish, our soul is eternal. The bodies were burnt soon after death and the ashes sprinkled in holy rivers. The concept of death varies from culture to culture.

❑ ❑ ❑

Chapter 17

Teacher in Me

I had no teacher in my life to guide and inspire me. Perhaps that is why teaching became a passion for me. When I got attachment to a teaching hospital, it was a wonderful opportunity for me to take clinics for undergraduate students and train the postgraduates. More than three-hundred residents worked with me and several surgeons came as observers. Their associations are a precious treasure for me.

Whenever I go abroad, I contact my students. During one of my visits to London, Dr. Krishna Patil was driving me, in his Mercedes Benz car, from Croydon to his home in Surrey. I was thinking about his remarkable journey from a village in India to becoming a consultant robotic and laparoscopic urological surgeon at Royal Surrey County Hospital, Guilford, Surrey, UK.

He came from a farmer's family in a small village named Bastawade near Kolhapur. He could not go for medical education and so he took a degree in Ayurvedic medicine called BAMS (Bachelor of Ayurvedic Medicine and Surgery). At that time there was a provision for these young students to take a condensed course and become allopathic doctors. He decided to become a surgeon after MBBS, worked with me in 1978, and got MS in General Surgery. Later he decided to specialise and did MCh (Magister Chirurgiae) in Urology under Professor Ajit Phadke. He married a fellow-doctor working in the same hospital, and went to the Middle East. While working in Saudi Arabia, he took leave, and went to the UK where the couple eventually settled to work as consultant surgeons. He had special interest in robotic surgery and his wife became a paediatric urologist.

The family lives in a house in Surrey where they have maintained a simple lifestyle. The couple and their children ran the New York Marathon to raise money for charities. His son, along with his four English friends, bought an old ambulance, repaired it and drove it around sixteen countries before giving it as a gift to Mongolia. They also raised £ 10,000 for charity. Dr. Krishna Patil has visited East Africa to render health services to the poor and the needy. He has been visiting Dervan near Chiplun in Maharashtra state, where he performs urological procedures for the poor at the Walawalkar Trust hospital.

He gave a guest lecture in memory of Dr. Dwarkanath Kotnis during our state conference at Solapur. "*I consider myself blessed that I got inspiration to tread the ethical path, concern for the neglected and spirit of excellence from the late Dr. Phadke and from Dr. Shrikhande,*" he said before starting his lecture.

Krishna Patil represents an example of the social mobility which India is witnessing in all fields.

(Dr. Kotnis from Solapur was one of the five physicians sent to China to provide medical assistance during the second Sino-Japanese war in 1938. He married a Chinese girl. He died in China and is regarded as a symbol of Indo-Chinese friendship. Chinese leaders have maintained the tradition of meeting the Kotnis family during their official visits to India since 1950).

The real success in life is not what we achieve but how we have invested our time to mould, inspire and instil values in those who come in contact with us. It is not how much reputation we have earned but how much we have helped others to grow. The biggest joy in life is to leave behind a legacy.

A German doctor wrote, "*I joined medicine to serve the sick. I had high quality education in my country but I was missing something. In you I met the teacher I was searching for. Science and human touch is a wonderful combination.*"

I was invited to conduct a three-day workshop by the department of surgery, at a medical college at Visakhapatnam on the east coast of India. The head of the department of surgery wrote, "*It has been a very memorable event not only for me, but for all of us at the Dept of Surgery and the students at the medical college. Very often your name is mentioned during our meetings. Everyone was spellbound by your lecture and surgical demonstration.*"

"*In addition to the professional skills, an in-depth discussion took place on professor and student relationship, and your warmth and attitude towards your trainees captivated our minds. I also mentioned that your attitude towards your patients is much more than a mere business relationship as seen these days. I told them that you consider the operation theatre as your temple and the patient as a God.*"

"*Your lectures are discussed by the student circles here. Your message that a surgeon is required to go beyond the horizon of a skilled worker to earn the confidence of the patient and to mitigate his sufferings was appreciated by the students. They tell me that you have impressed them for a whole lifetime.*"

Dr. D. Subhash Chandra
10th May 1988

A medical student wrote a letter, "*I am a postgraduate student of General Surgery studying at Kasturba Medical College, Manipal, Karnataka. Sir, I had the fortune of reading your article on 'Techniques of Gall Bladder Surgery' and have been benefited by it immensely both theoretically as well as practically. After following your technique we have come out of some difficult situations. How lucky your residents must be to have seen you at work!*"

I had gone to Belgaum, where I had spent my childhood, for a conference where I was felicitated for my contribution to the development of gastro-intestinal surgery in India. I was surprised to learn that a small act on my part had worked as a catalyst and resulted in shaping an outstanding career. Dr. Mahadev Dixit, leading cardiac surgeon of India, told the teachers of the medical university about our association which I had forgotten and this is what he said:

"It was year 1980 when I was to appear for General Surgery final MBBS examination when I met Dr. V. N. Shrikhande as my external examiner. Till then I was a local boy having grown up in the small town of Belgaum. We were told that examiners were strict and unless we did well, we would not pass. With heart in my mouth I entered the examination hall. I was allotted one long and three short cases. Dr. Shrikhande and another examiner from Delhi took my exam. They were professional examiners because they put me at ease and started building up questions from basics till recent advances. Once I felt at ease, I was able to answer all their questions. They were impressed. In the afternoon session involving specimens and instruments, they again took my exam. This time too, I did well. Dr. V. N. Shrikhande was so impressed with my performance that he told me that I should meet him in Bombay as soon as I finished internship and that he would help me to become a surgeon."

"It was at that moment that I decided to become a surgeon and go to Bombay and under his guidance pursue my surgical career. And that is what I did exactly. Till that moment I had not realised what I would do after MBBS."

"In fact, he got me a house job in General Surgery at G. T. Hospital, Mumbai where I worked for three-four months. He was an excellent surgeon and ethical and humane in his behaviour."

"Luckily I got a surgical post, and did MS in general surgery. Later on I was trained by Dr. Nemish Shah, pioneer cardiac surgeon at Bombay Hospital, did M.Ch and then he arranged for my training in England. I returned to India and worked with Dr. Devi Shetty at B. M. Birla Heart Research Centre, Calcutta for seven years after which I returned to my native Belgaum to start the cardiac surgical programme."

"If I had not met him I do not know what I would have done. Firstly, I would not have gone to Bombay and secondly, maybe

I would not have become a surgeon. I consider myself fortunate that I met Dr. V. N. Shrikhande, who left a lasting impression on me and changed my destiny."

"Dr. Shrikhande, a big 'thank you' for all your guidance and help and keep motivating us because you are a beacon of light in this world which is turning dark. We all wish you much more happiness, good health and energy to lead the new generation. God bless."

(The Department of heart surgery has grown tremendously and at present it performs 140-160 open heart procedures per month. The department has completed more than 20,000 open heart surgeries which include bypass surgeries, valve surgeries and congenital surgeries. The Heart Institute at K. L. E . Society is known all over India. Many of the trained surgeons in his MCh (CVTS) program, have started their own centres across the country.)

The only role I had played was to appreciate a good student during his examination, the way Professor Charles Rob had appreciated my performance when I appeared for the Fellowship examination in London in May 1959 and suggested that I could contact him if I needed any help. If I had gone to work with him, different opportunities would have come my way, but I was determined to return to India and serve the society. What Dr. Rob had done for me in England, I did for Dr. Dixit in Belgaum in 1980.

There is no need for great events to happen to change the destiny of an individual.

A surgeon wrote, *"Twenty-five years ago on this date you inaugurated my clinic and I wish to share the memories flooding my mind."*

"I lost my father after an attack of pancreatitis in 1971 in Parbhani. My father was forty-two and I was eleven years old. I decided to become a doctor and specifically a stomach surgeon

at that time. The family had to face financial difficulties, but that taught us a lot. I got my M.S. in 1986. Everyone in college had heard about your work in abdominal surgery."

"I was lucky to work as your resident in Bombay Hospital. We were impressed by your analytical mind, clinical approach, surgical excellence and human touch. I am walking on the ethical path shown by you and am now nicknamed the 'Dr. Shrikhande of Marathwada'. I was the first recipient of the Parbhani Ratna Puraskar. I would simply call it a 'Parees-Sparsh'...(Midas touch)."

Krishna Katneshwarkar
5th April 2013

(Pancreas is a soft gland situated deep inside the upper part of abdomen. It produces digestive juices which are collected by fine ducts which join the main duct which opens in duodenum, a part of small intestine next to stomach. If that duct gets blocked with a gall bladder stone or due to excessive alcohol intake, the obstructed gland becomes tense, inflamed and even bursts and then the digestive juices start digesting the patient's internal organs. In severe cases 20% patients die in spite of best efforts.)

xxx

An observer to Shrikhande clinic, a senior surgeon, wrote in the visitors' book in November 1987, "*Meeting Professor Shrikhande has been a landmark in my professional career and also a turning point. I admit perhaps I was not on the right track. His philosophy and teaching will ever remain a source of inspiration in my professional career.*"

Some years later, when I had gone to this surgeon's city for a lecture, I visited his home. His wife touched my feet (a gesture of reverence) with tears in her eyes and said that I had brought happiness to their family. Her husband no longer chased after money, but enjoyed helping the poor.

Many people believe that the attitudes established from childhood remain forever. This is not true. Man has the ability to respond while animals have been programmed to react. An Alsatian reacts the same way today as it did thousands of years back. Recently I read that MRI studies have shown that thoughts can change even a structure in the brain! I do not know whether this is true.

A young surgeon who came as an observer wrote, "*One of my relations is a well-established surgeon who has a hospital with 100 beds. I will be appointed the day I join the hospital. I came to see your work for a few weeks and have learnt that a surgeon can reach heights of excellence without compromising on ethical standards. I have told my father that I will not join our relative's hospital. I would like to follow in your footsteps.*"

A resident wrote,

"Respected Sir,

Pardon me for taking the liberty to address this letter to you. But I couldn't resist the urge to write, because today is a different day for me. From tomorrow I shall be on my own, trudging along the road, destiny bound. Just like a child knows that he may fall, yet he walks so also I shall continue to march ahead, come what may. It was but known, that one day I shall have to leave the protective portals of an Institution and the benevolent care of my teachers and guides. But there has been a lurking fear of the unknown ahead. But now the mind is prepared at least to some extent, to take the bull by the horns.

This change has come about by working with you and knowing you. I have learnt not to expect everything to go on smoothly all the time, but to be prepared for deviations, More important, I have learnt that the secret of life is in continuing to pursue, with the firm belief that the end result shall always be positively good.

In closing I would like to say Sir, as I forge ahead in my career and if I do extremely well I shall remember you and even if I do not do well I shall remember you, because you are the symbol of both struggle and achievement. You are a towering example of a person who has scaled the peaks of success on his own might."

What greater contentment can a surgeon expect in life? The path has been circuitous and unusual and many believe that it does not work.

The ethical path that a surgeon is expected to tread and which I have followed has worked so successfully for me that I want many more to experience such enriching moments in life.

Not all the students trained by me have carried on the traditions of our noble profession. There is a law of wastage in nature; one seed out of many, one photograph out of many, one poem out of many clicks well. I am happy that some are doing outstanding work and bringing laurels to the profession. A student who looks very ordinary may become a role model tomorrow.

I was a guest speaker at the annual conference of the Association of Medical Consultants. I was asked to speak on, "Is success a bane or boon?" I ended my talk with a slide:

Pillars of Success

What will matter?
Not what you bought, but what you built
Not what you got, but what you gave
Not your success, but your significance
Not what you learnt, but what you taught.
What will matter is
Every act of integrity,
compassion, courage, or sacrifice
that enriched, empowered, or encouraged
others to emulate your example.

I am lucky that I could train so many surgeons. The show must go on!

❑ ❑ ❑

Chapter 18

Diseases Brought Strangers into My Life...

Keshavrao Date

My patient Dr. Hemchandra Gupte, Mayor of Bombay, referred Shri Keshavrao Date, a celebrated actor of yesteryears, for consultation. When he entered my room I told him how fortunate I felt to meet such a celebrated personality, whose movies I had seen as a collegian 20 years earlier. He was reluctant for surgery which was considered major those days, but agreed to it after I advised him.

He offered me consulting fees which I refused. He had served the theatre and cinema with great distinction at a time when artistes were poorly paid. They stayed in small apartments and led very simple lives.

Date had suffered an unpleasant experience with hospitals and consultants during his wife's terminal illness. No one had explained why she died unexpectedly. When he consulted a chest physician for his asthma, the first question that was asked to him was, "Can you afford my consultation fees of Rs 30?" Date felt sad and insulted with this question that was asked even before the doctor had discussed his health problem. Date had everything going against him to become an actor. He did not have an impressive personality, he was short, his voice was unattractive, and he suffered from asthma. All his deficiencies became irrelevant because he modulated his voice, developed command over facial expression and looked a towering personality when he entered the stage. He is regarded as a role model of excellence in the field of drama and film even today, after the passage of over fifty years.

He told me that success had to be handled with humility. Actors got addicted to applause and adulation, but when the curtain fell and the theatre becames empty, the artiste also tend to feel empty and depressed.

I always feel encouraged meeting those who have succeeded despite shortcomings. Keshavrao Date was among the first celebrities in my life, and I felt great. I operated on him for enlarged prostate and later for inguinal hernia. He never made money but enriched our lives. We became close friends and I treasure the memory of our association. He had sent me Diwali greetings with a handwritten note, "From one artist to another"!

Jal Pardiwala

An elderly gentleman was admitted in a critical condition, with septic shock following rupture of the colon due to diverticulitis. Excellent management, and operations in stages saved his life, and he lived for many years in good health. Later on I learnt that Jal Pardiwala was the grand old man of Indian athletics and was the recipient of honours from Switzerland, Finland, and USA.

(What is a septic shock? Bacteria causing infection enter the blood stream and damage every organ in the body. Heart rate goes up, blood pressure falls, lungs can't perform adequate oxygenation of blood, kidneys can't throw out waste products, intestine cannot digest food and brain function goes down. Draining the pus and antibiotics to destroy the bacteria can save the life.

In diverticulitis, some elderly people develop small pouches on the lining of the large intestine that bulge out from the weak spots in the muscular tube. Diverticuli are common in people whose diet is deficient in fibre leading to constipation and increased pressure within the colon. It is a disease of modern civilisation! About 20 per cent of diverticuli give rise to complications like bleeding, repeated attacks of pain or they burst due to infection. The affected portion may need removal but if the patient's condition is serious, pus is drained, the healthy portion of colon above the diseased part is brought out through the abdomen so that the faeces drains out into a bag attached to the abdomen. Diseased portions are removed at a later date and then the ends of the colon above and below are stitched together.)

I liked Pardiwala because of his inspiring story of struggle and his selfless social contributions. Born in poverty in village Pardi, in the state of Gujarat, he studied in a Parsi orphanage, and became a respected sports teacher at the national level in India. He gave his life for his profession and country without any expectation of returns. He was a product of an era when sports was not linked with money. He nurtured high ethical values in his distinguished career. He believed that those who feared defeat, never won. They count the risks but not the rewards when facing difficult situations.

I have no interest in sports but I found a common thread in our thoughts. We both believed that positive thoughts were essential for achieving great results in life; talent alone was not sufficient and the desire to excel was essential for achieving the impossible. I believe that like-minded people come together. Otherwise how could a man like me, who has no interest in sports, and a great sport teacher become friends?

The Parsis form the smallest community in India, a country which gave them shelter when they left Persia and arrived on the western coast in the state of Gujarat. India has given shelter to many displaced people for centuries. Parsis have maintained their distinct identity but their contribution in the fields of education, health, industry, judiciary, science, and philanthropy continues to be remarkable.

His residence was at a walking distance from my place. He would drop in, climb two floors and spend some time with me, with a glass of water! I miss his first words, "Kem Dikra (Hello young man)!" and his smiling face. Pardiwala passed away in 2002, but his daughter Mithu Jesia looks upon me like her father and never forgets to greet me on Hindu festivals, Parsi New Year day and my birthday! She remembers how her father impressed upon her the adage, "From the depth of humility can one rise to the height of greatness."

Justice Menon

I had gone to give a lecture at a surgical conference in Calicut. My surgeon friend, who had organised the conference, took me to Munnar, a beautiful hill station in Kerala after the conference. The place was like heaven on earth. I was requested to give a lecture to the staff but when I rose, the mike was very high and could not be adjusted to my short height. Such small difficulties are common in India. I stood on a wooden platform and said, "Every giant is a pygmy standing on the shoulders of previous generation's achievements." This sentence was received with a big applause.

After the question-answer session, my host wanted me to meet a man of great distinction who was spending his retired life in a bungalow on a hill. He was Justice M.S. Menon, former Chief Justice of Kerala High court. He was past eighty at that time.

It was a beautiful house on the top of a hill built during the British Raj, surrounded by tea estates and greenery. As I entered the house, I saw his photo with Pandit Jawaharlal Nehru. I was very curious to know how the meeting had gone with the Prime Minister. He said that his meeting had been very short. He was a great admirer of Nehru; his book *Discovery of India,* was a reflection of his sensitive mind and easy command over the English language.

Justice Menon was a living encyclopaedia of the events of his time, and it was no wonder that a week before, the former Chief Justice of India had come to meet him. I did not know how three hours passed. As a young man in 1930, he had worked as a secretary to Rabindranath Tagore for a short time in Europe.

His memory was sharp and he had so many enriching experiences to share that I wondered whether he had written his autobiography. He said, "Many requested me to do so. Autobiography is a risky proposition. It is tempting to show the world what you think they should believe about you, but which you know is not true. Only a transparent man like Mahatma Gandhi could write one."

He narrated some examples of autobiographies of well-known individuals which contained a lot of lies. He knew persons of great eminence whose autobiographies were full of falsehood. One technique was to refer to personal associations with great men who had died, and therefore with no possibility of contradiction.

Apparently, in one autobiography, the had author stated– the cabinet took a decision to send the author for an important mission abroad. The Prime Minister sent him a message to meet him on the way to the airport. When the author met–the Prime Minister, he put his hands on the author's shoulders and said that the government had entrusted a very important mission in his hands and that he was sure that he would do an excellent job. And that the author looked run down, and should not ignore his health. Justice Menon told me that there was more imagination than truth in that narration!

Meeting Justice Menon was so enriching an experience that I went all the way to meet this man on two more occasions. Spending time with him was like reading a book.

We kept in touch with letters, in one of which he wrote, "I was hoping that I will be able to see you once again on the high ranges before I disappear on the toppling wave of time. You are one of the grandest men I have ever met in a long life of 8 decades and over. Persons who attended your lecture say that they have never heard such a speech as the one you delivered at the Tata Tea Hospital in Munnar." In another letter, he wrote, "I shall be 88 years of age in June next. The end I trust, will not now be long delayed. Even now I am feeling like one who treads alone some deserted banquet hall, whose lights are fled, whose garlands dead and all but he departed." Justice Menon's language I felt was hypnotising!

These rare individuals have made living a delightful experience.

Hrishikesh Yadav

I never knew the credentials of Mr. Hrishkesh Yadav when I operated on him at my clinic. I learnt about this famous mountaineer through visitors who came to the hospital. He was the leader of the first successful Indian civil expedition to Mount Everest, from the northen side. He had spent fifteen days at a height of 24,000 feet without oxygen during the Kanchanjunga Expedition. He invited me to a function where 117 cyclists launched a Manali to Leh expedition in 2009. He organised and led the first Himalayan Expedition in which 10 visually-impaired and hearing-impaired persons scaled a 17,000-feet peak.

I continue to meet him. I was invited as a chief guest to a function organised by Giri Mitra, an organisation of mountaineers, at the Shankmukhananda Hall on July 17, 2011 to felicitate mountaineers of great distinction. Mark Inglis, the mountaineer who climbed Mt Everest on artificial legs, was one of the dignitaries present on the dais. The hall was completely packed with young men and women standing in every small place available. The atmosphere was charged with enthusiasm and festivity.

Our state of Maharashtra is studded with mountains which have protected the land from the attack of invaders in the past. Mountain climbing has become a passion among the youth in the recent times.

I started my talk with, "I cannot believe that a man who has not climbed any mountain is the chief guest for today's function. How can I miss this opportunity to be among the VIPs? Though I have met many in all walks of life, they were all under anaesthesia!

Today we are witnessing a unique event in the history of mankind, as unique as man walking on the moon. Mark Inglis made history on May 15, 2006 by climbing Mt. Everest on two artificial legs. He had lost his both legs when he was caught in a blizzard while trying to reach the peak of Mount Cook, the highest mountain in New Zealand. He survived for thirteen days in a temperature of–20 degrees centigrade. He lost 31kg. Mark Inglis was depressed but rallied his spirits and did something impossible to imagine. He not only climbed Mount Cook in New Zealand but also Mount Everest. Mark Inglis said he did not climb with his legs but by the power of mind.

Viktor Frankl has written a book on his experiences in the concentration camp in Europe. He learnt that the human body could survive impossible hardships. He believed that he survived because he had a mission to give meaning to life.

Mark Inglis established a charitable trust to supply prostheses to thousands of people in Cambodia who lost their limbs due to land mines. All these people on the dais whom we are going to felicitate, have exhibited a deep social concern in spite of their limitations and reputations." My talk was well received but more importantly, I returned home an inspired man. My association with Hrishikesh Yadav has enriched my life.

Only those who risk going too far can display how far they can go.

— T.S. Elliot

Pandit Ramnarayan

While I was scrubbing for an operation, my secretary told me that Pandit Ramnarayan needed an urgent admission for surgery, that all the rooms in the clinic were full, and that she was unable to convince the relatives about her inability to help them. Ravi Desai, my friend and our manager, spoke to the relatives and assured them that a room would soon be arranged. I did not question him because Ravi was a man to handle a crisis. Musicians, sportsmen and actors are known and recognized all over, but it was my ignorance that I had not known Pandit Ramnarayan, the sarangi maestro of international repute.The number of artists and music lovers who came to inquire about his health made me realize Panditji's stature. Ustad Alla Rakha, the renowned tabla player, came to visit him directly from the airport with a large bouquet of flowers!

How did Ravi Desai manage the difficult task of arranging a special room for Panditji? He approached a patient in a special room and requested him if he could shift to a general facility with two other patients to make place for Pandit Ramnarayan. The patient, himself a music lover, gladly offered to shift, but on one condition- that he would like a photograph with the maestro; a precious memento to grace his drawing room! Everything went well, Pandit Ji expressed his gratitude while he posed for a photograph, the patient was thrilled and we were happy!

I have enjoyed my many years of association with Pandit Ramnarayan. Every meeting is an enriching experience, a confirmation that all great men are humble and simple. Panditji is conferred with the Padmavibhushan, the second highest civilian award of the country for his unparalleled contribution to Indian music and has performed at the most prestigious concert platforms in the entire world, but continues to remain detached from all of it. Even at the age of 87, he practises daily and is alert to not miss any detail of value.

His son, daughter and grandson are all excellent musicians following the rich tradition of Indian classical music. His elder brother, late Pandit Chaturlal, was regarded as a genius of a tabla player by the greatest of musicians. Once, I was in Udaipur for a lecture and Panditji happened to be there. We visited a small village where I saw about 20 – 25 young boys playing Sarangi. I was told that there were many such traditions of music in many parts of our vast country- that there were many gems scattered all over.

Late Sir Yehudi Menuhin, the legendary violin maestro, was Panditji's admirer and close friend, and has written–"*The Sarangi remains not only the authentic and original Indian bowed instrument, but the one, which most poignantly and in the hands of Ram Narayan, most revealingly expresses the very soul of Indian feelings and thought. I can not separate the Sarangi from Ram Narayan, so thoroughly fused are they, not only in my memory, but in the fact of this sublime dedication of the great musician to an instrument which is no longer archaic because of the matchless way he has made it speak.*"

My profession has given me a unique opportunity to come in contact with talented, extraordinary individuals from many fields.

Pandurang Shastri Athavale

Another patient who made a deep impact on me was Pandurang Shastri Athavale. When he was in my hospital, recovering after surgery, he received a letter from Costa Rica from Dr. Geiko Müller-Fahrenholz, Professor of Peace and Ethics at the Peace Foundation, University of Peace, created by the UN General Assembly in 1980.

"*An article by Mr. Majid Rehnama acquainted me with your work. It was also through Mr. Rehnama that I received your address. First let me say that my wife and I are very fascinated indeed by what we learned about the Swadhyaya Movement.*"

"*Obviously you have been able to invoke great strength in the poor people so that they were able to reconstruct their communities. We are deeply grateful that this is possible; for in this part of the world we see a great deal of utter dependency, not only in a material sense but even more so in a spiritual dimension. As if the poor had lost faith in themselves and their divine strength.*"

"*Therefore, after talking to some friends who are equally concerned we began to ask ourselves whether you might be prepared to spend a week or so with us in Costa Rica in order to help us discover our own approach.*"

I wanted to know more about Shastriji. I read an article by Majid Rehnama, an Iranian intellectual connected with United Nations and now living in Paris, entitled 'Swadhyaya, The Unknown, The Peaceful, The Silent Yet Singing Revolution of India'.

Mr. Rehnama had come to India to see the different developmental programmes and was so impressed with the Swadhyaya movement that he is reported to have said that this unique experiment in human development without any economic assistance had been more attractive than anything achieved by the conventional programmes with large amounts of funding.

I had to change my impression that Pandurang Shastri Athavale was one of the spiritual leaders with a large following.

He was a great social reformer who founded Swadhyaya movement in 1954 based on selfless love for the poor, giving dignity to oppressed masses and made them see God within every person, every tree, every flower. He never went to any school but was taught in Sankrit, a system prevelant in Ancient India.

By temperament I am not inclined to go near any spiritual or religious gurus but on some occasions I went to Gujarat and visited villages to see the work continued by his followers.

At Umergaon, in Gujarat, I saw the biggest mass of humanity, about a million, gathered to celebrate the function named Emancipation of Man. After the function was over, no traffic system would ever have worked given the volume of people. I walked for a distance of about three miles in a massive crowd at night time in darkness. Almost all were rural folk. There was no stampede, no shouting, no rubbish thrown on the ground or streets, not a single purse was stolen, and no woman was molested. In a country known for indiscipline, the police had no worries. This was a miracle!

But every function of Swadhyaya is unique for its discipline, co-operation, smiling faces and enthusiasm. I was lucky to witness this miracle.

One of my patients, a youth leader, went to Sardar Vallabhbhai Patel, Home Minister of India, in 1949 with a delegation, and expressed his frustration and anger at the inability of the leaders to keep their promises of a better India.

The Iron Man of India gave a patient hearing and told them, "To achieve anything in life you have to take people with you. Show me whether you can influence five people in your lifetime." I have remembered this statement ever since.

The development of man is one of the most creative activities in this world and the question uppermost in my mind was how Shastriji could achieve this miracle. He talked with the masses in simple conversational tone that we must live in harmony with the environment in a social, economic and ecological way.

The Swadhyaya movement has purchased large barren lands and converted them into lush green areas.

Even a tree has a divine element and a man who looks after that tree once a month or once every two-three months, becomes a priest and therefore it is his sacred duty to look after that tree with affection. With such words of Shastriji, it was no wonder that the maintenance of tree plantations was superb. He coined a new term *sagarputra* (sons of the seas), for the fishermen and *bhoomiputra* (sons of the soil) for the farmers. I saw cleanliness in homes of his followers. A large number of women have also joined his movement.

Is it possible to do such good activity without using the concept of God? An individual can do a lot of good work without believing in a man-made god but what about the masses?

Gandhiji said, "Man's body is a temple of God. Respect the temple." Pandurang Shastriji gave the same message and it worked. He told people that everyone must make one's life sacred, noble and useful. He convinced people to be grateful for the great gift Almighty had given to them in the form of life. He was honoured with the Ramon Magasaysay Award, considered as Asia's Nobel Prize, in 1996. for community leadership, and also the Templeton Prize for Progress in Religion in 1997. Other recipients were Billy Graham and Mother Teresa. I happened to be in London and I attended the ceremony when HRH Prince Philip honoured him in Westminster Abbey.

He reminded the people that God existed in other human beings too, and therefore we must respect each other. This is the whole concept of Swadhyaya—understanding one's relation to oneself and also to the outside world.

I had the unique opportunity to travel on some occassions with Shastriji by car, train and air, and I have vivid memories of hundreds and thousands of men, women and children in colourful clothes, lining the roads, rail platforms, airports and sea ports, with flowers, and in a festive mood waiting to have a look of Shastriji. For reasons I do not know, he considered me as his brother! How it all happened is beyond me.

Wing Commander Rakesh Sharma (Retd.)

I had a patient who had developed a small tumour in his pancreas. It was secreting insulin. *(Pancreas produces digestive juices which reach the intestine via a duct. It also produces insulin which goes directly into the blood stream. Insulin production is stimulated when the blood sugar level goes up after taking food. Insulinoma is an extremely rare disease where pancreas goes on continuously secreting insulin even when blood sugar level goes down. The only treatment is the surgical removal of the tumour. Normal blood sugar level varies between 80 to 180 mg/dl but in this case it is recorded as low as forty! Patients can go into a coma.)*

His low blood sugar made him eat all the time, as a result of which, he gained a lot of weight. Even when he was waiting in my consulting room, he had to eat. Luckily I could find the exact location of the tumour during the operation. He was instantaneously cured after surgery. The embarrassing necessity to eat all the time had now ceased and he was happy to be normal, as any average individual.

He was the chief of Hindustan Aeronautics Limited (HAL). He invited me to spend a weekend at his guest house. We get such invitations often but the pressure of work leaves no time for such small breaks. When I expressed my difficulty he said, "Do you know Mr. Rakesh Sharma? He works with us and you will love to meet him." I was keen to meet the only astronaut from India and therefore I picked up the first opportunity to spend a weekend with my patient. He had arranged a dinner in my honour and everybody was keen to meet me but I was more keen to meet Mr. Rakesh Sharma.

I spent so much time that evening with him that his wife Madhu said to me, "Dr. Shrikhande you have taken charge of my husband for the whole evening."

I replied, "You have taken charge of him for life, please spare him for one evening for me!"

There was loud laughter among the crowd which had gathered to meet and listen to a surgeon who had done a rare successful operation on the CEO.

I wrote a letter to Rakesh Sharma:

August 28, 1988

It was a great privilege for me to have such a long talk with you during my visit to Ojhar last month. You are the first Indian to go farthest away from our mother planet and that is why you are so close to our hearts. Individuals like you, who explore and expand the unknown horizons, are the torch bearers of human progress and achievements.

All genuinely great individuals are humble and unassuming, and therefore I was not surprised when I saw the compassionate and unassuming aspect of your personality despite your achievement. I have spoken about you to a large number of my friends, and I hope my children will one day get a chance to meet you in person.

— Yours sincerely,
Dr. V N Shrikhande

I am reminded of Sir Winston Churchill's statement, "Never in the history of human conflict was so much owed by so many to so few." He was referring to the sacrifices made by the Royal Air Force in keeping Britain a free country. I only hope our politicians, intellectuals and others in civilian life know what sort of hard life people lead to keep us independent. The humanitarian work of the Air Force and Armed Forces, in recently evacuating hundreds and thousands of stranded people in Uttaranchal state, is unparalleled. In the recent catastrophic floods in Kashmir, the Indian Air Force evacuted more than 1,25,000 people by air.

I came to know after meeting Rakesh Sharma, that for a fighter pilot, alone in a plane, personal performance was vital. In space flight, everything is computerised. I asked him how he trained his thoughts. "Very simple, do not worry about something on which you have no control."

He had to learn Russian as the communication during the flight was in Russian except when Prime Minister Indira Gandhi asked him in Hindi, "*Vahanse Bharat kaisa dikhata hai*?" (how does India look from there?) Prompt came his reply, "*Sare jahanse acchha*" (the best in the world). His reply was spontaneous.

He said about his experience of space flight, "During my eight day space mission, at first I marvelled at the beauty of my home country. Slowly my mental horizon expanded and I saw the Earth as my home planet. This feeling intensified when I viewed the Earth against a black, uninviting and frontierless vacuum."

"I saw myself not as an Indian working along Soviet cosmonauts, but as an individual involved in peaceful human activity in space. It is not that I lost or surrendered my national identity; instead, I rejoiced in the fact that my country's rich and centuries old tradition and culture has conditioned me to look beyond man made boundaries and prejudices."

"I also realised that one does not have to undertake a space flight to come by this feeling of oneness, that this could be understood by all of us, at an intellectual level and with equal intensity, right here on our mother planet—Earth."

He became a test pilot and had a mishap. He wrote to me on 29 Oct 1988, "I am writing to acknowledge with gratitude your warm good wishes for my recovery from the injury sustained in the recent flying accident. Right now I am in the slow and painful phase, that of getting the ankle mobilisation going."

"I am quite confident that I will be good as new after a few months. My escape may have been extremely lucky but to me it means that if I am still alive, my mission in this world is still not yet over as was so nicely written by Richard Bach."

He is invited for lectures all over the country and donates the fees to the charity. He however makes exceptions. He was one of the speakers at a well-attended function to celebrate my 75th birthday.

His message in his talk, "*We belong to a great country. The youth must work hard to bring our country to our former glory. We have no trust in our generation and therefore the young must do work by setting a personal example. They will have to rediscover India and her values, question intelligently how the culture of wastage has adversely affected their life, compare them to our ancient values. Do not become acquisitive. Learn the essence of contentment."*

Dr. Gunter Schallor

It was by chance that I met Dr. Gunter Schallor, a surgeon from Germany. It was my profession that brought me in contact with this remarkable individual. What amazed me most was his intellectual clarity, logical mind and interests in instrumentation, philosophy and history. We became close friends. He had patents for inventing instruments for laparoscopic surgery. He stayed with me for three days. His lifestyle was simple; his only luggage was a small suitcase.

I stayed with him in south Germany and had lots of things to discuss. I remember that day clearly as we had heard the sad news of Princess Diana's death in a car accident in a tunnel in Paris.

A couple of years later, I was to go to Vienna for a surgical conference. He was very happy at the prospect of our meeting. He phoned me on two occasions indicating how keen he was to meet me. He said, "I will take a short holiday, we will walk a lot in the Black Forest, discuss many matters and enjoy beer." When I expressed my inability to visit him he informed me that he would go to England for a short visit instead.

A month later I had a letter from his girlfriend that brought tragic news of his death. As he was on his way to England, he saw a vehicular accident on the road. He stopped his car to help the injured when unfortunately another car came and hit him ending his life. In her letter, Dr. Ingrid wrote, "Very rarely in our life, we meet intellectuals who have compassion in their soul. He was one among them. He was looking forward to meeting you."

He made a will that no money should be spent on his funeral but his savings should be sent to India to any deserving hospital. His death left a sad feeling in my mind that had I gone to Germany, he would not have died! That is life and that is destiny.

Tatyasaheb Shirwadkar (Kusumagraj)

On March 5, 1999, I was getting ready to go to Lucknow where I was invited as a chief guest for an Army Surgeons' conference. Just as I was about to leave for the airport, I got a message that Kusumagraj was not well and that I should go to Nashik as soon as possible, since my advice was the only he would listen to.

I returned to Mumbai on the 7th evening and went to Nashik from the airport by car. He was drowsy, but as soon as I took his hand in mine and said, "Tatyasaheb, I am Dr. Shrikhande, I have come to meet you." Everybody was surprised to see a change in his facial expression. He asked, "How was the talk in Lucknow?" His chest was full of thick secretions which were sucked out with the help of a chest physician, and he felt better immediately. He had been advised to get admitted to a hospital but had refused. I stayed at his house overnight. March 8, was my birthday. He gifted me a shawl, a bouquet of flowers, a statue of a classical dancer and a copy of the English translations of his poetry book. He said, "I will sign it when my hand is free from this intravenous drip."

His friends told me that he was constantly expressing a desire to leave this world, and that I should tell him not to say such things because the world still needed rare individuals like him. While taking his leave I said, "We are all going to depart one day, but we shall again meet on February 27 (his birthday) and March 8!" We shook hands with smiles on our faces, but I knew that he had no will left to go on.

I returned to Mumbai. On March 10, when I was operating in Bombay Hospital, the news came of his passing away. He was the first civilian in Maharashtra to get a state funeral attended by thousands of mourners. On that day, the taxi and auto drivers in Nashik, refused to charge any fares to the mourners. It was a rare tribute to a great poet, a giant in the field of literature, respected and loved by people from all strata of society.

The last moments of his life, he asked from his helper Shantabai for a pencil and paper and wrote.

On the Final Threshold

Beloved,

That moment has come
When you have to stay behind in this last travellers' lodge.
Now I will move ahead in the directionless dark, nothing
But the glow of the star light which you have given to me
Through our lifelong companionship
And which I have stored up to the brim.
With every step, the overflowing drops will show me the way ahead
Nay, do not worry, that glow will not end
Till that ecstatic moment of the journey's end when the
past, present and the future
Would melt into nothingness like the sand
Engulfed by the ebbs and flow of water along the seashore
Despite knowing this, why those tears?
A few drops on the threshold ... along the traveller's path

After writing this he was so tired that he handed over the paper and pencil, to Shantabai. He requested her to open the windows and said, I am on my way and closed his eyes forever.

(It has been my privilege to have a few suggestions from my friend Dr. Ajay Vaidya of Panjim, Goa an ophthalmic surgeon who is known for his vision and passion for art, literature and theater.)

❑ ❑ ❑

Chapter 19

Do I Believe in Luck?

What role luck plays in a person's life is a thought that often crops up in my mind during introspective moments.

I had survived an attack of typhoid in 1943 when chloromycetin was not available. I had a relapse, a fever that lasted forty-eight days. Mine was an unusual case of recovery as complications like bleeding and perforation of intestines commonly led to death during those days. I have lost some friends to typhoid.

I had another brush with death as an adult. After finishing work in a diagnostic camp in a small town, I was on my way to Pune (a city one hundred miles from Mumbai) with three senior consultants. Forty years ago the roads weren't as good or as safe, and the cars had no seat belts. I had chosen to sit in the front seat but at the last minute, it was a senior surgeon who sat there, next to the driver. We were close to Pune when the first rains of the monsoon hit. I remembered my childhood love of enjoying the feel of raindrops on my face, and expressed a desire to sit near the window. There was a double rainbow in the sky and the earthy smell made me think of a good single malt.

Even as I was taking all of this in, I saw one car coming from the opposite direction. It suddenly took a turn to the right where there was no road. I could sense the imminent crash and reflexively turned on one side to avoid injury to my chest. I heard a big bang, a shower of broken glass and the resultant chaos. The surgeon sitting on the front seat was unconscious and bleeding from his nose. The driver was in pain with a broken, trapped leg. Another consultant had been thrown on the road but couldn't disentangle his leg from the car. I was relieved to find out that I could move my fingers. My swollen left wrist was a sign of fracture but I had no abdominal pain, could move my head and legs without difficulty, and was still able to breathe well. I thanked destiny for getting out alive.

I got out of the car to see four dead bodies lying on the road, with one man gathering mangoes that had spilled out from the opposite car. He was in a state of confusion and shock, keeping busy with an activity that nobody would think of in that situation. The ambulances showed up to take my unconscious, bleeding colleague and other injured passengers to a nearby hospital. The former never completely recovered and I still don't know what quirk of fate made him take the front seat I had initially wanted to sit in. I was thus saved from serious, potentially fatal injuries.

When my wife and children (my eldest daughter was eight years old and my youngest son only sixteen months) came to meet me in the hospital, I maintained a smile on my face and told them that I would be home within a few days. I was in a lot of pain but thankful for not being in a morgue and happy that my family was at ease.

Two years later, I was in Dhaka as a WHO consultant. We were experiencing a continuous downpour of rain. I was in the car when I saw a double rainbow. My previous experience of this made me a bit uneasy. The river at the side of the road was swollen, with forceful gushing waters, there were dark clouds and thunder and I couldn't help but feel unsettled by the eerie atmosphere. Even as I thought about it, our car started going down the muddy, slippery slope. I was now face to face with imminent death for the second time. Why had I come all this way to die in a distant land where my body would perhaps never be traced? As the car neared the river, the middle part of its bonnet hit a tree, and we ground to a sudden halt. We waited for a few moments, but it didn't tilt. A big crowd had already gathered on the road fearing the worst. We jumped out of the vehicle and our shoes sank in the mud. The onlookers helped us climb up onto the road, and refused the money we offered them in thanks. They simply praised Allah and said that they were relieved that a tragedy was averted. I was again grateful to destiny for keeping me alive. This feeling intensified when the newspapers the next day were full of photos of others who hadn't been so lucky in the floods. Over twenty passengers had perished in a bus mishap.

Needless to say, I hate to see double rainbows in the sky!

During a surgical term in 1950, we were informed that Sardar Vallabhbhai Patel had passed away. Later in the day I went with my friends to join the grieving mass of humanity who had gathered to give a tearful farewell to the Iron Man of India. He had achieved the stupendous task of integrating 650 princely states into the Indian Union. Many do not know that only 20% of the railway from Bombay to New Delhi was through Indian territory, the rest ran through the independent states with their own rulers and army! Some experts had predicted that India would certainly disintegrate and chaos would rule. Sardar Patel proved them wrong.

The crowd was so huge that we lost contact with each other. I was on French Bridge, near Opera House. I am short and got caught up in the massive crowd that was trying to move ahead. I got squashed from all sides and was virtually lifted up from the ground. I was in the air for some time which was a frightening experience. It was a great relief when I touched the ground. I was sweating but could breathe. The bodyache lasted for some days. It was easy for me to appreciate how people die in a stampede when the mob becomes unruly at religious gatherings in India or at soccer stadiums in Europe and Latin America.

In 1959, while in England, I had finished the day's work including two emergency operations by 10 pm and joined a resident's party where I consumed only a pint of beer. I left town to go to Cambridge to join four friends for a ten day holiday in my recently purchased blue Ford Anglia. I enjoyed driving, it was my first car, there was hardly any traffic on the way and everything was going as per my plans. The sound of the rolling wheels on the smooth road had a soothing effect and my eyelids started feeling heavy. I would roll down the window to get a blast of cold air on my face to keep myself alert.

I was on the outskirts of Leicester when I saw the red traffic signal. I took my foot off the accelerator and pressed on the brake but to my horror I had gone through the red light! The deafening sound of a car swerving across the road to avoid a collision woke me up. It was a miracle! The alert driver's quick response averted the crash. My feet were trembling and I told myself, "Never again." I stopped the car at the wayside and slept for two hours before going on to Cambridge. I experienced that one could fall asleep within the blink of an eyelid. Exhaustion and alcohol even in small amounts is a fatal combination.

My First Heart Attack

I got up from sleep with sudden chest pain and I knew that my heart was demanding rest at the age of sixty-two after a hectic life of three decades. I had four doctors at home—my wife, daughter, son-in-law and son- and the cardiac ICU 200 yards away! Luckily I got emergency treatment within the golden hour and neither stenting nor bypass was necessary.

I had led a disciplined life, maintained my youthful weight, and exercised regularly, but the stress of professional work was my constant companion. I had taken good health for granted for too long but here was a wake-up call. Spare time was no longer a future goal. The time was now.

The heart attack was a turning point in my life. The anxiety that I might get a heart attack had now gone. I was surprised that I was not scared but felt sorry that I may miss the joy of living the only life I had. A clean conscience was my main asset. I had practised without greed and operated on many poor free of charge. I had no faith in life after death, no reward or punishment of rebirth.

I had received far more than I ever imagined or deserved. No other profession but surgery would have given me an enriching experience of a healer, scientist, artist, philosopher, teacher and humanist.

I was facing the reality that there might not be a tomorrow. I told my son that work should not stop, no rituals should be performed. My photograph should be given with the news in Marathi and English language newspapers because I was known all over the country. Patients, well-wishers and friends should not send Diwali/Christmas greeting cards for me. But luckily I completely recovered and was back to work within four weeks.

The Second Attack

I returned from Finland where I had gone to see the midnight sun. On my return, an emergency was waiting. A consultant surgeon was admitted with acute abdominal pain. The surgery was planned for Monday but four major operations were already on the list that day. So I operated on the surgeon for intestinal obstruction on Sunday.

The next day while having a bath I got a second heart attack. I was again lucky to get immediate help. The angiography showed that a bypass was necessary. I withstood the procedure well.

I realised why people felt depressed in the ICU. Completely cut off from the outside world, I would not know whether it was day or night. There was a feeling of profound weakness. There were serious patients on life support, some deaths, and continuous new admissions. Doctors and nurses running around all the time and the constant sound of gadgets and innumerable tubes imprisoning the patient made every movement painful.

I was very happy to leave the ICU and shift to a room from where I could see the Mumbai skyline, hear traffic and see heavy rain beating against the window panes. I was put on tranquilisers because my sleep pattern had completely changed and it continued to harass me even after my return to home. Sleep had never been a problem for me; I could take excellent naps even in noisy Mumbai traffic. But now I found myself struggling with insomnia. I increased the dose of sedatives but even then my eyes would remain wide open throughout the night.

My fear of facing sleepless nights made the situation intolerable and so one night I took three tablets of sedatives when I saw my trembling hand. It shocked me because I was used to steady hands and sound sleep for seven decades. There was a fear in my mind of not being able to sleep without the tablets, and a bigger fear that even with tablets I may not succeed. I decided that the absence of sleep for a few more days would not kill me.

I remembered a young college girl from the Middle East who met me in a train in London. She spoke in broken English and it so happened that the address she was looking for was near the station where I was getting off. She was an arts graduate and was interested in dramatics. During the conversation she told me that she had enjoyed good sleep for the first time in her life in London. The place where she came from was a place of friction with violence, shooting, machine guns and tanks rolling down the streets.

I had heard how people in England suffered nights of agony during bombing in the Second World War. I met a surgeon in St.Petersberg who told me of his mother narrating the suffering of citizens during the German siege of a thousand days. Hunger, disease and cold claimed hundreds and thousands of lives. Millions of people have died in Europe, China, Japan, Vietnam, Bosnia, Palestine and Myanmar. There are over four million people living in subhuman conditions in the slums of Mumbai. What right had I to worry about my sleep when I was in a very comfortable room looked after so well in a secure homely place?

This realisation made me feel small with my petty fears. I threw those tablets away and decided not to touch them. That night I could sleep only for one hour but without the tranquilisers. Over the next few days my sleep steadily improved and the tranquilisers had gone back in the cupboard.

We increase our stress in life by wrong expectations. We ought to be more greatful about how fortunate we are as compared to millions all over the world.

Pulmonary Edema

In October 2010, I was to undergo a health check-up mainly for loss of appetite. Sometime after the C.T. Scan I developed breathlessness. I had to sit up and restlessness and fear overpowered me. My colleague Dr. Kishore Adyanthaya, put me on a wheel chair and rushed me through the corridor of Bombay Hospital. I was taken to the lCU in a lift. I experienced what it was to be desperate for air, and I was face to face with death. The oxygen mask did not help and I knew that it was the end, as my last breath had not taken in any oxygen. I heard a loud thud that I learnt later was the oxygen being pumped into my lungs with pressure. The water accumulated in the lungs was squeezed out by applying pressure on my lungs—that was when I experienced the joy of inhaling air. But a chain of thoughts crowded my mind. Would I need a ventilator and how long? Luckily I could breathe on my own. We breathe over 20,000 times a day but the moment I took an effective breath that day, is carved into my mind with gratitude and joy. Only one breath separates life from death, said an illiterate woman, Bahinabai, a great poet from rural India.

(A dye injected during CT Scan to picture the abdominal organs with clarity can overload the circulation. The heart with a narrowed valve is unable to cope with the extra load of circulating blood, leading to a fluid collection in the lungs, leaving no space for the air to enter. Only oxygen under pressure pushes the fluid out of the lungs and revives the patient.)

Doctors knew that the aortic valve in my heart had become thick, rigid since the bypass operation. The condition is frequently seen in old age, but it was not affecting my activities.

A few days later when I was still in the hospital, I suddenly had the feeling of an impending disaster with heart failure, and was revived in the ICU. Doctors use the term near-death experience but without understanding how it really feels.

I felt that death would be kinder than this suffering.

An angiography showed that the bypass surgery done on me eight years earlier had worked well, that the internal mammary, which are small arteries used to bypass the blocks, had now grown into beautiful large blood vessels. Nature is indeed remarkable. A small service lane had now become a broad highway.

The narrowing of the aortic valve was now a death sentence for me. I decided to undergo surgery, a safer risk than the hanging sword of cardiac failure even at rest. The suggestion to avoid surgery was considered because I had already undergone operation once. Reoperation made any surgery technically difficult as the structures in the chest get fused to each other and dissection is not easy. I was almost eighty, a well-controlled mild diabetic with a pacemaker for a complete heart block.

I have been active throughout my life and to accept that I should slow down would have been unthinkable for me. Only three events were likely. I might die on the operation table, a blessing of a painless death. The next possibility was to get well with a new valve and enjoy some more years of active life, after going through the storm of painful recovery at my age. The third possibility which bothered me was that I might have to suffer life support management, might become incapable of living a rational existence ever again. I had told my doctors and relatives that in such a situation, I should be allowed to die with dignity.

The thoughts of the end became my companions when the countdown for surgery started. The day before the operation I thought that it was perhaps the last evening of my life. The sense of finality was experienced at every moment, when I brushed my teeth, was lifted from my bed, left the ward, was taken by the elevator, and entered the operation theatre. I thought that my body may go in a similar way to the electric crematorium in a few hours. The thought did not disturb me.

I chose Dr. Aniruddh Trivedi, from Bombay Hospital for my surgery. I had seen him operating and his meticulous post-operative care. He came to my room before the operation, and sought my blessings by touching my feet—a unique experience for anybody. I felt blessed. I will remain ever grateful to him and his team, for bestowing me with an excellent quality of life for over four years now.

I had followed the highest traditions of the medical profession, training many young surgeons and enriching many lives. This feeling gave me tremendous strength. When the anaesthetic was being injected, I remembered a quote by Tukaram, the great saint-poet of the 17th century, "It was worthwhile undergoing a life of such a rigour, of highest integrity, so that the last moments on this Earth could be filled with contentment."

I was told that the aortic valve was badly damaged and was successfully replaced. The surgery lasted for eight hours because of a defect in the clotting of blood. The post-operative period, as expected, was tough. The breastbone had to be divided for the second time. It was a source of constant pain. I was tied down with many tubes connected to the body. Coughing was an ordeal. Gradually one by one the tubes were removed from the body and when the last tube was removed, life without tubes was wonderful.

In the ICU, I lost all sense of time. There was a continuous stream of nurses, physiotherapists and attendants bringing tea and breakfast. Technicians would come at 6.30 am to collect blood so that the report would be ready for the doctors who came in at 8 am As a senior surgeon working in the hospital for thirty years, I got privileges which I would never have received elsewhere.

Itchy skin was a terrible problem. Moisturising creams were not effective. The skin of the palms and soles would peel off. Using a bed pan and passing motion lying down was a terrible experience. I would show my helplessness to the attendant waiting to remove the bed pan. I felt sorry for the sweeper whose only job was to bring and remove the bed pans from under the patients' beds.

The embarrassment of exposing my body in the presence of nurses who worked with me soon disappeared.

I also appreciated the doctor for his sense of humour. When my kidney function improved, I was told that I could donate my kidneys for transplant!

I lost a lot of my muscle mass and it was with great effort and pain that I could get up from bed. My legs would wobble while standing.

As I was lying on the hospital bed, I became aware that some birds were still managing to survive in Mumbai. Through the window I saw people walking briskly on the sidewalks, young men and women playing hockey, football and cricket. Children full of laughter running, falling down and still continuing their play. And in the ward were old patients with fractured hip bones after a simple fall. It made me realise the beauty of strong and elastic bones.

As we start growing in age, we realise what a splendid gift youth is—going up and down the staircases, running, eating full meals without bothering about blood sugar, operating continuously for eight to ten hours without exhaustion, occasionally enjoying enough alcohol without any tummy upset, reading without watery eyes, hearing even whispers, enjoying sound sleep and intact teeth.

During my stay in the hospital, I could interact with ward boys, sweepers, technicians, and barbers who were mostly from rural India. The ward boy who served me tea early in the morning was always cheerful, wore a red *tilak* on his forehead and would recite devotional songs. His wife had no formal education, but his two daughters were in school. The family would look forward to one day in the week when all the neighbours would sing devotional songs (*bhajans*) and narrate stories from the epics and mythology. The family lived in a small tenement. Everyone would get up early, wash their clothes and children would go to a nearby school. The family saw TV once a week for any interesting movies.

Singing devotional songs was a divine experience for his family and even the daughters would eagerly await the program. Such faith in prayers and devotional songs is far better than the excitement of uncultured night life and use of stimulants and sedatives.

Any faith that creates contentment is superior to tranquilisers. Human civilisation is in search of contentment and happiness because the world is in the grip of depression. Medicines and pursuit of pleasures cannot create contentment. It comes from within, when one lives a meaningful life with gratitude.

One young nurse's story is worth recalling. She had to be up at five in the morning, walk for twenty minutes along a poorly-lit road, full of potholes to catch the train from the suburbs where she lived so that she could report for duty at 7.15 am. When she had an evening duty, she would reach home at 10 pm. Her father was an auto-rickshaw driver. Her mother had educated herself through the Open University and taught young boys and girls at home. The brother was pursuing a computer diploma and her sister was employed in an organisation as a telephone operator. The family stayed in one room. They had the privilege of having their own toilet. Millions of Indians live in this way. Their whole life is a struggle. It is these hardworking individuals who are taking the country ahead despite the corruption at all levels (which is even greater at the higher levels).

I was waiting for the monotony of the tasteless diet food served in the hospital to be over. I had no appetite, but I had to force the food into my mouth to maintain my vitality and to ensure that my wounds healed well.

The universal smell in any hospital ward-a mixture of ether, spirit, medications, wound dressings, half-eaten food plates, urine pots and bedpans-was depressing, but I knew that it would soon be over. I was far luckier than a ninety-year-old patient in the adjoining room who was bedridden in the lCU for six months. He was in a vegetative state with his mouth open and had to be taken out on a wheel chair for a stroll. Somebody from the family would come and visit him regularly, but he did not recognise them. I was happy that somebody cared for him. Why was medical science so cruel as to keep the man technically alive when he was unable to experience the joy of living? It is a difficult ethical dilemma in modern era where prolonging life has become possible.

Science does not define the quality of life; it can only prolong life. The family was very rich and the relatives were insistent that everything possible must be done for the patient. There is a big difference between everything possible and everything reasonable. The unfortunate patient had no say in the matter.

It so happened that the room opposite mine was sealed by the Mumbai police when President Obama visited Mumbai in December 2010. He had come to give a lecture in a college near the hospital. I could see his motorcade passing along the road from the twelfth floor of our hospital. Everyone hoped that his stay in the country would be safe and that the sealed room should remain so until he departed for Delhi.

I am alive despite so many near-death experiences. I remember that when I was in England, open heart surgery carried high mortality. It is good to be old now than sixty years ago! Four years after the surgery, I am very active and for that I am grateful every day.

When I recall the health mishaps in my life, I feel that we die in accidents, but also live by accidents. A scientist has said, "A great truth is one where the opposite is also true."

Every time I missed death, I felt convinced that there was a purpose behind my miraculous survival.

❑ ❑ ❑

Chapter 20

Courage in the Face of Death

My daughter Neena (Anjana) has a pen friend from Germany, Gaby, who lives in a village near Cologne.

In May 2007, I had the opportunity to meet her father Horst Jablonski, a man in his 70s, whose life was a series of tragedies that he bore with equanimity. As a child, he lived on a big farm, but war broke out and the entire family was forced to flee. Thus started their long ordeal to escape for safety. He saw people being killed and heard the cries of girls who were raped by the attacking soldiers. They had to walk in temperatures of –20°C. People died of cold, some by drowning when the ice underneath gave way. They heard gun fire and bomb explosions all around. Ultimately they got shelter in a village where he worked with a rich farmer. He was made to slog and was served a loaf of bread and soup that often contained worms.

The war ended. He got a job in a hotel, polished shoes and cleaned the bar. Somehow the boss of the hotel was impressed by him. He learnt to drive a truck. He learnt to be a salesman. He was working so well that his boss wanted him to marry his daughter. But he knew he could not marry such a rich girl and maintain his self-respect.

He left his job and started a tour bus company, first for small distances and then for long trips. As things were settling down, he developed a throat cancer in 1987, and was successfully treated. He bought a plot of land and for the first time he had a house of his own. Unfortunately another calamity struck him. He developed muscular weakness, became invalid and ultimately started using a wheelchair. Breathing difficulties led to pneumonia and a tube had to be placed permanently in his wind pipe. In 2003 he got a heart attack and underwent a bypass surgery. The relentless march of progressive muscular weakness continued and he was placed on a mechanised bed where his hands and leg movements were controlled by computerised pulleys. He moved about on a self-driven electric wheelchair, which is how I saw him in 2007.

He was nattily dressed, wore Ray Ban sunglasses, his black hair was slicked back and he had a contented expression. One could not believe that he had recently developed herpes zoster on his right arm, was in great pain and on cortisone.

He knew that the end was near and was making farewell rounds to express his gratitude and to meet friends.

I spent one night with the family. He wished to have a group photograph as we were in his house. He came to see us off to the bus which was parked about a kilometre away. He wished us goodbye with a smiling face and while his family remained with us till the bus started, he went back home. I was watching him for a long time—a lonely man who could not move his muscles, who had suffered tragedy after tragedy, driving on that empty road. I gazed after him till he disappeared around the bend. Tears rolled down my face because I knew I would not see him again. He passed away a few months later.

He had taken photos in the white jacket which he wanted to wear for his funeral. He took photos with his grandchildren because he knew that the end was near. He was getting repeated chest infections and was admitted to a hospital in April 2008. The next day a pacemaker was installed but the heart did not respond and he passed away. The funeral was the biggest the small village had ever seen. People had taken leave to give him the last send-off.

I was told by his daughter, how in spite of his condition, he maintained a sense of humour, enjoyed life, good food, good music and an occasional drink. One meeting taught me what books would have failed to convey.

My thoughts go back to my time as a young doctor undergoing surgical training in 1954–57. There was a patient called Keroba lying on the veranda of the government hospital's general ward which was packed with poor patients.

Keroba was a unique example of how to live and accept impossible situations of physical disability. He was engaged and was travelling to meet his fiancée staying in a village two hundred miles away from Bombay, but met with a car accident. The driver and his two friends had minor injuries but Keroba had a serious injury in the back. Both his lower limbs were paralysed and he lost control over the urinary bladder and rectum.

When he realised that the damage was permanent, he told his fiancee to forget the engagement and get married to someone else. He assured his weeping fiancee that in his next life they would be husband and wife. In those days management of paraplegics was very crude. He developed ulcers on the back. There was a constant smell of urine and faeces around him and so he was kept in a corner bed of the ward in the verandah next to the toilet block. In spite of his unfortunate condition, I never saw him unhappy. He would sing devotional songs and make others smile with his funny stories.

One day he told me that he had seen the decoration of lights on Republic Day. I thought that the hospital had taken him in an ambulance to see the beautifully lighted city. All that he had done was sit up by holding the pulley on the bed and see some lights through the window. He looked so happy. Was he making a show or was it his attitude? These thoughts would trouble me every time I went for a ward round. My term was coming to an end. He wished that I should give him a book as a present so that he could keep it as a souvenir, but destiny had other plans. In the heavy monsoon, he got a chest infection which could not be controlled. One day during a round, I saw his face covered with a bed sheet, breathing, coughing, but still not complaining. Two days later I got a night call that Keroba had died.

I went to the ward in the heavy rain. The night nurses, ward boys and sweeper were standing around the cot with tears in their eyes. Normally when such patients (a big burden on the staff) die, there is a sense of relief, but Keroba was an exception.

One sweeper said that Keroba was God. I could not stop the tears rolling down my cheeks. It was the passing away of a very remarkable individual who faced his crippled, dependent, miserable life with a smile on his face until the end. He taught us how to live and how to die! It is now more than fifty years since his death. I still remember his face whenever I meet people who grumble about the small inconveniences in life. He had nothing in his life for which he should have been grateful. I often recollect a young man of 40 in my ward in UK who greeted me with a smile "Doc, how are you?" only 4 hours before his death. These memories have moulded the way I look at the art of living.

❑ ❑ ❑

Chapter 21

My Family

I married Dr. Suhas Bokil after my return from the UK. Our families were introduced through a common friend. Her father, a very intelligent yet simple person, was an engineer respected for his integrity and retired as the Chief Commercial Superintendent of the Centrail Railway. Her mother was a graduate in those days, and the daughter of a doctor. Suhas had stayed in a hostel in Pune, had an excellent academic career, and her parents had an independent house in Pune. She gave her consent for the wedding even after I'd told her that as a surgeon, I would have to wait for a long time to settle down in life, and that we would be staying in a joint family with my parents and brother and his family in a small apartment in Mumbai. She never once complained about my limited income or our simple lifestyle.

She had a diploma in Obstetrics-Gynaecology, but did not complete the postgraduate course because of family responsibilities. Our daughter, Seema, fell ill when she was barely 3 years old and Suhas had to leave her job at the Railway Hospital, but she continued to assist me during surgeries at Colony Nursing Home and Shrikhande Clinic. However, a few years later, our son, Shailesh too was unwell, for which she had to fully stay at home. Suhas sacrificed her career, but the family did well.

We are blessed with three daughters and a son, all of who have had excellent academic careers. Our eldest daughter, Anjana, had a very good academic record and had the option to pursue post graduate studies in many disciplines after completing her MBBS. But she opted to play a very different but perhaps more important role of providing a support system looking at the larger picture. Along with her husband, she looks after the entire family and Shrikhande Clinic. Our son-in-law, Dr. Anand Nande, was my finest student, and is a Professor of Surgery at the Bombay Hospital Institute, apart from his continuing work at Shrikhande Clinic. He is also a Sangeet Visharad (a qualification equivalent to a bachelors degree in Hindustani classical music), trained under renowned vocalist, the late Pandit Dinakar Kaikini. Had Anand not become a surgeon, he would have become a vocalist of national fame. A few years ago, in the memory of Pandit Kaikini, he has started to teach music on Sunday evenings, whenever possible. He continues to be a solid support to the entire family.

They have two daughters. Anushree, who has been a bright student, completed her 12th standard in Science, but surprised many outside the family when she opted to pursue her true passion for writing rather than continuing with the family's medical legacy – a decision we fully support. She has Creative Writing (and Media Studies) Bachelors and a Creative Writing Masters from Edge Hill University in the United Kingdom. She is a freelance editor, does work for Leadstart Publishing and Wordit CDE, and is a writer for various magazines, blogs, literary websites on books, writing, football, film, TV. She has had short stories, literary essays, and poems published on various platforms. Anushree has recently returned from Spain where she was an English conversational assistant staying in a Spanish host family for 10 months. She is currently experimenting with the impact and challenges of flash and shorter fiction, as well as working on her first novel. Their second daughter, Anjalika, has also had a brilliant academic career, finishing her undergraduate masters in Theoretical Physics and Applied Mathematics at the University of Birmingham in July 2014. She is currently pursuing a PhD in Theoretical Physics at Harvard University. Both Anushree and Anjalika have played badminton for their respective school and university teams, and have a keen interest in music and art.

Our second daughter, Madhavi (Seema, and after marriage, Sanyukta Khot), with a bright academic career, has a BSc.Tech in computer engineering, and is married to Group Captain Dhananjay Khot, a fighter pilot in the Indian Air Force. Both of them met while pursuing their BSc Physics degrees at Ruparel College, Mumbai. Dhananjay joined the Air Force, while Seema continued with her higher studies. They got married in 1991. Dhananjay had a miraculous escape after he ejected from a MiG plane which caught fire over the Rajasthan desert in October 1991. He has had a bright career, and continues to serve the Air Force and the nation with great dedication.

They have two daughters. Sanjana is a very intelligent and logical girl, and is studying computer science in the United Kingdom, while Shivani, who is highly gifted in the arts, has just completed her 12th grade in science, and will pursue an international master's programme in Animation in Pune. Seema, along with their two daughters, has lived in various places across the length and breadth of the country, joining Dhananjay on his innumerable postings; often in remote areas. As a result, Sanjana and Shivani have attended 10 different schools, gaining a vast exposure at a young age. Seema has wholeheartedly shouldered the social responsibilities inherent in military life. She has also been working in the field of education and computers, whenever possible. She now works as a freelance web-developer.

Dhananjay, apart from being a first rate pilot, plays the sitar, and is an excellent speaker. His speech on the occasion of my 75th birthday celebration is still remembered by many. He had said:

Every landing is a kiss of death
Every take off is birth
Because I fly
I know not hate, I envy no man on Earth!

Our third daughter, Vasanti, with her infectious enthusiasm, plays a multifaceted role, balancing her passion for music with various responsibilities of the clinic and the family. She has a natural talent for music. She is a commerce graduate and later did a Masters in Hindustani classical music. She pursued vocal music under the guidance of the well-known classical vocalist, Smt. Shruti Sadolikar-Katkar, but unfortunately developed an atrophy of one of her vocal cords. Thereafter she has taken up the Sarangi (an ancient Indian bowed instrument that comes closest to the human voice, although very tough to master) and is being trained by Padmavibhushan Pandit Ram Narayan, the legendary Sarangi maestro of international fame and repute. She has recently started to perform and her performances have been well appreciated.

Our son, Shailesh, was good at cricket and successfully represented his school and city teams, but decided to be a doctor and a surgeon. He is now the Chief of the G.I. and HPB Department, and a Professor of Surgical Oncology at the Tata Memorial Centre, the leading cancer hospital in the country. Shailesh was awarded an honorary F.R.C.S. England in London on March 10, 2015. Till recently he was known as my son, but now I am known as his father. I feel blessed that my son has imbibed the core values of compassion, sincerity and integrity, and has earned a good name at a young age. All India Radio had interviewed us for the unusual occurrence of three surgeons in one family. We are lucky to have five doctors in the family, where we had none in the past. Shailesh's daughter, Josephine, is 7 years old, his son, Arjun, 5 years old, and they currently live in Germany.

I have a sister and a brother. My elder brother, Neelkanth (we call him Kumar), a renowned structural engineer, has established a consulting firm of great repute, and is ably assisted by his two sons – Ravindra, a structural engineer and the Managing Director, and Rajeev, a chartered accountant and the Joint Managing Director. My sister-in-law, Smt. Nalini, has supported their family including our parents. Her father was bestowed with the Padmashree by the President of India, Dr. Rajendra Prasad for the electrification of a part of the eastern railways. My younger sister, Indrayani Kolhatkar, is an arts graduate in sociology. She represented her college in badminton. Her husband, Balasaheb Kolhatkar, has a diploma in electrical communication engineering and has worked in the field of instrumentation. He lost his father when he was only a few months old, but his mother looked after the family through all the hardship. The couple selected Nashik, where they guide challenged children and individuals in distress. They are an outstanding example of how to lead a purposeful life even after retirement.

❑ ❑ ❑

Chapter 22

Along the Final Bend

The departure gate is not far. I have no load of baggage to carry. There is no security check, there are no immigration formalities. I will be on a journey without destination. I do not need foreign exchange or a visa. The expected time of departure is not known and till then I am free to enjoy whatever time is available for me. I am in a reflective mood.

I was in Goa at the age of seven when I saw a ship approaching the Panjim harbour—first, there was only smoke rising in the sky, later the mast and then the ship. That was the day I learnt that the earth was round. I saw the novelty of radio, ballpoint pen, tap water, wide roads, telephone, television, electric type writer, planes without propellers (jet plane), computers, cell phones, tablets. I can now see and talk to people living thousands of miles away!

I have lived in a remarkable era of human history. When I was 16, India became free after hundreds of years of subjugation. Many Indians had felt that democracy could never work in India with her diversity, poverty, illiteracy and backwardness. But the prophets of doom were wrong. India is now addicted to democracy.

I have remained an optimist. The most beautiful sight for me is that of small boys and girls in uniform, from slums, villages, remote corners of our vast subcontinent, going to school. There is a justifiable concern about the falling standards in education, but I predict that from these multitudes of neglected masses would rise tomorrow's leaders of change. The more I travel, the more I realise that there are a number of jewels scattered all over the country, waiting to be discovered.

Man took his first steps on the moon on 20 July 1969 when Neil Armstrong said, "That is one small step for a man, one giant leap for mankind." Man is an animal and, with the attitude of might is right, has survived on this planet. Nelson Mandela, while taking the oath to become the President of South Africa, gave the message of love and forgiveness in the presence of his oppressor. Martin Luther King, Nelson Mandela, Burma's Aung San Suu Kyi are walking on the same path as that of Mahatma Gandhi. I was lucky to see Gandhiji in real life.

I have travelled in my grandfather's bullock cart as a child and also seen India's successful Mangalayaan mission. How lucky I feel to have witnessed so many momentous events in my lifetime!

Medicine has made great strides. I experienced incredible good fortune to be old in this era, when I successfully withstood major open heart surgery for a deformed aortic valve at the age of eighty.

The disappearance of a family physician is a great calamity faced by the sick. More than 90% patients who contact consultants and attend hospitals could be easily looked after by general practitioners, but the comment, 'He has only MBBS degree, is a sad reflection of society's mindset today. And to think my family was looked after well by a general practitioner, the late Dr. M. P. Vidvauns, for over forty-five years!

I still remember what was stressed at home and school- "Early to bed and early to rise, makes a man healthy, wealthy and wise". There is tremendous wisdom in this simple teaching. Also importance was given to regular exercise, simple, disciplined life, chewing the food well, eating vegetables and fruits, etc. Now this simple but important advice is given by highly qualified consultants after series of investigations in modern hospitals! And the society complains that medical treatment has become unaffordable!

Society must realise that modern lifestyle diseases are best prevented by individual efforts rather than cured by doctors. Self centered individuals who lack concern for others carry a curse of unhappiness. Medicine is helpless to comfort these patients.

I have worked in teaching hospitals where eminent doctors gave part of their time to look after the poor without any remuneration; there was no parallel to this service facility in any other profession. Modern hospitals have to work as an industry, and industry must make profits. Unfortunately, when medical education too has become a money amassing industry, how can medical services become affordable to the sick? A society promoting educational institutes that do not inculcate human values, should not expect doctors with humane values.

I have realised that my valuable assets were my striving for improvement and seeking solutions in difficulties. They worked as a trigger for creativity and confidence. Every small step ahead increased my confidence and made my drawbacks gradually irrelevant. Curiosity was my GPS. Curiosity is a driving force for improvement and creativity.

It is my experience that any average person who resolves to improve a bit every day will reach heights beyond even his own imagination. Many decades later I learnt that this is the principle behind the Kaizen (zero defect) philosophy from Japan. An observer from Germany who spent three months with me and is now a professor of surgery, wrote to me, "Now I understand the significance of your question—'What have you learnt today?' I ask the same question to myself and my students."

How do I judge improvement? As an experiment at the age of 69, I wanted to see if my handwriting could be further improved. It was very easy to judge that it indeed had. Such an experience was invigorating because I had proved wrong, the assumption that with advancing age the hands do not remain steady. At my age of 84, I can still carry two full cups of tea from the kitchen to the dining room without spilling a single drop! It is what you believe in that matters in life. A former resident could not believe that the skills which he saw when he was my resident 30 years ago were still undiminished. Life becomes boring if there is no improvement or novelty in whatever activities one pursues. 'Improve everyday' is my mantra for everyone.

The passion to improve continues!

My patients have taught me how to live, why to live and also how to die. Any sensitive surgeon has no choice but to become a philosopher and accept things that he cannot change. But at the same time, he also has to be an optimist and make efforts for things that he can change. Acceptance and efforts are the two principles for a balanced, meaningful life. And these are the lessons my profession has taught me.

My profession gave me opportunities to observe the wonders of nature within the human body and the society around me. I have enjoyed the status that the society gave me for my work and that has given meaning to my life.

I am often asked, what is the secret of success?

Contribute something valuable to society which will benefit posterity.

Success cannot be measured, it has to be experienced. It is not a destination or a one-time achievement, but a journey. Those who decide their destination in form of money, property or status pursue a mirage and do not know where to stop like in Tolstoy's *How much land does a man need?*

I was touched by a poem circulating through emails written by a young girl dying of cancer in a New York hospital:

You'd better slow down. Don't dance so fast.
Time is short. The music won't last.
When you run so fast to get somewhere.
You miss half the fun of getting there.
When you worry and hurry through your day,
It is like an unopened gift... Thrown away.
Life is not a race. Do take it slower.

I had gone to Valencia, Spain in 2008 where I had lunch in La Pepica, a restaurant on the beach. It was made famous by Ernest Hemingway whose large photo was conspicuously exhibited. Thoughts raced through my mind: Why did he commit suicide? Why do so many celebrities in the film and fashion industry in

India and abroad commit suicide? What a well-known Korean model wrote before ending her life in a Paris apartment at a young age of twenty years throws light on her state of mind, "Depressed and overworked, the more I gain, the more lonely it is!" Life is a wonderful gift, but death without a witness and without a cause, is a double tragedy.

These individuals were symbols of success, but defeated from within. I know so many successful individuals who have felt barren, unhappy and frustrated in the evening of their lives.

The futility of all the worldly possessions that the patients experience during suffering at the end of their lives must have reinforced my balanced outlook in life. Greed breeds unhappiness. Beauty created in a beautician's saloon does not last, external pleasures are temporary. Anything that evolves from within lasts forever and that is success.

That is the reason my father continues to be my hero; he wanted me to be an extraordinary surgeon for an ordinary man. I did not fail him.

Some years ago a well-known advocate who was operated by me quoted a judgment my father gave sixty years ago:

'One moon is enough for our Earth
One good child is enough for a family
One good friend is enough in life and
One good evidence is enough in a court of law.'

One life is enough for me. I have enjoyed my long life and remain grateful!

❑ ❑ ❑

Appendix

A Surgeon, Teacher, Philosopher...
....Who touched our lives.

The 75th birthday of Dr. V. N. Shrikhande was celebrated by organising a scientific program, 'Current Standards in Digestive Surgery—An Update for General and GI surgeons' in 2006. A booklet was published about the same.

The foreword reproduced below was written by the doyen in anaesthesia, the late Professor Dr. Y. G. Bhojraj.

Dr. Y. G. Bhojraj was the first Indian to get FFARCS in 1953. He was offered a consultant's post in the UK, but returned to India to join KEM in 1954 where he worked till his retirement in 1974.

He joined Bombay hospital in 1954 and was appointed as the Emeritus Professor in Anaesthesia at the Bombay Hospital Institute of Medical Sciences in 1995.

He is remembered because of his pioneering contributions to the development of major surgical specialities in India.

My association with Dr. V. N. Shrikhande actually started with a chance meeting in Dr. A.V. Baliga's operation theatre at Patel chambers at Opera House, sometime in the year 1962. This very first meeting with him somehow left a lasting memory in my mind for various reasons.

Dr. Baliga was performing a major abdominal surgery. I noticed somebody standing behind me, and he introduced himself, saying that he was a surgeon and that he had come to see Dr. Baliga operating. I introduced him to Dr. Baliga and it seemed that Dr. Shrikhande had already taken Dr. Baliga's permission and Dr. Baliga was expecting him. Dr. Baliga advised Dr. Shrikhande to wash up for the operation so that he could see the surgery better.

The reason I remembered my first meeting with Dr. Shrikhande was that here was a young surgeon, already a consultant at a teaching hospital, keen and earnest to learn from the legendary surgeon. I believe that it is only those who remain students throughout their lives, who can be good teachers. Dr. Shrikhande more than justified my first impression by being recognised as one of the best teachers in surgery in later years.

A few more years later, Dr. Shrikhande called me to administer anaesthesia to one of his patients for a major abdominal surgery. The patient was admitted in a small private nursing home and the operation theatre was small and very poorly equipped. By this time I had become sufficiently senior to be called by senior surgeons who conducted their major surgical work in very well equipped prestigious hospitals. I was rather skeptical and uncomfortable to do this major abdominal case for Dr. Shrikhande in this small private nursing home. At the end of the operation however, I must admit that my fears were unfounded. The surgery went on very well and I was no longer uncomfortable to conduct major surgical procedures at that small nursing home for Dr. Shrikhande.

I still remember some of the major operative procedures I conducted for Dr. Shrikhande at this place. Once there was a pancreatico-duodenal procedure which even at a major well equipped hospital is always considered as a very major procedure. The second was a huge thyroid tumour with a compression deviation of the trachea and the third was a mixed parotid tumour. The last one was done without the nerve motor stimulator and each branch of the facial was clearly dissected and was left unharmed.

Very soon Dr. Shrikhande's work increased and he had to have a nursing home of his own which he did at Hindu Colony, Dadar.

The first operation was on the daughter of my student and I was the anaesthetist. I found this place particularly very well equipped and very well staffed. I continued to work for Dr. Shrikhande for a few more years as I had to cut down my own work on medical grounds. I stopped doing anaesthesia for Dr. Shrikhande except for occasional specific cases.

Dr. Shrikhande got attached to Bombay Hospital in 1979 and soon earned a reputation as an excellent general surgeon.

Dr. Satyendra, Dr. Kishor Adyanthaya and Dr. Anand Nande were his associates.

No wonder therefore that very soon Dr. V. N. Shrikhande was appointed as the Head of the Surgical Department when Bombay Hospital earned the recognition as a teaching institution and came to be recognised as The Bombay Hospital Institute of Medical Sciences. This recognition was possible because of the standard of excellent teaching and academic work done by the staff members and untiring work of Dr. B. K. Goyal who ultimately became the first Dean of the institution.

One thing I could observe all along was inspite of his increasing work at Bombay Hospital he maintained his base at his own nursing home at Dadar.

Unlike in Bombay Hospital, most of his patients at Dadar were from the middle and lower middle class. They came to his nursing home by buses and trains and taxis with hope and prayer as one would enter a place of worship and they left the nursing home with great satisfaction. Dr. Shrikhande's work at Bombay Hospital definitely earned for him much more recognition all over the country but I always felt that his heart was at Dadar in his own nursing home.

Justice Chandrashekhar Dharmadhikari, a retired judge of Bombay Court, had once said, "Bhojraj I think there is a North and South divide in Bombay; as in every activity, the south is affluent, north is not."

The doctors of my generation, the legends of those times, such as Dr. G. M. Phadke, Dr. S.G. Joshi and Dr. V. N. Shirodkar never abandoned their middle and lower middle class patients in spite of their commitments to some institutions in South Bombay. The doctors of the next generation who maintained the tradition of these giants were doctors such as Dr. Ajit Phadke, Dr. K. Ramamoorthy, Dr. A.V. Bavdekar, Dr. Nandu Laud and Dr. V. N. Shrikhande. These are the people I know. They never left their bases at Dadar and the middle-class patients remained their main commitment in life.

I however started getting reports that Dr. Shrikhande was not very readily available and was spending more and more time outside Bombay. His well-wishers approached me and requested me to advise Dr. Shrikhande to give a thought to their concern.

I had a detailed discussion with Dr. Shrikhande about this matter. I was also concerned about this problem. During this discussion however, I learnt a lot of things about Dr. Shrikhande and he rose very high in my estimation. I realised that Dr. Shrikhande was not only an excellent surgeon, but wanted to do much more for the society in which he lived. He told me why he was away from his work in Bombay and what he was trying to achieve. This is what he said in his own words, "So many surgeons from outside Bombay visit my nursing home to see my work. This is more beneficial to them because here they learn how even a major surgery can be done in a private nursing home. The surgeons who visit, have to work in a similar ambience in their respective nursing homes, they thus develop more confidence and they do not need to send the patients to Bombay. I believe patients must get treatment near their home. It is not possible for either the patients to come to Bombay or for all surgeons to come to Bombay to see and learn the surgical procedures. I have decided therefore that I should devote more and more time to visit these small cities and towns and give talks and to demonstrate some surgical procedures to the local surgeons. In other words, to create more and more surgical centres in smaller places and thus make it possible for a large section of population to receive surgical aid locally. Over a period of time I have seen very good results of this program and many sophisticated and major surgical procedures are now successfully being done. I feel that this effort on my part, though small and limited in its scope is bearing results and this gives me satisfaction. My visits abroad are to keep myself abreast with all modern developments in surgery and this gives me satisfaction and I also make personal contacts with the renowned surgical personalities who would accept our students for training. So many of my students have benefited from this scheme and returned as full-fledged consultants.'

On listening to Dr. Shrikhande I had no reason to advise him in this matter. On the contrary, I had nothing but appreciation for what he said and what he was doing. When I was listening to Dr. Shrikhande somehow I remembered an interview which

Mr. Narayana Murthy MD of Infosys and one of the most respected industrialists of India gave to an American journalist. After a prolonged question-and-answer session, the journalist said, "Mr. Murthy I want to know your political ideology."

The reply which Narayana Murthy gave to him was remarkable. He said, "To start with I was a communist then I changed over for sometime to a socialist but now I am a compassionate capitalist."

On being asked to elaborate Murthy replied, "As a capitalist I believe in creating and accumulating wealth, but being compassionate, I believe not in hoarding it for myself but in distributing it to my partners who helped me to create this wealth. This helped my partners not only to help themselves but also to help me create more wealth."

Mr. Narayana Murthy somehow reminded me of what Dr. Shrikhande said two decades ago. If only you replaced the word 'wealth' from Mr. Murthy's reply for 'surgical skill and knowledge' in Dr. Shrikhande's reply the similarity becomes evident. In both there is emphasis on acquiring and distributing and not accummulating.

Dr. Shrikhande, because of his papers and talks at various conferences, became very well known as an excellent speaker and he soon was one of the most sought-after speakers, not only in Maharashtra but all over the country. Besides his professional colleagues, he seems to be very happy in the company of his friends who come from all walks of life. The circle of friends include renowned literary figures, renowned musicians, social workers, and so on. He has a very good sense of humour and it is very easy to make him break into a happy and hearty laugh.

In the entire write-up about Dr. Shrikhande I have deliberately not spoken about his great achievements in the surgical field. However, there is one crowning achievement I must mention here. Not to mention it here will be a big lapse on my part. His surgical work got the ultimate recognition when he was called to operate on the 'First Citizen of India' namely the President of India, Shri Shankar Dayal Sharma. In choosing Dr. Shrikhande for his operation, the President of India chose to ignore the established practice of rushing down to a foreign country. It was a matter of great honour for Dr. Shrikhande to be selected to operate on him and to be called all the way from Bombay to operate on him in Delhi, the capital city.

In my conversation with Dr. Shrikhande, I always heard him talking about his parents from whom he imbibed human values, love for work ethics and enthusiasm. His father was a sessions court judge who had a reputation not only for excellence in his judicial work but also for his integrity and high ethical standards for which he was held in high esteem. This was a matter of great pride for him.

I came across a book whose author dedicated his book in the following words. "I dedicate this book to my parents who gave me some of the best genes and to all those who allowed me to flourish them." Well I got my answers to Dr. Shrikhande's outstanding achievements.

Finally let me strike a personal note. My mother who was in her nineties, a very frail woman, hardly weighing 35 kg developed a strangulated femoral hernia. She was admitted in Shrikhande Clinic at Dadar in critical condition. It was Dr. Shrikhande who operated on her and saved her life. It was a very challenging job for both the surgeon and his anaesthetist Dr. Satish Gupte who did a marvellous job and saved her life. I will remain grateful to both of them forever.

On the occasion of his 75th birthday, his students are holding an international scientific conference. Such an event is of rare occurrence, which reflects both on the teacher and the students. I am sure it will be a great success and it is my earnest wish and my blessings that Dr. Shrikhande may continue to do excellent work, both in the medical and social context for many more years to come.

Dr. Y. G. Bhojraj

The following poem was contributed by Dr. Mrs. Kshama Valsangkar, consultant anaesthetist of Solapur, wife of Dr. Satish Velsangkar, who worked with Sir for 2 years in 1982.

To Sir, with Love

I stepped out of my nest, shy and naive,
I sought for a helping hand, and Sir, it was there...your very hand!
Tricks of trade and a lot from books...you taught me, Sir, as others do.
What was so special...something in You? A good Samaritan! That was you!!
Fun it was, Sir, to watch you work, with that pair of gifted hands,
Striking therby melodious tune, cheering up dischorded souls!
You may not know, Sir, what you have done...to your students...by a Midas Touch...
Noble profession, and not business...in your footsteps, here I trot!!
Through storms and hurricanes, to a right path—
You are Sir, my North Pole Star!!
Wish you, Sir, life hale and hearty,
I pray for you, to God Almighty!
To you, Sir, with Love,
To you, Sir, with Love

A Source of Inspiration

"I am happy to be a part of the momentous occasion—the 75th birthday celebration of Dr. Shrikhande. I had the good fortune of being a student of Dr. Shrikhande since 1964 at the Grant Medical College and a resident doctor and PG student at the G.T. Hospital. I have the further good fortune of being able to continue to tap his wisdom up to the present day.

When we talk of Dr. Shrikhande the images that are evoked are that of a great surgeon, a passionate teacher, a philosopher, a humanist, a compassionate doctor, a consistent friend, a reliable guide and an outstanding human being—a man from whom I imbibed ethical values. May you continue to inspire many more generations of students and serve as an icon and a role model that you truly are."

Dr. Lalit Kapoor,
Managing Trustee of Association
of Medical Consultants, Mumbai

First Amongst Equals

"The topic of discussion among anaesthetists in the operation theatre is naturally the surgeons but it is not the surgeon's surgical skill that is discussed first but how good a human being he is.

Whenever such things were talked about I would always mention Dr. V. N. Shrikhande.

I had the privilege of working with him for a number of years in G.T. Hospital. The first thing he would instill in his residents were good manners, good behaviour and the essential qualities that make a good human being. He taught by personal example He had excellent rapport with anaesthetists, ward sisters, operation theatre nurses, sisters and ward boys. So much so that before assigning any surgical work independently to his registrar he would first inquire from me about the resident's behaviour in the O.T. Even today, when any anaesthetist mentions that a particular surgeon is very polite or understanding and is from Mumbai the first thought that comes to my mind is that he must be Sir's resident.

Many a time surgical procedures used to get over very late in the night. He was the only consultant who used to worry about our safety and would ensure that we were escorted by either his residents or by himself. He received best cooperation from everyone and it was no wonder that his unit used to do the maximum number of cases. Normally the air-conditioning would be switched off at 1 p.m. but when Sir was doing oesophagectomy, it would go on till the surgery got over.

In 1998 he was invited to deliver the Dr. Dilip Kusurkar Oration in Pune. I had met him in Mumbai several years ago. He made it a point to find my telephone number and invited me personally for the function. That day he talked about various people who had a role to play in his illustrious surgical career. He mentioned his teachers, colleagues, O.T. and ward staff and of course anaesthetists. He said that without good anaesthetists excellent surgery was not possible. I remember his statement: "Every surgeon gets the anaesthetist he deserves just the way people get the governmment they deserve." Among the anaesthetists he particularly mentioned my name. I felt very proud and so emotional that my eyes were full of tears. After the lecture there was a buzz among the anaesthetists who showered me with congratulations. They had never heard any surgeon praising the anaesthetist from the podium. Yet, here was such an eminent surgeon like Dr. V. N. Shrikhande doing just that.

I feel honoured that I had the privilege and the opportunity to work with a person of a great stature like Dr. V. N. Shrikhande. I had worked with many surgeons at J. J. Hospital and G.T. Hospital for more than two decades. He really is first among equals."

Dr. Veena Gadkari
Anaesthetist, Pune

A Rare Example in a Commercial World

"I have had the pleasure to meet, to know, and to develop lasting friendship with Sir and he has always showered me and my family with his love and blessings over the years.

I first met Sir when I first joined G. T. Government Hospital as a House Physician in 1964 when he was an Asst. Honorary Surgeon. In the three years I was at G.T. Hospital, I developed an admiration for Sir as an individual for his simplicity, for his humane values, and for his humility. My father was admitted to G.T. Hospital with urinary retention and posted for surgery for an enlarged prostate in 1968. One day prior to surgery he suddenly collapsed but eventually recovered. Sir came up to me and with his hand on my shoulder said to me, "If you feel I am a junior, call in a senior surgeon and I will assist him." I insisted that Sir should do the surgery. Everything went off smoothly but I can never forget that gesture.

He had recently joined the hospital, he was not busy and he was young. He was at a stage in life when everyone is keen to operate to make an impression. I will not dwell very much on Sir's calibre as a surgeon but everybody in G.T. Hospital spoke highly of his dexterous hands. My father, mother, sister and my wife have all been operated upon by him purely because of the implicit trust and confidence I have in his competence. Undoubtedly Sir is a Surgeon of class, a Surgeon with a Heart, and a Surgeon of the Poor as exemplified here. After performing surgery on several of my patients when I phoned him for his fees for the surgery he told me, "You know the patient better and if he is in a position to pay, let him go ahead, if not ask him to pay the nursing home charges and forget my fees."

A gem of a human being with no greed for money, but full of care and concern for the poor. A God-fearing person, a dedicated doctor and above all, a good human being with high ethical values and social concern."

Dr. Andrade Mario
C.M.O. at G.T. Hospital
In private practice at Mazgaon since the 1960's

Against the 'Run of Play'

"The title of the piece is borrowed from the world of sports, where a game turns on its head because unexpected events take place. The expression could be applied to human affairs and individuals as well. For example when a person who by way of all available evidence is destined for a bright future fails or someone with no pretensions of reaching high ground suddenly achieves success, the events would be termed as being against the 'Run of the Play'.

A surgeon for example is supposed to have a certain robust and imposing personality, an ability to inspire confidence by a demeanour that these physical attributes bring about and a certain boldness sometimes bordering on adventure leading to unexpected happy results. There is also an element of glamour around a surgeon like around a lead actor in a film or a play with a motley crowd of actors performing secondary role.

What if a person had none of the above and yet turned out to be an outstanding clinical surgeon of his time good enough to be chosen to operate on the President of this country? Slight of build, simply dressed, saddled with a speech impairment and with no great command over the sophisticated phraseology of the English language. He was not raised in the upmarket quarter of the city, without a Godfather to pull strings or any semblance of a network in this uncaring, cruel, and competitive city. When a man rises almost like a phoenix to the higher reaches of the world it could be said that the event was against the 'Run of the

Play'. Such a man is Vinayak Nagesh Shrikhande. I purposely do not write his degree nor use a prefix before his name. To me they are irrelevant.

He epitomises empathetic conversational reach, not articulatory skills. He connects with his patients and also his colleagues through a bond which is transparently caring but his style does not include the modern 'back-slapping' camaraderie. ln his later years he probably has rolled in money, privileges, honours and has considerable clout among the powerful. But these are only ornaments mounted on a man who only wanted to relate to his fellowmen, in which he succeeded so handsomely. That he wielded a knife in his profession is an accident. He could have wielded a pen as well. True, he wielded his knife skillfully, frequently but also conservatively because the knife sharpness was honed in the furnace of ethics, that very furnace where most of his contemporaries got singed if not burnt. V. N. Shrikhande emerged unscathed with only his knife sharpened. Success, as is its character brings forth floating friends but also lurking under its belly are detractors and adversaries, ready to criticise if not strike. The protagonist of this piece, I suspect, adores both."

Dr. Ravin Thatte
M.S. F.R.C.S. (Edin)
Formerly Professor and Head Plastic Surgery
Lokmanya Tilak Hospital Sion, Mumbai
Awarded Hon. F.R.C.S. Edin.

(The citation for honorory F.R.C.S. read: He has made plastic surgery simpler for the developing world and has also knocked on some fundamental issues involving flap circulation and the treatment of cleft palate.

He is the only Asian who has received this Honour. He is also the only non-North American who has been invited to write an editiorial in the American Journal of Plastic Surgery.)

❑ ❑ ❑